THE PHAIDON ATLAS

OF CONTEMPORARY WORLD ARCHITECTURE

TRAVEL EDITION

Foreword

The Travel Edition of *The Phaidon Atlas of Contemporary World Architecture* presents the best works of architecture completed in the last five years in an ultra-convenient mini format, perfect for the holiday or business traveller.

A companion to the Comprehensive Edition of *The Phaidon Atlas of Contemporary World Architecture,* this book features the same selection of 1,052 projects. It includes work from countries as geographically, climatically, economically and culturally diverse as Argentina, Botswana, Denmark, Egypt, Guinea, Israel, Jordan, Lithuania, Mozambique, Turkey and the USA. The building types represented range from the super-scale, such as the US$2.2 billion Kuala Lumpur Airport by Kisho Kurokawa in Malaysia (1998), to the delicate minutiae of Jae Cha's timber and polycarbonate church in Bolivia (2000).

Organized geographically, the Travel Edition features a single image per building and a short text to help the traveller recognize it. Each project entry gives the name of the building and its architect, the location and the address, if accessible, as well as the telephone number, where appropriate. There is also a system to indicate which projects are open to the public. In addition to the 41 regional maps from the Comprehensive Edition, there are an additional 28 new city orientations to facilitate the location of buildings in built up areas.

This book provides a unique opportunity to visit 1,052 works of contemporary architecture in 75 countries. The Travel Editon of *The Phaidon Atlas of Contemporary World Architecture* is an essential companion on the travels of all those interested in gaining a first hand understanding of contemporary architecture around the world.

ntents

Introduction

Like the Comprehensive Edition, the Travel Edition of *The Phaidon Atlas of Contemporary World Architecture* divides the world into six regions – Oceania, Asia, Europe, Africa, North America and South America – each identified with a specific colour code. The featured buildings are generally presented in the geographical sequence set by *The Times Atlas of the World*. The data bar at the top of the page indicates the larger geographic region. Each region also contains detailed maps to indicate the sub-regions of countries or groups of countries. The sub-regional maps are interspersed throughout each region according to the density of architectural projects. Where there are five or more projects in one city, there are also city orientations indicating their location.

Each page contains a maximum of three projects. Every project entry includes a photograph of the building, the name of the architect, the name of the building, the address and telephone number where appropriate, the project number which is also featured in the Comprehensive Edition and a short narrative description. The project entry also includes the year in which the building was completed and a three-letter code indicating the building type.

Place Names

Local name forms are used throughout the book, where these pre-exist in the Roman alphabet, and are recognized by the country concerned. For places in languages that do not use the Roman alphabet, *The Times Atlas of the World* transliteration or transcription has been used. Although local forms for place names are given priority, some English-language conventional names are used where the English form exists in common use.

Building Type Abbreviations

Each building has been allocated with a thre letter code for comparative purposes.

COM Commercial Buildings
Includes banks, conference centres, exhibiti centres, factories, nightclubs, offices, resear facilities, restaurants, shops and wineries

CUL Cultural Buildings
Includes art galleries, artists' studios, arts centres, band stands, concert halls, cultural centres, glass houses, libraries, lookout tower media centres, memorials, museums, studios and theatres

EDU Educational Buildings
Includes colleges, research facilities, schools, student housing and universities

GOV Government Buildings
Includes embassies, government facilities (such as border controls, coastal authorities), law courts, parliament buildings and town halls

INF Public Infrastructure
Includes bridges, motorway structures, power stations, water pumping stations, stairs and waste facilities

PUB Public Buildings
Includes community centres, fire stations, lavatories and medical facilities

REC Recreation Buildings
Includes entertainment centres, parks, zoos, recreation facilities (such as golf clubs, saunas camping cabins and pop music venues)

REL Religious Buildings
Includes bell towers, cathedrals, cemeteries, chapels, churches, crematoria, pilgrim hostels, memorial centres, monasteries, synagogues and temples

RES Residential Buildings
Includes apartment buildings, multiple housing developments, social housing and single houses

SPO Sports Facilities
Includes stadia, gymnasia, swimming pools, cricket pavilions and archery pavilions

TOU Tourism Buildings
Includes hotels and tourist attractions

TRA Transport Buildings
Includes airports, boat piers, bus stations, canal facilities, port facilities and railway stations

ce Name Abbreviations
e abbreviations listed below are those used
he building address.

	Alberta
T	Australian Capital Territory
	Alaska
	Alabama
R	Arkansas
Z	Arizona
C	British Columbia
A	California
O	Colorado
T	Connecticut
C	District of Columbia
E	Delaware
L	Florida
GA	Georgia
A	Iowa
	Illinois
N	Indiana
KS	Kansas
KY	Kentucky
A	Louisiana
MA	Massachusetts
MB	Manitoba
MD	Maryland
ME	Maine
MI	Michigan
MN	Minnesota
MO	Missouri
MS	Mississippi
MT	Montana
NB	New Brunswick
NC	North Carolina
ND	North Dakota
NE	Nebraska
NH	New Hampshire
NJ	New Jersey
NM	New Mexico
NS	Nova Scotia
NSW	New South Wales
NT	Northwest Territories if used in the context of Canada, or Northern Territory if used in the context of Australia
NV	Nevada
NY	New York
OH	Ohio
OK	Oklahoma
ON	Ontario
OR	Oregon
PA	Pennsylvania

QC	Québec
QLD	Queensland
SA	South Australia
SC	South Carolina
SD	South Dakota
TAS	Tasmania
TN	Tennessee
TX	Texas
UK	United Kingdom
USA	United States of America
UT	Utah
VA	Virginia
VIC	Victoria
VT	Vermont
WA	Washington if used in the context of the United States of America, or Western Australia if used in the context of Australia
WI	Wisconsin
WV	West Virginia
WY	Wyoming

Key to Symbols
To ascertain the accessibility of every building, each owner, occupier or architect was asked a series of questions. The following symbols indicate the answers given. In some cases the occupier has discouraged viewing, but the building may be visible from the street. In all cases we ask you to respect the privacy of the occupiers. Airports and train stations are sometimes indicated on the city orientations to facilitate the location of projects.

☐ Exterior and interior can be viewed during normal working hours
■ Neither the exterior nor the interior can be viewed
◪ Exterior can be viewed. Interior cannot be viewed
◪ ✎ Exterior can be viewed. Interior can be viewed by appointment only
✎ Exterior and interior can be viewed by appointment only
○ Railway Station
✈ Airport

Opening times are subject to change and access may be limited. While every care has been taken to ensure accuracy throughout this book, it is advisable to check the times and dates of opening prior to visiting or making travel arrangements.

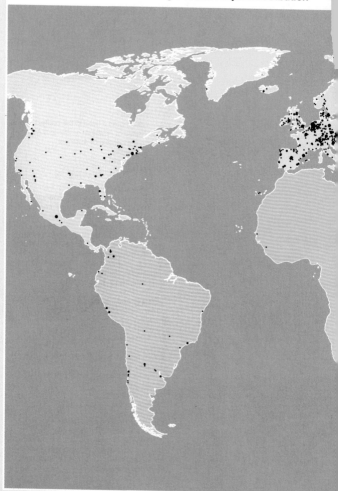

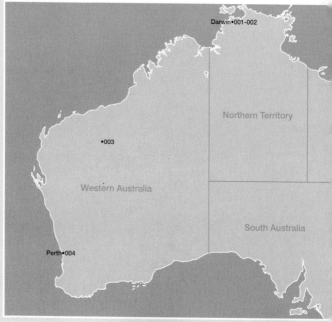

Darwin•001-002

Northern Territory

•003

Western Australia

South Australia

Perth•004

Troppo Architects

Pee Wee Restaurant
East Point Road, East Point,
Darwin, NT 0800
Tel +61 8 8981 6868

001   □ COM 1998

Situated on a tropical foreshore
overlooking Darwin Harbour,
this dining pavilion opens up,
via pivoting glass louvres and
doors, to the north and south –
allowing cross-ventilation while
deflecting strong prevailing
east–west winds. Its shed
aesthetic is inspired by adjacent
military huts.

opo Architects

zak House
nner Road, Lake Bennet,
chelor, NT 0845

2 ▮ RES 2001

ended to promote a sense of
mping out', the Rozak House
mprises three linked units on
vated platforms – a series of
rrugated-steel-roofed
rrandahs with timber-decked
ors. Screens promote cross-
ntilation and, combined with
htweight, heat-reflective
aterials, provides shading.

oodhead International

**arijini National Park Visitor
entre**
anyjima Drive, Pilbara, Karijini
ational Park, WA 6751
el +61 8 9189 8121

03 ☐ CUL 2001

spired by the 'Kurrumanthu',
monitor lizard, the curved
alls of richly weathered steel
ominate the scheme; lower
ofs and frameless glazing
hance the effect of a building
rowing from the landscape.
he dark interior re-presents
e landscape to visitors.

ary Marinko Architects

oll House 2
alkeith, Perth WA 6009

04 ▮ RES 2002

vast hipped roof gathers a
ain building and secondary
esidence around a central
ourtyard, the former with a
maller court of its own which
nsures light penetration into
he heart of the structure. The
ouse presents an unassuming
ontage to its suburban street
ocation, enlivened at night by
ovocative lighting.

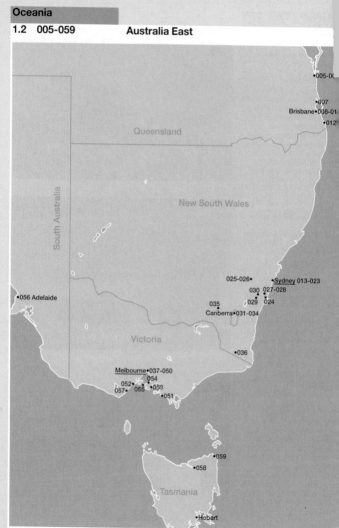

Queensland

•005-0(

•007
Brisbane•008-01
•012

South Australia

New South Wales

025-026•   •Sydney 013-023
030 027-028
•029 024
035
Canberra•031-034

•056 Adelaide

Victoria

•036

Melbourne•037-050
054
052• •053
057• 055
•051

Tasmania

•059
•058

•Hobart

rry Hill Architects

gilvie House
unshine Beach, QLD

05 ■ RES 2001

Approached through a low-level
water court and galleries on the
landward side of the plot, this
residence culminates in a series
of layered and intersecting living
and dining 'boxes', which frame
a swimming pool and the ocean
from its spectacular headland
site. Finely detailed timber
screened facades moderate
the climate.

Bligh Voller Nield with John
Mainwaring & Associates

**Sunshine Coast University
Library**
90 Sippy Downs Drive,
Sippy Downs, QLD 4556
Tel +61 7 5430 1234

006 □ EDU 1998

A permeable, extended
verandah connects the library
buildings, with their sawtooth
roof-forms reminiscent of
Queensland woolstores. This
walkway, with its hardwood
screens, symbolically reaches
into the wider community.

Andresen O'Gorman Architects

Moreton Bay Houses
Moreton Bay, QLD

007 ■ RES 2001

References to Japanese
courtyard houses are brought
to Queensland by these paired,
timber-framed residences,
which form a palm court
between them – the largest
'room' in their sequence of
double-height spaces. Detailed
sliding slatted screens, pebble
beds, and white-glass panels
and doors complete the effect.

m3architecture

**Micro/Health Laboratory,
University of Queensland**
103 Gatton Campus, Brisbane,
QLD 4343
Tel +61 7 3365 2776

008 ☐ EDU 2001

This two-level teaching facility
engages with its 1970s brick
campus surroundings via
contrasting effects achieved
through the use of just two brick
types. The contrasting, clinical
interior uses deep window
recesses to provide solar
protection.

Donovan Hill Architects

C House
Brisbane, QLD

009 ■ RES 1998

Firmly grounded on an
elaborately layered concrete
base, the suburban C House
rises from a landscape of
ledges, plinths, walls, stairs
and pool to culminate in a large
external room, around which
smaller spaces unravel. This
final, dramatic space is roofed,
yet open to the subtropical
Brisbane climate.

Peter Skinner and Elizabeth
Watson Brown

St Lucia House
3 Hiron Street, St Lucia,
Brisbane, QLD 4072

010 ☐ RES 2000

In a reversal of the subtropical
tendency to move living areas
outside, this dwelling pulls a
living room/verandah into its
core. A promenade links its five
interlocking split levels to each
other and to the courtyard. The
resulting zigzagging sightlines
bring these five zones together.

Andresen O'Gorman Architects

Rosebury House
Brisbane, QLD

011 ■ RES 1998

Sited in a steep bushland gulley under a significant tree canopy, the Rosebury House acts as a rigorously crafted 'inhabited landscape', by opening up its three pavilions – set along an extended axis – to the north, capturing both light and views. Entry, at lower level, is through a courtyard overlooked by the living areas.

Rex Addison

House and Studio
Taringa, QLD

012 ■ RES 1998

The house's floor levels have been raised to head-height, to allow continuation of the landscaping below, and inverted hipped roof planes fold around existing trees on this plot in the architect's childhood garden. Tilted gables draw light inside, where adjustable plywood panels are incised with patterns based on the overhead foliage.

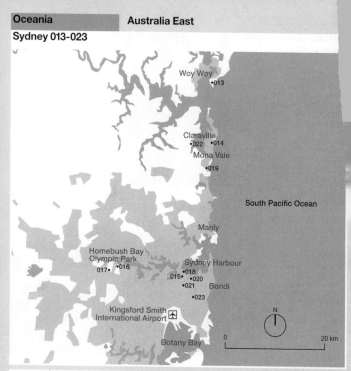

Woy Woy
•013

Claraville
•022   •014
Mona Vale
•019

South Pacific Ocean

Manly

Homebush Bay
Olympic Park
017•   •016

Sydney Harbour
•018
015•   •020
•021   Bondi
•023

Kingsford Smith
International Airport ✈

N

Botany Bay

0   20 km

Alexander Tzannes Associates

Kronenberg House
7 Patricia Place, Kilcare,
NSW 2257

013   ▮ RES 1998

When unoccupied, metal
louvres enclose this residence,
giving it the appearance of a
solid, silver tree-house – but
inhabited, it opens up as a
timber and steel platform below
a 'floating' monopitch roof. A
simple metal handrail separates
the inhabitant from the ocean
below, and the bush to the rear.

Craig Rosevear Architects

Archer House
251 Whale Beach Road,
Whale Beach, NSW 2107

014 ■ RES 2001

An open living pavilion over an enclosed sleeping/bathing area, this house interprets a simple concept in a sophisticated manner: the hovering roof anchors the upper pavilion to its hillside site and unites external and internal living areas. An outdoor terrace with open fireplace overlooks the ocean.

Renzo Piano Building Workshop

Aurora Place
88 Phillip Street, The Domain,
Sydney, NSW 2000

015 □ COM 2000

Both this 16-storey residential building and the 40-storey office tower are wrapped in a white-glass facade. The office tower's floor space increases with height to give harbour views, and the residential block has deeply recessed balconies overlooking the nearby botanical gardens.

Stutchbury and Pape

Olympic Archery Building
Bennelong Road, Olympic Park,
Sydney, NSW 2127
Tel +61 2 9714 7300

016 □ SPO 1998

The power and grace of archery are manifest in these nine box-like pavilions arrayed under a soaring planar roof canopy, anchored by tapering concrete buttresses and slender red tensile columns. The timber-clad cubicles accommodate administration, storage and toilet facilities.

Durbach Block Architects

Olympic Amenities Building
Cnr Sarah Durack and Edwin
Flack Avenues, Olympic Park,
Sydney, NSW 2140
Tel +61 2 9714 7300

017 ☐ PUB 2000

These three amenities 'hubs' –
housing water fountains, pay
stations and telephones, feature
bright primary colours and
bulging translucent fabric
canopies. These roof forms are
borrowed, and distorted, from
the more sober, adjoining steel-
framed stadium structures.

Lippmann Associates

Andrew 'Boy' Charlton Pool
Mrs Macquaries Road, The
Domain, Sydney, NSW 2000
Tel +61 2 9358 6686

018 ☐ SPO 2002

A replacement for a 50-year-old
Sydney Harbour icon, the new
facility takes advantage of its
spectacular site with a series of
pools arranged all on one level,
allowing views across the bay.
Visitor entry is through a
progression of low, gravel- or
pool-topped spaces, tucked
away at upper level.

Alex Popov Architects

Rockpool Housing
Surfview Road, Mona Vale,
NSW 2103

019 ▮ RES 1999

With these 17 shallow-vaulted
residences, overlooking Mona
Vale beach, the architects have
combined the intimacy of
freestanding houses with a
sense of community. The two
groups of dwellings are
simultaneously divided and
united by a pedestrian spine
and communal garden areas.

gelen Moore

tair Apartments
Kings Cross Road, Kings
ross, Sydney, NSW 2011

20 ❚ RES 2001

he use of a structural grid of
oncrete shear walls dominates
he striking north facade of this
6-storey residential tower
straddling a major arterial road
unnel. Secondary towers –
projecting out of the built form
to the south – create
apartments that are open to
light and views on three sides.

Harry Seidler & Associates

Horizon
184 Forbes Street, Darlinghurst,
Sydney, NSW 2010

021 ❚ RES 1998

Taking advantage of a planning
anomaly prohibiting height
restrictions, this residential
tower rises to 43 storeys, its
apartments' 360° views over
Sydney Harbour enhanced by
boldly curving balconies. It is
flanked by two low townhouse
blocks, which frame gardens,
a pool and a tennis court.

Stutchbury and Pape/Sue
Harper

Reeves and Hunt House
Hudson Parade, Clareville,
NSW 2107

022 ❚ RES 1999

The house's split-level zones
are arranged around two sets
of blank concrete blade walls,
which form its southern and
eastern elevations, while the
northern and western facades
are glazed. The parasol roof
surface is folded to admit winter
sun and to shade in summer.

Francis-Jones Morehen Thorp

Scientia, University of New South Wales
Anzac Parade, Kensington, Sydney, NSW 2033
Tel +61 2 9385 1000

023 ✎ EDU 1999

This building was inspired by the notion of people gathering under a tree. It comprises a timber-and-glass portico flanked by sandstone plinths housing performance areas, with ceremonial spaces in contrasting glass-and-metal-clad 'boxes' above.

Engelen Moore

Rose House
Saddleback Mountain, Kiama, NSW 2533

024 ▯ RES 2000

Balanced on a grassy slope, this house is a glass box wrapped in a silvery metal sheath and approached centrally by a concrete bridge striking off from ground level. On either side, parents' and children's zones are separated by service cores to the east and west respectively.

Drew Heath Architects

Bush Hut Private Library
Blackheath, NSW

025 ■ CUL 2000

Located in the Blue Mountains west of Sydney, this 'cathedral to literature' unites a spine wall of 4,000 books with six perpendicular blades of double-sided bookshelves. The building volumes sit below a dramatic swooping roof – combining low, framed mountain views with the need for tall ladder access to the bookshelves.

Drew Heath Architects

Zig Zag Cabin
Wollombi, NSW

026 ■ RES 2002

Conceived in a single sketch, this weekend country retreat intended to offer a camp-like experience is a simple fibreboard-and-pine-clad box on a timber deck, with bold 'zigzag' window openings. It has three sleeping areas and an outside sink below deck level, served by a rainwater collection tank located uphill.

Harry Seidler & Associates

Berman House
Joadja, NSW

027 ■ RES 1999

The L-shaped plan of this residence clearly distinguishes public and private wings, using open-plan and cellular arrangements respectively, beneath a sinuous, curvilinear roof. A balcony extends vertiginously over the cliff face, while stone retaining and screen walls anchor other parts of the building to its rugged site.

Glen Murcutt

Kangaloon House
Kangaloon, NSW

028 ■ RES 2000

The house's cross-section is extruded east–west, with a steeply pitched roof deflecting strong southerly winds and sheltering living areas – all of which engage with and open on to the northerly aspect. The curved profile of the hallway is washed by light from its north-facing skylight, producing a serene circulation zone.

Glen Murcutt, Wendy Lewin and
Reg Lark

**Arthur and Yvonne Boyd
Education Centre**
Off Illaroo Road, Bundanon,
NSW 2541
Tel +61 2 4423 0433

029 ✆ EDU 1999

The communal spaces of this
centre – hall, dining room and
verandah – are united under a
soaring roof plane. The smaller-
scale dormitory areas that
extend along the site's ridge are
pod-like units articulated by
sun-screening concrete blades.

Glen Murcutt

Fletcher-Page House
Kangaroo Valley, NSW

030 ■ RES 2000

A translucent volume and a thin
roof plane are stretched along
the site contours, while a series
of openings – manipulated as
habitable spaces, with benches
and shading – allows views of
the landscape both from and
through the house. The
southern living room wall fully
retracts, engaging even more
closely with the setting.

Ashton Raggatt McDougall and
Robert Peck von Hartel
Trethowan

National Museum of Australia
Lawson Crescent, Acton
Peninsula, Canberra, ACT 2600
Tel +61 2 6208 5000

031 ☐ CUL 2001

The various strands – land,
water, space and building –
refer to the convergence of
cultures within Australia.
Ribbon canopies, pathways
and a crescent-shaped building
footprint comprise the scheme's
architectural elements.

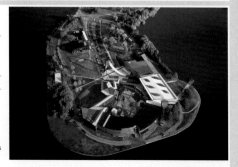

Denton Corker Marshall

Anzac Hall
Treloar Crescent, Campbell,
Canberra, ACT 2612
Tel +61 2 6243 4211

032 ☐ CUL 2001

Embedded into rolling ground around the existing domed Anzac monument, this new memorial hall – beneath its low, double-curved roof – has walls which are radial to the dome in plan, creating a dramatic fan-shaped space. It also anchors a major axis in the national capital.

Durbach Block Architects with
Sue Barnsley Design

Commonwealth Place
Parkes Place, Yarralumla,
Canberra, ACT 2600
Tel +61 2 6271 2888

033 ☐ CUL 2002

Situated beside Lake Burley Griffin, its gently concave 'town square' mirrors the dome of New Parliament House, with a grand ramp linking it to the Great Lawn of Old Parliament House. At night, illuminated slots in its stone wall form an abstract visual 'gateway'.

Hirvonen-Huttunen Architects
and MGT Architects

Finnish Embassy
12 Darwin Avenue, Yarralumla,
Canberra, ACT 2600
Tel +61 2 6273 3800

034 ☐ GOV 2002

This building houses a glass-atrium three-storey secretariat, an office wing clad inside and out with stainless steel, a timber decked residence and a wooden sauna. The result is a building that is Nordic in roots, yet fundamentally Australian.

Oceania

Australia East

Garner Davis Architects

Wagga Wagga Civic Centre
Cnr Baylis and Morrow Streets,
Wagga Wagga, NSW 2650
Tel +61 2 6926 9100

035 ☐ GOV 1999

The complex consists of two plazas which are linked by an internal arcade, punctuated by angled skylights, that provides access to a library, galleries, and community and council spaces. Elevations fronting a lagoon are smooth, while those to the plazas are fragmented.

Collins and Turner Architects

Bombala Farmhouse
Bombala, NSW

036 ■ RES 1998

This building in the Monaro Plains is an extrusion which has twisted upon itself to give a north-facing main living area and a smaller, southward-looking 'night zone', connected about a central freestanding services pod. The house utilizes passive climatic control, with diagonal cross-ventilation.

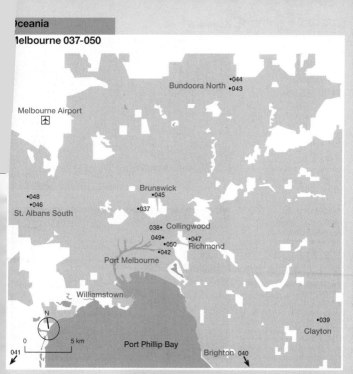

Bundoora North •044
•043

Melbourne Airport ✈

Brunswick
•045

•048
•046
St. Albans South •037

038• Collingwood
049•
•050 •047
•042 Richmond

Port Melbourne

Williamstown

N

0 — 5 km

041•

Port Phillip Bay

•039
Clayton

Brighton 040•

Denton Corker Marshall

The Melbourne Gateway
City Link Tullamarine Freeway,
Flemington, Melbourne,
VIC 3031

037 ☐ INF 1999

In a heroic city 'portal', a
canary-yellow boom cantilevers
70 metres out across the road
from a curvaceous orange
sound wall, and 39 red canted
columns rise opposite. The road
sweeps into an elevated ellipse-
shaped tunnel that hovers
above the motorway route to
and from Melbourne's airport.

Denton Corker Marshall

Melbourne Museum
Carlton Gardens, Carlton,
Melbourne, VIC 3001
Tel +61 3 8341 7777

038 □ CUL 2000

Set opposite the existing
nineteenth-century city
museum, this new facility
groups research and Aboriginal
centres, an IMAX cinema, and
a children's area as volumes
along a light-filled atrium – itself
containing an aviary and indoor
garden, beneath soaring roof
planes.

Denton Corker Marshall

**Art and Design Building,
Monash University**
900 Dandenong Road, Caulfield
East, Melbourne, VIC 3145
Tel +61 3 9903 2707

039 ✎ EDU 1999

In this latest addition to the
Caulfield Campus, teaching
facilities and studio apartments
for visiting artists are distributed
between two separate wings,
linked by an elevated walkway.
The building's exterior presents
an undulating aluminium wall to
its congested highway setting.

Sean Godsell Architects

**Woodleigh School Science
Faculty**
Golf Links Road, Baxter,
VIC 3911
Tel +61 3 5971 1108

040 ✎ EDU 2003

The repetition of ironbark and
oxidized steel columns forms
a protective outer layer to this
teaching facility, housing an
aquarium, greenhouse and
classrooms. Embedded into its
gently sloping site, the building
forms the eastern edge of a new
quadrangle.

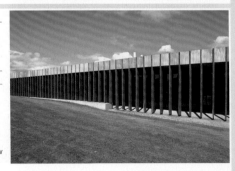

Sean Godsell Architects

Carter Tucker House
61 Horwood Drive, Breamlea,
VIC 3227

041　▮ RES 2000

Emerging from sand dunes,
this house groups three levels
of accommodation within a
timber-battened facade, parts
of which convert from wall to
ceiling plane as they open out
to a horizontal position. The
result is a constantly changing
gridded pattern of sunlight in
the open-plan living spaces.

Wood Marsh in association with
Pels Innes Neilson Kosloff

Malthouse Plaza
111 Sturt Street, Southbank,
Melbourne, VIC 3006
Tel +61 3 9654 6422

042　☐ CUL 2002

This arts centre fuses together
exhibition, dance and set-
production facilities – enclosed
by a single folded surface of
rusted steel. The workshop is a
shed, dance studios are clad in
orange plywood and glass, and
the gallery houses white-walled
exhibition rooms.

Wood Marsh in association with
Pels Innes Neilson Kosloff

RMIT Building 220
Bundoora Campus, Plenty
Road, Melbourne, VIC 3083
Tel +61 3 9925 2000

043　☐ EDU 1998

Building 220 features convex
and concave faces covered
with aluminium panels, which
change hue from dull brown
to vibrant orange depending
on daylight conditions. These
contrast with rock-textured,
rusticated concrete to echo
the surrounding landscape.

John Wardle Architects in association with DesignInc Melbourne

RMIT Biosciences Building
Bundoora Campus, Plenty Road, Melbourne, VIC 3083
Tel +61 3 9925 7391

044 ☐ EDU 2001

Laboratories are framed by T-shaped concrete and blackened steel sunshades – an element that repeats as a glazing motif, timber sections and a pergola. Vertical light monitors alternate with laboratory modules, creating courtyard niches.

John Wardle Architects

RMIT Printing Facility
Brunswick Campus, 25 Dawson Street, Melbourne, VIC 3056
Tel +61 3 9925 9441

045 ☐ EDU 1999

This building reveals its inner workings through glazed curtain walls – and jointing between pre-cast concrete panels on its west elevation evokes the exacting nature of image registration in the printing process. The facility defines a new edge to the western perimeter of the campus.

Lyons Architects

Sunshine Hospital Redevelopment
176 Furlong Road, St Albans, Melbourne, VIC 3021
Tel +61 3 8345 0283

046 ☐ PUB 2000

This hydrotherapy facility and ward block has a brightly coloured southern facade, stretch-patterned to engage with the adjacent freeway, which curves out to create a new public entry. Inside, faceted bay windows function as both seats and shelves for patients.

Edmond & Corrigan

Niagara Galleries
245 Punt Road, Richmond,
VIC 3121
Tel +61 3 9429 3666

047 ☐ CUL 2002

Clad in black-and-white metal
decking with a red underside
and yellow fenestration, this
striking addition extends out
over the rear of the Victorian
terrace that houses the original
gallery. Ideal light conditions for
viewing and storing art are
created via tilted south-facing
openings.

Lyons Architects

**Victoria University Online
Training Centre**
St Albans Campus, Willis Street,
Melbourne, VIC 3021
Tel +61 3 9365 2282

048 ☐ EDU 2000

A compact two-level building,
with a metal skin which is cut
and folded out at points to
form angled, hooded openings
admitting natural light. The
facade's panels are imprinted
with a pixelated image, derived
from colours and forms within
the surrounding landscape.

Katsalidis Architects

Ian Potter Museum of Art
University of Melbourne,
Swanson Street, VIC 3010
Tel +61 3 8344 5148

049 ☐ CUL 1998

The street frontage – a striking
ensemble of steel, glass and
concrete, which wraps round
the adjacent 1940s building –
conceals six large exhibition
spaces arranged around a
towering central stair. Black
steel blades drop from a
skylight, screening the top floor
office and research space.

LAB Architecture Studio in association with Bates Smart

Federation Square
Corner of Swanson and Flinders Street, Melbourne, VIC 3000
Tel +61 3 9655 1900

050 ☐ COM 2002

Occupying an entire urban block, this development houses national exhibition and broadcasting facilities, restaurants, shops and commercial spaces within its complex geometry. An open-air amphitheatre for 15,000 people completes this project.

Lyons Architects

Chisholm Institute of Technical & Further Education
Bass Coast Campus, Wonthaggi, VIC 3995
Tel +61 3 5672 1844

051 ☐ EDU 2001

This small education facility uses triangular and diagonal forms for its footprint and for both the central courtyard and the ceilings of its surrounding corridor. Through rescaling the light industrial shed and domestic porch, it resists immediate rural associations.

Kerstin Thompson Architects

Leopold House
Maloneys Road, Lake Connewarra, Leopold, VIC 3224

052 ◼ RES 2002

The house's two main elements – to the east and west – containing living quarters and work and guest areas respectively, are clad in black-stained, rough-sawn cedar boarding below an origami-like roof. As a result, this linear building tends to 'disappear' into its ridge-top site.

...tus

...hnology Building,
...'s College
...tain Road, Epsom,
...1003
...524 8108

... EDU 2001

...d by a heavy pre-cast
... wall clad in local
...e – relieved only by a
...white-glazed crucifix –
...ding screens its campus
... adjacent elevated
...y. It accommodates
...achinery, information
...echnology areas.

...s Patterson Limited

...t Benedict's Street
...nedict's Street, Newton,
...d 1001

... EDU 2001

...site of a historic stables
..., this rental space
...the utilitarian nature of
...uctures in both its siting
...a courtyard and its
...romatic palette of zinc,
...oncrete and plywood.
...raped stairways and
...aled skylights add a
...al note to the project.

...ture +

...Museum of Arts and
...s
...street, Porirua,
...ton 6006
...4 237 1511

... CUL 2001

...s title from a Maori term
...ulating 'enclosure,
...ory and storehouse', this
...varehouse now provides
...useum accommodation
...lery, arranged around a
...block. The building is
...a screen of steel louvres.

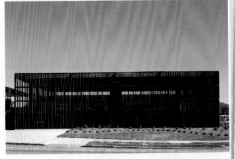

Gregory Burgess Architects

Burraworrin Residence
Flinders, VIC

053 ■ RES 1998

Burraworrin ('Magpie'), a house
for three generations of one
family, is conceived as two
curved wings clad in radially
sawn timber, which splay out
from a central entrance below
projecting roofs. Curves are
echoed in the built-in furniture
and ceilings, and an 8 metre
high lookout surmounts the
whole ensemble.

Sean Godsell Architects

Peninsula House
Mornington, VIC

054 ■ RES 2002

Surrounded by a dense scrub
of tea trees and wrapped in a
translucent veil of eucalyptus
battens, the interlocking spaces
of this dwelling open out, via
vertically swinging panels, to
the surrounding dunescape.
Its materials, including oxidized
steel, will give an appearance
of continuing change as they
weather over time.

Denton Corker Marshall

Emery Residence
Cape Schanck, VIC

055 ■ RES 2002

This sleek elongated tube of
a dwelling resists both the
elements and the traditional
beach-house typology, being a
decisively internalized building
engaging with the landscape
through carefully selected
views rather than external
spaces. Its interior is divided
by freestanding elements and
sculptural supports.

Oceania

Australia East

Ashton Raggatt McDougall with Phillips Pilkington

Marion Cultural Centre
287 Diagonal Road, Marion,
Adelaide, SA 5043
Tel +61 8 8375 6855

056 □ CUL 2001

The centre transcribes itself in the form of a massive built version of the word 'Marion', within which a library, art gallery, performance space and café are linked yet independently accessible. In the process, it seeks to address the issue of art and architecture in suburbia.

Kerstin Thompson Architects

West Coast House
Apollo Bay, VIC

057 ■ RES 1999

Disappearing into its bushland site with extensive glazing yet forming a monumental buffer wall to the ocean-front, this sharply geometrical beach-house resists blending into its surroundings. The dwelling is complemented by a camouflage-like palette of materials, which will weather in deference to the landscape.

David Travalia Architect

Design Centre of Tasmania
Corner of Brisbane and Tamar Streets, Launceston, TAS 7250
Tel +61 3 6331 5506

058 □ CUL 2002

This extension to the existing Price Hall was designed to create an internationally recognized identity for Tasmania. The galleries are set in stepped sequence around a courtyard. Inside, a glazed link connects to the old building and U-shaped alcoves form spaces for display or storage.

Oceania

Ken Latona

Bay of Fires Visitor Lodge
Mount William National Park,
TAS 7250
Tel +61 3 6391 9339

059 ✏ TOU 1998

The lodge comprises two strips of accommodation – containing guest rooms and communal facilities – bisected by a path ending in a deck. Solar-powered lighting and fans, composting toilets and a hand-pumped water supply system seal the environmental credentials of this project.

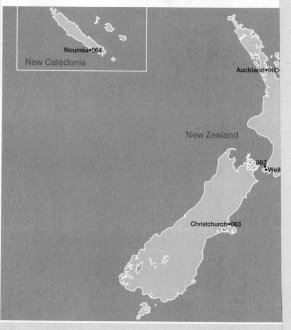

1.3   060-064   New Zealand and Southeast Paci

Nouméa•064
New Caledonia

Auckland•060

New Zealand

062
•Well

Christchurch•063

Oce

Archit

New
St Pe
23 Mc
Auckl
Tel +€

060

Enclo
conc
roads
strikir
this b
from
moto
heavy
and b

Archi

Site
3 St
Auck

061

On th
build
echo
farm
arour
mone
glass
Mest
over-
whim

Arch

Pata
Cult
Norr
Welli
Tel +

062

Takir
enca
repo
1970
new
and
'spir
clad

Thom Craig

Craig House
Wroxton Terrace, Fendalton,
Christchurch, South Island

063 ▮▮ RES 1999

This black-stained
weatherboarded residence
provides a series of spaces –
both inside and out – designed
to cope with changes in living
patterns. A multipurpose living
space on the ground floor is
surmounted by two equal-sized
rooms on upper levels,
separated by a central
bathroom and storage core.

Renzo Piano Building Workshop

**Jean-Marie Tjibaou Cultural
Centre**
Rue des Accords de Matignon,
Tina, BP 378-98845 Nouméa
Tel +687 41 45 45

064 ☐ CUL 1998

The scheme, incorporating
open-air terraces and clearings
for performance and exhibition,
is based on the tapering-rib
huts of the Kanak people
indigenous to New Caledonia.
The traditional palm sapling is
replaced by laminated iroko,
which will weather similarly.

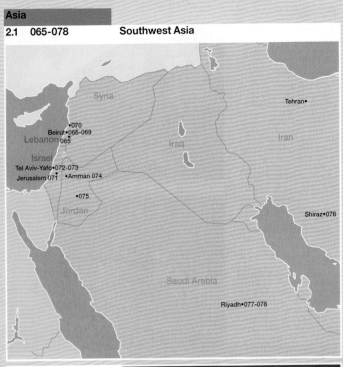

Syria

Tehran•

•070
Beirut•066–069
Lebanon 065

Iran

Israel

Iraq

Tel Aviv-Yafo•072–073
Jerusalem 071   •Amman 074

•075

Jordan

Shiraz•076

Saudi Arabia

Riyadh•077–078

Simone Kosremelli

Nancy's Farm
Maasser ech Chouf

065 ■ RES 2002

A stone barrel-vaulted living area – reminiscent of shepherds' shelters – separates a southern living block from a northern service area incorporating a large kitchen for the preparation of organic produce. Stairs either side of a pergola lead to the roof, which affords stunning Mediterranean views.

Bernard Khoury Architects

B018 Nightclub
Lot 317, Quarantaine, Beirut
Tel +961 1 580 018

066 ☐ COM 1998

Ceding the ground plane of this troubled city to history, Khoury's jazz club burrows beneath the site of a 1976 massacre to offer a subversive underground experience, including anthropomorphic bar-stools and a seating console doubling as a table to dance on. Rich mahogany and the colour red are everywhere.

Bernard Khoury Architects

Yabani
Lot 21, Damascus Road, Beirut
Tel +961 1 211 113

067 ☐ COM 2002

Another subterranean experience from Khoury, this Japanese restaurant and music club signals its street presence only with an 18 metre high glass-floored, aluminium-clad drum. This turret houses a reception-room elevator, which transports guests down to a nether realm of unseen pleasures and intoxications.

Bernard Khoury Architects

Centrale
Lot 615, Saint Maron, Beirut
Tel +961 1 575 858

068 ☐ COM 2001

The contemporary, in this conversion of a historic building in Beirut, consumes the new – with a carefully crafted space-age capsule straddling a new rooftop bar, and the war-ravaged historic fabric clad externally with steel mesh. An ominously private meeting room contrasts with the intimacy of the bar.

Raed Abillama Architects

Apartment Building AWB 654
Beirut

069 ■ RES 1999

Two cluster blocks of eight-storey accommodation are shoehorned into a narrow irregular urban site – the angles generated by their clash being absorbed into the circulation zones – and set back at the rear to allow sunlight to reach the ground floor. Large balconies permit the extension of dining and living spaces.

Raed Abillama Architects

House ZEK 17
Dbayeh

070 ■ RES 2003

Carved out of a mortar-damaged stone villa, this project adds a contemporary block for the children of the family, linked to the old house by a dematerialized living zone that encompasses an interior courtyard and front porch. A new circulation core and master and guest bedrooms occupy the original house.

Guggenheim Bloch Architects

The International School for Holocaust Studies
Yad Vashem, Jerusalem 91034
Tel +972 2 644 3400

071 □ CUL 2000

Accessed via a sunken pillared grotto, this stone- and glass-clad reconciliation centre comprises classrooms and research spaces disposed along a central axis. It terminates in a stepped seating court, and a cross-axis orientated towards the Judea mountains.

Mario Botta

**Cymbalista Synagogue &
Jewish Heritage Centre**
University Campus, Tel Aviv
University, Tel Aviv 69978
Tel +972 3 640 8020

072 ☐ REL 1998

Two brick towers – beginning
as square-planned and
transforming into drums –
dominate this 'house of
assembly'. The visitor reaches
either of the twin 'sacred or
'secular' auditoria beneath them
via a richly finished, yet
uncluttered, lobby.

Zvi Hecker

Palmach Museum of History
10 Levanon Street, Ramat-Aviv,
Tel Aviv 61650
Tel +972 3 643 6393

073 ☐ CUL 2002

Notions of upheaval and
resistance reminiscent of the
underground Israeli-nationalist
Palmach movement are boldly
represented in the museum's
angular forms. An auditorium,
youth centre and cafeteria are
housed within their colliding
concrete and limestone wall
planes.

Sahel Al-Hiyari

**Consultation Space for a
Psychologist**
Amman

074 ■ COM 2000

Light became paramount in
the renovation of this 1920s
house, as the client required
adjustable windows, shutters
and light fixtures to provide
different spaces for individual
clients. Internal sliding panels
allow for flexibility of space
contrasting with permanent
fixtures carved from local stone.

Sahel Al-Hiyari

Bilbeisi House
Jordan Valley

075 ■ RES 1999

The courtyard and main living areas of this residence are linked visually, spatially and structurally in a fusion unusual in this type of building – an effect extended by the external upper-floor living room, with its monumental square pillars. The house combines 'rusticity' with a sophisticated handling of space.

Mehrdad Iravanian

House No. 3
Shiraz

076 ■ RES 2002

The exterior surfaces of this house are interrupted by its expressed services – the walls are layered with louvres, mesh and brackets on which to stack firewood – which erupt from the otherwise carefully controlled volumes. Internally, 'ordinary' elements such as unmilled trees and broken stone are used in an extraordinary manner.

Foster and Partners

Al Faisaliah Centre
King Fahad Road, Olaya,
Riyadh 11491
Tel +966 1 273 2000

077 □ COM 2000

Saudi Arabia's first skyscraper, the 267 metre high 'Star Dome' tapers from a square footprint enclosing an octagonal core, to a lantern apex with stainless-steel finial and a golden glass sphere housing the country's highest restaurant. Its base houses a luxury hotel and a banqueting hall.

Asia

Moriyama & Teshima Architects

National Museum of Saudi Arabia
King Abdul-Aziz Historical
Centre, Riyadh 11481
Tel +966 1 402 9500

078 ☐ CUL 1999

Built to mark the centenary of
Saudi unification, this museum
draws on the Najdi building
tradition of massive adobe walls
and passive environmental-
control devices such as arcades
and courtyards. The design
culminates in a limestone
entrance wall.

2.2 079-096 Central and South Asia

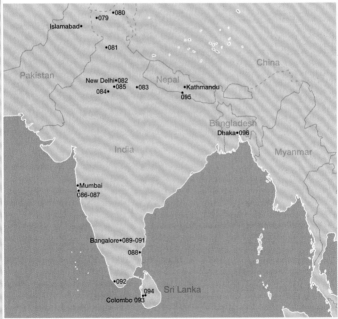

Ahed + Azem Partnership

**Professional Development
Centre**
Konodass Gilgit, Northern Areas
Tel +92 57 05811

079 ◼ EDU 2000

Organized as a single building
that turns to follow the contours
of its 5-hectare mountainside
site, there are classrooms to the
north, while the south facade is
lined with laboratories and
seminar rooms. Interiors are
punctuated by light wells, a
series of double-height spaces
and splashes of colour.

Arup Associates and Arup
Group

Druk White Lotus School
Shey, Ladakh 194101, Jammu
and Kashmir
Tel +91 19 822 672 55

080 ☐ EDU 2003

Located in the cold Himalayan
desert, this educational facility
is arranged around courtyards –
to maximize sunlight – as part
of a traditional nine-square
Buddhist *mandala* layout. Grey
stone and oiled wooden posts
and beams provide a
complementary richness.

Sameep Padora and Associates

Ambassador Resort
T P S 94, Chadiyari, Manali
175131, Himachel Pradesh
Tel +91 19 022 522 35

081 ☐ TOU 2003

The renovation of this hotel
unifies its disparate elements by
playing with geometric shapes
and spaces. The threat of
earthquakes is dealt with by
incorporating horizontal timber
strips in the masonry walls as a
flexible buffer. Balconies tucked
under the roof pitch overlook a
mountainous panorama.

Raj Rewal

Parliament Library
Pt Pant Marg, New Delhi 110001,
Dehli
Tel +91 11 230 341 82

082 ✎ GOV 2002

Recalling ancient Indian
temples and palaces, the
library organizes activities into
symmetrical polygonal blocks
and skylit atria. The lower floors
utilize a structural grid of
prefabricated concrete coffers,
while the upper areas are
covered by shallow domes
supported on steel lattices.

Raj Rewal

Gas Training Institute
24, Sector 16a, Noida 201301,
Uttar Pradesh
Tel +95 12 025 153 53

083 ☐ EDU 1998

Classrooms, laboratories, an
auditorium, a canteen, an
industrial workshop and even
a hostel for visiting students are
all grouped around a series of
interlinked landscaped
courtyards. The facades feature
Rewal's trademark sandstone
lattice, or *jali* – derived from
historic Rajasthani residences.

The Barefoot Architects

Barefoot College
Tilonia Village, via Madanganj,
Ajmer 305816, Rajasthan
Tel +91 14 632 882 05

084 ☐ EDU 1998

Founded in 1972, the Barefoot
College aims to provide a
sustainable alternative to India's
urban contractor system, and
has hand-built its own premises
using locally available materials
and scrap metal. In addition,
students at the college have
built up to 250 mud-brick
shelters in surrounding villages.

The Architecture Alliance

Children's Retreat
Damdama Lake Drive,
PO Damdama, Sohna, Haryana
Tel +91 44 626 0097

085 ✆ PUB 1999

Seeming to grow out of the
rocky terrain, this centre for
engaging children with nature
uses strong primary forms
which are clustered in naturally
formed 'bowls'. Dormitories,
dining and teaching facilities
and an amphitheatre all follow
the contours of the land.

Rahul J Mehrotra

Shanti
Jirad, Alibag, Maharashtra

086 ▮ RES 1998

A 'weekend house' set in the
hilly Mumbai hinterland, this
dwelling uses sloping roofs
of iron sheets – a continuation
of 'frontier' and nomadic
antecedents – supported by
and fastened to the floors and
walls. Guest accommodation is
divided from the main house by
a courtyard, to which both may
be opened up.

Rahul J Mehrotra

House for a Film Maker
Kihim, Alibag, Maharashtra

087 ▮ RES 2001

The house's services fill a
central thick wall – running
between a living room with
forest views and a private realm,
whose bedrooms overlook a
garden. The wall is surmounted
by convex surfaces of mirror-
like metal cladding on a steel
frame. Internally, cane mats and
wooden surfaces offset this
industrial aesthetic.

Anupama Kundoo

Wall House
Petite Ferme, Auroville 605101,
Tamil Nadu
Tel +91 41 326 224 33

088 ⌀ RES 1999

A walled atrium marks the
entrance to this house, dividing
a narrow block containing
private areas from a guest wing
with a rooftop bathing pool,
reached by a bridge which
spans the entrance. Handmade
bricks contrast with smooth
concrete and steel-framed
windows.

Chandavarkar & Thacker

**The NS Raghavan Centre for
Entrepreneurial Learning**
Bannerghatta Road, Bangalore
560076, Karnataka
Tel +91 80 265 824 50

089 ⌀ COM 2002

This complex of meeting
rooms and conference facilities
is partially buried while allowing
visitors to walk over virtually
the whole building. Extending
Balkrishna Doshi's iconic
Institute of Management, it
continues the former's extensive
use of local granite.

Mathew & Ghosh Architects

Benjamin House
Srinivagilu Extension 1st Cross,
Viveknagar, Bangalore 560047,
Karnataka

090 ▯ RES 2001

The dwelling combines a
double-storey services block,
a single-storey living block and
a dynamic entrance promenade
flanked by a yellow plane that
becomes a partition inside the
house. The sloping roof slab of
its verandah appears to be
anchored to its fin-like pillars
rather than supported by them.

Mathew & Ghosh Architects

Bethel Baptist Church
29 4th Main Road Ashwini
Layout, Ejipura, Bangalore
560047, Karnataka
Tel +91 80 569 966 74

091　✆ REL 2002

Churchgoers enter on a
diagonal axis extending the
street into the site, from which
the gathering hall opens out
through large pivoting doors.
From beneath a suspended
mezzanine, they encounter
a dramatic altar set against
freestanding white walls.

Laurie Baker

Nav Yatra
Nooliyode, Vilappilsala,
Trivandrum 695573, Kerala
kaith@navyatra.org

092　✆ RES 2003

This community for people
with intellectual disabilities
comprises seven buildings
whose curving brick forms and
moulded roofs are designed to
ensure maximum circulation of
air and heat. At high level, a cut-
away roof forms a sheltered
terrace, with air vents doubling
as seats.

Madhura Prematilleke

Royal Bakery
202 Galle Road, Wellawatte,
Colombo 00600
Tel +94 1125 88 476

093　☐ COM 2000

This frontage of steel
scaffolding, signage and
sunshades protects the interior
of the ground-floor bakery and
preserves the aura of the old.
Once a quiet Sri Lankan *kad*, or
facade-less shop entirely open
to the street, the bakery is now
increasingly menaced by traffic
on the congested Galle Road.

Bernard Gomez

Sri Jayewardenepura Kotte House
Pahalawela Road, Kotte,
Colombo, 10100

094 ◻ RES 1999

The visitor's eye is drawn from the entrance to the central courtyard and the garden beyond, while the family rooms are located on the first floor. These upper rooms overlook the varied open spaces of this timber-framed modern 'manor house'.

Tadao Ando Architect & Associates

Siddhartha Children and Women's Hospital
Butwal

095 ◼ PUB 1998

A public/private health facility, consisting of exposed brick forms: a tower denotes civic purpose, parallel blocks contain the wards, and a perpendicular block houses consulting rooms. Colonnades and ample openings, in turn, protect the interiors from the hot sun.

URBANA

AS Residence
3/12 Block E, Lalmatia, Dhaka 1207, Dhaka
Tel +88 2 967 1500

096 ◻ RES 2002

Based on the concept of the Char Bagh, or enclosed four-part Mughal garden, this six-storey block devotes its spaces – largely open to the elements – to sitting, eating, sleeping and notions of spirituality. It also uses recycled materials: brick, teak, glass, copper, concrete, stainless steel and porcelain.

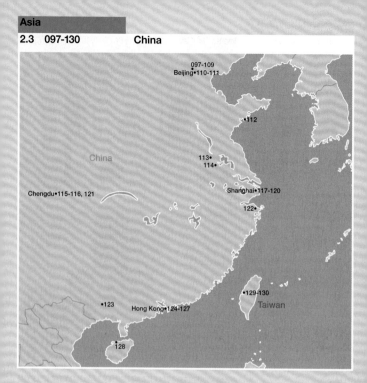

097-109
Beijing•110-111

•112

China

113•
114•

Chengdu•115-116, 121

Shanghai•117-120

122•

•129-130

•123

Hong Kong•124-127

Taiwan

•128

Commune by the Great Wall 097-109

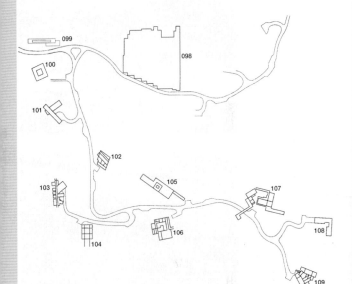

Zhang Xin

Commune by the Great Wall
Shifosi Village, Badaling,
Yanqing, Beijing 102102
Tel +86 10 8118 1888

097 ✎ RES 2002

In the shadow of China's Great
Wall, this private collection of
contemporary architecture
brings together 12 Asian
architects to provide dwellings
and a clubhouse for the client-
developer Zhang Xin. She was
awarded a special prize by the
2002 Venice Biennale as a
patron of architectural works.

Seung H-Sang

Commune by the Great Wall, Club House
Shifosi Village, Badaling, Yanqing, Beijing 102102
Tel +86 10 8118 1888

098   📡 PUB 2002

This Cor-ten steel-clad complex – comprising swimming pool, gallery, grocery store and management centre – uses materials and openness to connect to its site. Fountains, timber decks and reflecting pools surround the five long rectangular structures.

Gary Chang

Commune by the Great Wall, Suitcase House
Shifosi Village, Badaling, Yanqing, Beijing 102102
Tel +86 10 8118 1888

099   📡 RES 2002

The *piano nobile* of this dwelling is a long volume which, using mobile elements, can transform itself from a single room into a sequence of separate domestic spaces. Wrapped inside and out in timber cladding, it has many entrances – each with equal status.

Shigeru Ban

Commune by the Great Wall, Furniture House
Shifosi Village, Badaling, Yanqing, Beijing 102102
Tel +86 10 8118 1888

100   📡 RES 2002

A form of plywood, using a laminate of woven bamboo strips, has been adapted to form the framing system for this square courtyard dwelling. Cupboards and wall panels are strung together to create rooms and storage spaces.

Cui Kai

**Commune by the Great Wall,
See and Seen House**
Shifosi Village, Badaling,
Yanqing, Beijing 102102
Tel +86 10 8118 1888

101 ✆ RES 2002

The lower block of this two-part
residence is sunken, and, with
its planted roof, appears to
crouch in a thicket – while the
upper, bedroom wing is raised
on stilts to allow unobstructed
views. Bedrooms and
bathrooms can be reconfigured
to suit large or small groups.

Rocco Design Limited

**Commune by the Great Wall,
Distorted Courtyard House**
Shifosi Village, Badaling,
Yanqing, Beijing 102102
Tel +86 10 8118 1888

102 ✆ RES 2002

In this version of a traditional
courtyard house, a multi-
coloured glazed block of living
and dining areas sits askew
upon a white masonry base
containing private areas and
enclosing a planted court. A
service block forms a backbone
to this provocative composition.

Chien Hsueh-Yi

**Commune by the Great Wall,
Airport House**
Shifosi Village, Badaling,
Yanqing, Beijing 102102
Tel +86 10 8118 1888

103 ✆ RES 2002

Two monumental blade walls,
constructed from the same
stone as the nearby Great Wall,
define a narrow, double-height,
top-lit gallery, off which are the
living spaces. Those to the front
facade form three pavilions,
jutting out at different angles,
supported on concrete *piloti*.

Antonio Ochoa-Piccardo

**Commune by the Great Wall,
Cantilever House**
Shifosi Village, Badaling,
Yanqing, Beijing 102102
Tel +86 10 8118 1888

104　✎ RES 2002

Emerging like a giant, earth-
coloured boulder from its
mountainside setting, this
house draws visitors inside via
a tunnel beneath its mouth-like
balcony. Lower-level living and
sleeping areas lead into an
ascending sequence of open
and enclosed terraces.

Kengo Kuma & Associates

**Commune by the Great Wall,
Bamboo Wall House**
Shifosi Village, Badaling,
Yanqing, Beijing 102102
Tel +86 10 8118 1888

105　✎ RES 2002

Inspired by the way the Great
Wall absorbs the topography,
this house allows its site to flow
around and underneath it. Its
all-over bamboo flooring,
cladding and shutters, beneath
an emphatic oversailing roof
plane, lend the dwelling
delicacy and roughness.

Kanika R'kul

**Commune by the Great Wall,
The Shared House**
Shifosi Village, Badaling,
Yanqing, Beijing 102102
Tel +86 10 8118 1888

106　✎ RES 2002

Every space in this white-
rendered weekend villa has
direct access to decks or
terraces, including a large T-
shaped timber deck on the roof.
The dwelling thus unites
everyday domestic functions
with a keen sense of nature and
the outdoors.

Asia

Tan Kay-Ngee

**Commune by the Great Wall,
The Twins**
Shifosi Village, Badaling,
Yanqing, Beijing 102102
Tel +86 10 8118 1888

107 ✏ RES 2002

Two small L-shaped pavilions
oriented to command the best
views of the forest and Great
Wall, The Twins consists of a
single-storey block housing
kitchen and dining space and
a taller structure with double-
height living room and large
bedroom suites.

Nobuaki Furuya

**Commune by the Great Wall,
Forest House**
Shifosi Village, Badaling,
Yanqing, Beijing 102102
Tel +86 10 8118 1888

108 ✏ RES 2002

This house uses many devices
to connect to its surroundings:
a soft-seating area overlooks
the forest via a deck, and a
dining room has diners facing
outwards. A variation of a
traditional Chinese *kang* (a
balcony-bed) forms an indoor
terrace with folding doors.

Atelier Feichang Jianzhu

**Commune by the Great Wall,
Split House**
Shifosi Village, Badaling,
Yanqing, Beijing 102102
Tel +86 10 8118 1888

109 ✏ RES 2002

The mountainside forms a
narrow outdoor living area and
a creek flows through the glass-
floored entrance of this
ecological dwelling. The house
employs traditional rammed-
earth walls in laminated
plywood frames for its naturally
insulating outer skin.

Ai Wei Wei

Studio for an Artist
Beijing Province

110 ■ CUL 1999

This T-shaped house for an artist couple creates an effortless proximity between the ground-floor living/studio and upper-level study/bedroom areas. Constructed by local artisans in only 100 days, the house is a humble reminder that the purpose of architecture is to accommodate life, not vice versa.

Chang Yung-Ho

Villa Shan Yu Jian
Beijing Province

111 ■ RES 1998

Its stepping floor levels enable this weekend villa to mark out separate functional areas and to disturb its sloping farmland site as little as possible – all below a gently sloping roof punctured by three glass-cube guest rooms, which at night appear as three bright eyes. Facade-length window strips allow control of internal ventilation.

Atelier Feichang Jianzhu

International Conference Centre, Peking University
4 Lao Shan Lu, Lao Shan,
Qingdao 266000, Shandong
Tel +86 532 883 1188

112 ☐ EDU 2001

Rising from the steep slope of its oceanfront site, this linear series of stark, concrete-and-translucent-glass conference facilities steps up to a lookout platform. Five remodelled existing villas are now a hotel, their roofs made accessible as viewing terraces.

MADA s.p.a.m.

Father's House in Jade Mountain

Xi'an, Lantian, Shaanxi

113 ▮ RES 2003

Villagers spent two years collecting and grading stones from the nearby riverbed to fill the concrete-framed walls surrounding this two-storey residence situated in an L-shaped walled garden. The living areas have full-height windows with painted timber shutters, and the bedrooms overlook the valley.

Amateur

Library of Wenzheng College, Suzhou University

188 Yue Hu Road, Suzhou 215006, Anhui
Tel +86 512 6655 3161

114 ☐ EDU 2000

Following the Suzhou Garden tradition – in which people escape amongst elements of 'nature in a nutshell' whilst still in the city – four pavilions are suspended above a lake. These blocks slice the main structure at varying angles, contrasting with the placid water body

Jiakun Architects & Associates

He Duoling Studio

Shi Ting Village, Xipu, Pixian, Chengdu, Sichuan
Tel +86 28 8784 8249

115 ✆ CUL 1999

Referring in its form both to the ancient Chinese seal and, with its almost blind central patio, to the native 'sky-well' building type, this cubic structure is designed to bring exterior views to the inhabitant in an extremely controlled way. It orchestrates 'windows within windows' to achieve its effect.

Asia

China

Jiakun Architects & Associates

Lu-Ye-Yuan Stone Sculpture Art Museum
Yun Qiao Village, Xinmin, Pixian 611732, Sichuan
Tel +86 28 8792 6835

116 ✆ CUL 2002

The museum draws the visitor up via an entrance ramp – only to have them descend again into the building, where different lighting methods highlight the different areas. The journey into these concrete volumes allows the visitor to enter a pseudo-religious 'other world'.

Foster and Partners

Jiushi Corporation Headquarters
28 Zhong Shan Nan Road, Shanghai 200010

117 ▮ COM 2000

Foster's first project on the Chinese mainland is a 40-storey tower whose concrete core sits back from the Huangpu River to allow flexible, uninterrupted curved floor-plates to form terraces at three points. At the top is a six-storey winter garden.

Jean-Marie Charpentier

Grand Theatre of Shanghai
300 Renmin Boulevard, Shanghai 200003
Tel +86 21 6372 8701

118 ☐ CUL 1998

Based on a square, which in Chinese tradition represents the earth, this double-stage theatre and arts complex is roofed with a vast, upturned circular segment, symbolizing the sky. This gigantic canopy is held above a pillared entrance hall, whose glazed facades give a spectacular view of the city.

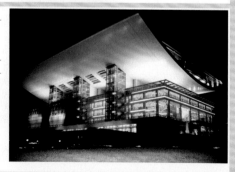

Skidmore, Owings & Merrill

Jin Mao Tower
88 Century Boulevard, Pudong,
Shanghai 200121
Tel +86 21 5047 6688

119 ☐ COM 1999

An 88-storey gothic needle with
overtones of pagodas, this
tower contains 50 office floors;
a Hyatt Regency hotel with
atrium and rooftop observation
point occupy the next 37 floors.
Sited amidst a theme park, it
could be seen as an exhibit
commemorating the grandeur
of the historical skyscraper.

Paul Andreu

**Shanghai-Pudong
International Airport**
Pudong New Area, Shanghai
201202
Tel +86 21 6834 1000

120 ☐ TRA 1999

Sited on reclaimed tideland, this
transport hub is fronted by a
pond reflecting air and ground
traffic – the latter organized by a
tree-filled square that structures
the flow of cars and trains.
Interior spaces follow on from
each other below a dynamic,
billowing roof structure.

Jiakun Architects & Associates

Red Era Entertainment Centre
30 Renmin Nan Road, Chengdu
610041, Sichuan
Tel +86 28 8555 8338

121 ☐ REC 2001

Located at the junction of two
busy roads, the functional block
of the Red Era makes an
immediate impact, with its full-
height skin of Persian blinds –
imposed in a redesign, part-way
through construction. These
give glittering glimpses of
internal life through carefully
placed windows.

Asia   China

MADA s.p.a.m.

**Library for Zhejiang
University, Ningbo Campus**
1 Xianhu South Road,
Ningzhou, Ningbo 315100
Tel +86 574 8822 9040

122 ☐ EDU 2002

Located at the centre of the
campus, the library subverts its
heroic form and position with
bright colours, Corbusian
skylights and window strips and
recesses. Inside, however, the
full-height atrium surrounded by
stacks and study-tables
reasserts the monumentality.

Denton Corker Marshall

Nanning Gateway
Inner City Freeway, Nanning,
Guangxi

123 ☐ INF 2002

To promote the image of a
'green' city, the architects
positioned a giant red steel
flower-like structure on either
side of Nanning's approach
road. One 'bloom' deconstructs
into a series of individual petals
as drivers crest the hill. This
device transforms the gateway
from a static to a dynamic
experience.

Foster and Partners

**Chep Lap Kok, Hong Kong
International Airport**
Lantau, Hong Kong
Tel +852 2188 7111

124 ☐ TRA 1998

A hilly island was levelled from
100 to seven metres high, and
expanded fourfold to
accommodate this terminal,
spreading out along a *feng shui*-
influenced Y-shaped plan. An
integral transport hub connects
its 38 boarding gates to a high-
speed rail and road corridor into
the city.

Denton Corker Marshall

141–149 Thomson Road
141–149 Thomson Road,
Wanchai, Hong Kong

125 ☐ COM 2002

From street level this skyscraper appears to consist of two equally high needle towers supported by a Kahnian 'servant' core; in fact the two 8-metre-square towers are different heights. The helix-like fenestration pattern is another surprise, making its slenderness appear almost organic.

Arquitectonica

Festival Walk
80 Tat Chee Avenue, Kowloon Tong, Hong Kong
Tel +852 2844 2200

126 ☐ COM 1998

This mall comprises a series of strata, with projecting volumes and louvred textures, while inside lie two large atria, 'The Glacier' which contains an ice rink, and 'The Canyon'. These themed spaces are connected by a third, 'The River', floored in blue terrazzo.

Arquitectonica

Cyberport
100 Cyberport Road, Telegraph Bay, Hong Kong
Tel +852 2514 3990

127 ✆ COM 2003

This 25-hectare complex contains meeting rooms, multimedia laboratories, a cyber library, fitness centre, cafés, lounges, bars and a retail-and-entertainment 'Cyber Centre'. The tonally varied dark glass facades soften to timber flooring and bold red walls inside.

Rocco Design Limited

Boao Canal Village
Boao, Hainan Province
Tel +86 10 6567 3333

128 ☐ RES 2002

Inspired by southern Chinese
river settlements, which feature
in seventh-century Tang-era
poetry, this development of 115
holiday villas (each with its own
dock and a waterfront view) is
organized around a newly
extended river and canal
system. Crisp white walls and
timber shutters here ensure a
contemporary aesthetic.

JM Lin Architect/The Observer
Design Group

Min Ho Junior High School
Chung Shin Lane 116, Min Ho,
Shui Li, Nant'ou 553
Tel +886 49 27 41138

129 ☐ EDU 2001

The domestic intimacy of the
nearby Elementary School is
here replaced with a more
mature metal-roofed 'academic
street', along which lie six
classroom blocks. A library
capped with a conical roof also
signifies its higher academic
status.

JM Lin Architect/The Observer
Design Group

Min Ho Elementary School
Chung Shin Lane 14, Min Ho,
Shui Li, Nant'ou 553
Tel +886 49 27 41140

130 ☐ EDU 2001

This school for boarders and
day students from rural
communities comprises six
classrooms, each with a steel-
and-timber-latticed pyramidal
lantern that can be raised for
ventilation on hot days, and a
shaded terrace for outdoor
classes.

North Korea

151
Seoul •131-138
•140-141
•148-149
142

South Korea

•144-145

•143   146-147•

150•
•139

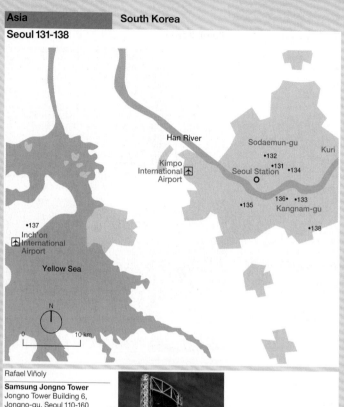

Han River

Sodaemun-gu

Kuri

Kimpo
International
Airport

•132

•131
•134

Seoul Station
O

•135

136• •133
Kangnam-gu

•137

Inch'on
International
Airport

•138

Yellow Sea

N

0   10 km

Rafael Viñoly

Samsung Jongno Tower
Jongno Tower Building 6,
Jongno-gu, Seoul 110-160
Tel +82 201 229 6067

131 ☐ COM 1999

The design is in three elements:
a two-level restaurant and
night-club 60 storeys above a
busy road junction; a giant
lower-level cornice extending
above a public plaza; and,
above the latter, a separate
volume accommodating offices.
Viñoly here tripled the height of
a part-constructed project.

Archium

Kim Ok-gil Memorial Hall
Daesin-dong 92, Sodaemun-gu,
Seoul 120-160
Tel +82 2 392 2622/3

132 ☐ REL 1998

Commissioned as a memorial
to Dr Kim Ok-gil, a leader of
the Korean modernization
movement, this series of
stepped rectangular panels fits
its narrow site and presents
contrasting facades of masonry
and glass. This configuration
gives an impression of space
lightly held in by its architecture.

Kim Jong Kyu

CAIS Gallery
Chungdam-dong 99-5,
Gangnam-gu, Seoul 135-100
Tel +82 2 511 0658

133 ☐ CUL 2001

A four-storey steel-plate wall
takes up the angled rear
geometry of this city-centre site.
Attached is a concrete box
containing the exhibition
spaces, hovering above
cylindrical columns to form a
stepped public gathering space.
The materials give the building a
hard-edged urban feel.

Seung H-Sang

Welcomm City
Jangchung-dong 190-10,
Jung-gu, Seoul 100-855
Tel +82 2 6363 4636

134 ☐ COM 2000

Comprising four Cor-ten steel
covered boxes – one for each of
the company's departments –
this headquarters for a Seoul
advertising agency uses its
geometry to bring sunlight and
ventilation to the rear of the
complex. The concrete podium
is used for public events and
exhibitions.

Jae Yong Lim

Dongbu Church
Bongchon-dong 1668-121,
Gwanak-gu, Seoul 151-050
Tel +82 2 877 0098

---

135 ☐ REL 2001

Hemmed in amidst dense
row houses on narrow curving
streets, this worship space
overcomes an additional site
problem – a 3 metre level-drop –
by introducing a sloping plane
from the entrance onwards. It
also utilizes local red brick and
white granite to match the
surrounding vernacular.

Hak Sik Son

OPUS Concert Hall Building
Shinsa-dong 566-31, Kangnam-
gu, Seoul 135-891
Tel +82 2 543 2027

---

136 ☐ ✒ CUL 1998

An L-shaped concrete-framed
structure with glass curtain
walls shielded by curved and
angular upper planes of
corrugated metal, this 150-seat
underground concert hall and
graphic design studio for a
recording-industry company
displays an exuberance that
belies its relatively small size.

Terry Farrell & Partners

**Transportation Centre,
Inch'on International Airport**
2850 Unseo-dong, Jung-gu,
Seoul 400-700
Tel +82 1 577 2600

---

137 ☐ TRA 2002

Symbolizing native culture and
flight, the steel-portal-truss roof
structure of this three-rail-
network interchange resembles
a crane in flight – a sacred bird
to the Korean people. Built on a
reclaimed island, it is a point of
orientation for the New Seoul
International Airport complex.

Kohn Pedersen Fox Associates

Dongbu Financial Centre
Daechi-dong 891-10, Kangnam-
gu, Seoul 135-523
Tel +82 2 3484 2368

138 □ COM 2002

With a 'layering' design concept
based on the traditional Korean
handicraft *shik-tak-bo*, in which
pieces of cloth are randomly
patched together, this 35-storey
tower comprises a sculptural
series of undulating diagonal
curtain walls. An entrance-level
bridge crosses a sunken
garden, flanked by a glass wall.

Space Group Architects

Kwangju World Cup Stadium
423-2 Pungam-dong, Kwangju,
Cholla-namdo 502-831
Tel +82 62 604 2002

139 □ SPO 2001

A facility that allows 43,000
spectators to exit in only six
minutes, and whose small
central area permitted World
Cup viewers the closest
possible view of the pitch, this
circular stadium is part of plans
to develop Kwangju. It is also
designed to host cultural and
trade-fair events.

Archium

Metallic House
Yanju-gun, Kyonggi-do

140 ■ RES 1999

Supported off its rocky site
on *piloti*, this steel-framed
residence – with its floating
roof above clerestory glazing –
comprises living/dining and
bedroom wings linked by a
timber-decked terrace, defined
by framing elements. Living
areas are extensively glazed,
while rear rooms facing a
nearby hill are clad in copper.

Lee Gangho

Karico Headquarters
Poil-dong 487, Euwang-city
Kyonggi-do 437-703
Tel +82 31 420 3114

141 ☐ COM 2001

The structure of this seven-storey headquarters – placed on axis to a new landscaped plaza – is of reinforced concrete, used sculpturally in places, with glass bands filling the horizontal lines in its facades. Around its outskirts, apartments and schools form the fringes of this large, urbanistic development.

Kim Jong Kyu + MARU

Dementia Clinic
Kwansan-dong 10, Doukyang-gu, Kyonggi-do 412-470
Tel +82 31 962 8360

142 ☐❚✎ PUB 1998

This clinic provides treatment and service areas on two levels articulated as distinct horizontal bands. A base of sliding glass and Cor-ten panels, and solid concrete, accommodates site level-changes; while an upper band has hinged Cor-ten shutters to ventilate the patient rooms.

Seung H-Sang

Dong Kwang Methodist Church
Geumkang-dong 418-1, 419-1, Iksan-si, Cholla-bukto 570-150
Tel +82 63 855 8158

143 ☐ REL 2002

A triangular chapel, sloping-sided tower and community hall enclose a grassed court and public square – all clad in Cor-ten steel on a base of natural stones embedded in concrete putty. The stones have been brought to the site by members of the congregation.

Seung H-Sang

Su Baek Dang
Keumnan-ri 20-3, Hwado-eup,
Namyangju-si, Kyonggi-do
472-842

144 ◾ RES 1998

Comprising 12 rooms, both internal and external, this predominantly white-walled residence for a businessman and his artist wife spreads horizontally along its mountainous site. 'Open room', 'big room' and 'special room' alternate with 'stone court', 'water court' and 'wood deck'.

Seung H-Sang

Dong Heon
Keumnan-ri 20-3, Hwado-eup,
Namyangju-si, Kyonggi-do
472-842

145 ◾ RES 2000

A painting studio in the grounds of Su Baek Dang, this stilted pavilion, clad in rough red Cor-ten steel, twists around existing Paulownia trees and provides restricted slit-window views of the nearby mountains. It sharply contrasts, in both materials and outlook, with its parent-dwelling by the same architect.

John Friedman Alice Kimm Architects

Adonis Golf Club Clubhouse
Maegok-ri san 1, Yangsan-si,
Kyongsang-namdo 626-840
Tel +82 55 371 3500

146 ☐ REC 1999

Anchored by its stone base, this clubhouse angles its roofs and glazing to the sky, while an internal art-gallery/circulation spine connects the scheme's limestone, lead-coated and copper-clad volumes. Three small 'tee houses', are scattered about the golf course.

John Friedman Alice Kimm
Architects

**Public Swimming Pool and
Visitor Centre**
Ok-dong 146-1, Nam-gu,
Ulsan-si, Ulsan 680-080
Tel +82 52 271 8818

147 ☐ SPO 2002

Bordering a large national
forest, the facilities are grouped
under curving roof planes –
the highest belonging to the
swimming pool with an
opaquely glazed facade.
Spaces open out through clear
glazing.

Byoungsoo Cho

Pine Courtyard House
Yongin, Kyonggi-do

148 ■ RES 1998

To counter the high-density
'filing cabinets' of so many
urban residential schemes, this
dwelling is organized around a
central *madang*, or courtyard,
on to which the apartments
open via their timber-screened
private balconies. An insulating
concrete outer wall forms a
sculptural screen and entrance
gateway to the street.

Keunwoo Cheon

Café en Rose
Seojong-myun 445,
Yangp'yong, Kyonggi-do
Tel +82 31 774 6398

149 ☐ COM 1998

Raised on stilts off its riverside
site, this irregular L-shaped café
incorporates trees growing
through holes in its external
timber decking, and a 30 metre
long curving red H-beam. This
striking element, which projects
over the deck area, appears
supported on a single white
tilted terrace column.

Asia

Kim Jong Kyu + MARU with Joh
Sung Yong

Uijae Museum of Korean Art
Unlim-dong 85-1, Kwangju,
Cholla-namdo 501-833
Tel +82 62 222 2034

150 □ CUL 2001

Commemorating the artist
Heo Baek-ryeon, also known
as Uijae, this museum deals in
contrasts: between its hall's
traditional exposed timber roof
and contemporary translucent
facade panels. It is set in the
exact spot where the artist
created his works.

Jae Yong Lim

Ilsan Residence 5
Madu-dong 937-1, Ilsan-gu,
Kyonggi-do, 411-350
Tel +82 31 904 9007

151 □ RES 2003

A provocative suburban house
which derives its complex
geometry from twisting its main
elements – a masonry boundary
wall that defines two external
courtyards, and a U-shaped
plan – against each other as it
rises. This twisting is expressed
on the exterior with cantilevered
forms and changes in material.

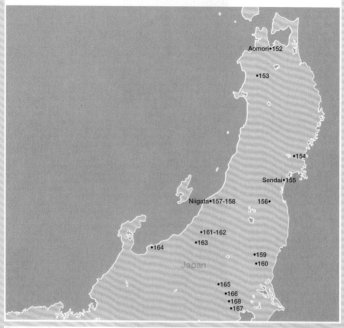

Aomori•152

•153

•154

Sendai•155

Niigata•157-158   156•

•161-162
•163

•164   *Japan*   •159
•160

•165
•166
•168
•167

Tadao Ando Architect &
Associates

**Aomori Contemporary Art
Centre**
152-6 Goshizawa, Yamazaki,
Aomori 030-0134
Tel +81 17 764 5200

152   □ CUL 2001

The rectangular Creativity and
Accommodation blocks and
the horseshoe-shaped Display
building, with its gallery and
outdoor stage, sit below steel-
framed reinforced concrete flat
roofs, designed to render the
low-lying centre invisible.

Shigeru Ban

Imai Hospital Daycare Centre
Odate, Akita

153 ■ PUB 2001

A tunnel-like structure is animated by dappled sunlight through a series of lightweight roof skins: an outer layer of steel and polycarbonate sheeting, a laminated-timber-band vault to form the inner skin, and a space frame connecting the two. The steeply pitched outer roof is designed to avoid snow build-up.

Kazuhiro Kojima and Mitsumasa Sampei/C+A Architects

Hakuou High School
184 Minami-tononishi, Wakayanagi, Miyagi 989-5502

154 ❚ EDU 1998

This two-storey complex gathers functions as diverse as classrooms and a sports court with bicycle park above a swimming pool, under one roof layout. The roof's pre-cast, pre-stressed concrete construction allows an adaptable interior, free of structural walls.

Toyo Ito & Associates

Sendai Mediathèque
2–1 Kasuga-machi, Sendai, Miyagi 980-0821
Tel +81 22 261 1585

155 ☐ CUL 2001

Seven steel floor decks are stacked on 13 hollow columns, which also carry services and information. At night its transparent outer skin leaves only the skeletal structure visible. This multimedia centre unites gallery, library and a centre for sight- or hearing-impaired people.

Maki and Associates

Fukushima Gender Equality Centre
1-196-1 Kakunai, Nihonmatsu,
Fukushima 960-0904
Tel +81 243 23 8301

156 ☐ CUL 2000

Sited on a steep slope facing
Kasumiga Castle, this training
centre made of a light upper
volume of steel and glass
floating upon a heavier brick-
clad base creates a link
between the upper and lower
parts of the town.

Jun Aoki

Fukushima Lagoon Museum
Maeshinden, Toyosaka, Niigata
950-3328
Tel +81 25 387 1491

157 ☐ CUL 1998

This museum is designed to
display the surrounding lagoon
to visitors via an entrance
bridge and spiral ramp, which
winds through the ring-shaped
structure, below a double-
layered tent roof, to the
observation gallery. A swimming
pool and video theatre are also
included in the building.

Itsuko Hasegawa Atelier

**Niigata City Performing Arts
Center**
3-2 Ichibanboridori-cho, Niigata
951-8132
Tel +81 25 224 7000

158 ☐ CUL 1998

The 'N-PAC' comprises a
2,000-seat concert hall, a 900-
seat theatre and a 350-seat
stage for traditional *Noh*
performances. It uses the
concept of an archipelago to
wind between already extant
structures on its 8 hectare
drained and reclaimed site.

Kengo Kuma & Associates

Stone Museum
2717-5 Nakamachi, Nasu,
Tochigi 329-3443
Tel +81 287 74 0228

159 ☐ CUL 2000

Planned as a series of additions
to traditional Japanese stone
warehouses, this museum
reinterprets the existing
masonry to form 'soft' walls,
with slatted and porous
arrangements of stone and
openings. Front- and back-lit
effects challenge the visitor's
response to the material.

Kengo Kuma & Associates and
Ando Architecture Design Office

Museum of Hiroshige Ando
116-9 Bato, Nasu, Tochigi
324-0613
Tel +81 287 92 1199

160 ☐ CUL 2000

Referencing the *Rain on
Travellers*, in which a cloudburst
is portrayed as a series of very
fine lines, the architect has
attempted to create this entire
museum from individual sticks
of cedar wood. Its long slatted
walls reinforce the importance
of nature in Hiroshige's artwork.

MVRDV with CLIP-architects

**Matsudai Snow-Land
Agrarian Culture Centre**
Matsudai, Niigata
Tel +81 25 595 6180

161 ☐ CUL 2003

This small museum building
also houses a restaurant and
shop as well as forming a
covered stage for an art festival
– by hoisting its square form up
on legs containing staircases,
which divides the museum into
six irregularly shaped areas.
It also continues upwards to
create an accessible roofscape.

Marin + Trottin Architectes/
Périphériques Architectes

Matsudai Small Tower
Matsudai, Niigata
Tel +81 25 595 6180

162 □ CUL 2003

Erected for the Tsumari Art
Triennale, this three-storey
galvanized-steel lattice
structure has an open base to
allow people and animals to
wander through, and two
enclosed middle levels
accessed by staircase. An
additional roof terrace may be
used by campers.

Jun Aoki

Snow Foundation
722-3 Yasuduka, Higashi
Kubiki, Niigata 942-0411
Tel +81 25 592 3988

163 ▮ ✎ CUL 1999

This centre for advice on how
to cope with severe snowfall is
a collection of polycarbonate-
wrapped ovoid forms set above
the snow line, its cladding
diffusing sunlight inside and
blurring views out. The
exceptions are a few framed
vistas, glimpsed through placed
clear windows.

Lapeña & Torres

Nizayama Forest Art Museum
364-1 Nizayama, Nyuzen,
Toyama 939-0631
Tel +81 765 78 0621

164 □ CUL 1999

Like a snake winding its way
between forest and rice fields,
this extension to the museum
uses a flag-bedecked pavilion
and metal-roofed stairways to
negotiate a series of outdoor
rooms. These 'gardens' are
enlivened with topiary hedges
of cedar and cypress and
channels of running water.

Office of Ryue Nishizawa

Weekend House
Usui-gun, Gunma

165 ■ RES 1998

A house turned in on itself,
this factory-produced, site-
assembled dwelling is lit solely
by three internal light courts –
augmented by glass walls,
shiny ceiling materials and
louvres, all of which 'supply'
outside views. It presents a
secure, windowless exterior of
galvanized corrugated steel to
its isolated surroundings.

Waro Kishi + K Associates/
Architects

Private House
Fukaya, Saitama

166 ■ RES 2001

A rectangular, tripartite plan of
bedroom block, living/dining
wing half a level higher, and
central courtyard and pool
focuses this residence inwards
– away from its semi-suburban
context. The court functions as
an outdoor living space,
separated from the rooms by
clear glass.

Shigeru Ban

Naked House
Kawagoe, Saitama

167 ■ RES 2000

In this polythene-clad shed,
the 'bedrooms' are four
moveable timber-framed boxes
on castors, which employ
traditional Japanese paper
honeycomb panels and *tatami*
mats. They measure 6 metres
square for an adult room, and
5 metres square for children –
the tops of whose boxes are
ideal for play and study.

Japan North

Riken Yamamoto

Saitama Prefectural University
820 Sannomiya, Koshigaya, Saitama 343-8540
Tel +81 48 971 0500

168 ✆ EDU 1999

The university consists of two parallel, 200 metre long laboratory and seminar-room blocks, the platform between them pierced by a number of light-permitting courtyards. A network of timber walkways links the platform to the flanks of the main blocks.

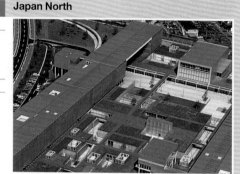

2.6 169-224 Japan South

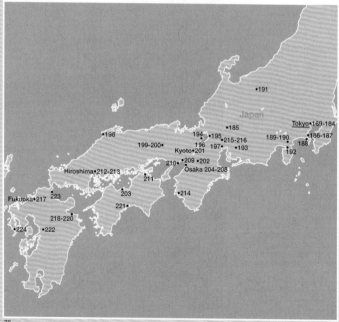

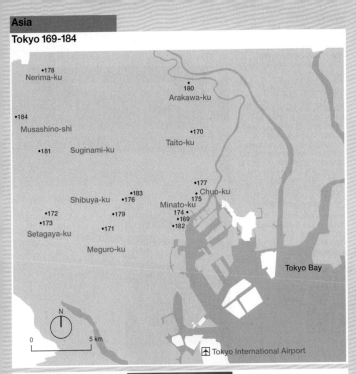

Nerima-ku •178

•180
Arakawa-ku

•184
Musashino-shi

Suginami-ku •181

Taito-ku •170

•177
Chuo-ku •175

•183
Shibuya-ku •176

Minato-ku 174 •
•169
•182

•172
•173
Setagaya-ku

•179

•171

Meguro-ku

Tokyo Bay

N

0   5 km

✈ Tokyo International Airport

Herzog & de Meuron

Prada Store
5-2-6 Minami-Aoyama, Minato-
ku, Tokyo 107-0062
Tel +81 3 6418 0400

169 ☐ COM 2003

The architects stacked this
shop and offices into a five-
sided block, its tubular-steel,
chamfered form wrapped in a
rhomboid grid of flat, concave
and convex glass panels – clear,
except for those covering
changing rooms. The unusual
shape accommodates a small,
moss-covered piazza.

Taniguchi and Associates

Gallery of Horyuji Treasures, Tokyo National Museum
13-9 Ueno Park, Taito-ku, Tokyo 110-8712
Tel +81 3 3822 1111

170 □ CUL 1999

Providing storage and display for the Horyuji Temple collection, this gallery houses storage in a dark, central masonry core, while exhibits are shown in six quadruple-height, glazed outer galleries. Top-floor curatorial spaces are lit by an open-to-sky courtyard.

Kengo Kuma & Associates

Plastic House
Nakameguro 5-19-4, Meguro-ku, Tokyo 153-0061
Tel +81 3 3401 7721 (architects)

171 ✆ RES 2002

This steel-framed residence sheathed in fibre-reinforced polyester wands has reinterpreted the Japanese tradition of translucent shoji-screened dwellings. It also features a plastic *tatami* platform, which admits light to a basement apartment via a light well.

Toyo Ito & Associates

Aluminium House
Sakurajosui, Setagaya-ku, Tokyo

172 ■ RES 2000

The extensive use of aluminium lends this house a remarkable slenderness: the flat ribbed-panel structure disperses loads, allowing members greater slimness than steel or timber. Aluminium's reversibility and durability mean structural panels act as finished external surfaces, and window frames as structural columns.

Toyo Ito & Associates

T House
Setagaya-ku, Tokyo

173 ■ RES 1999

Three pairs of concrete shear walls run the length of the site, with the dwelling's intervening spaces partitioned into room-sized rectangles by openable timber panels. Its street facade is a screen, on to which the shadow of a much-loved cherry tree falls, and up which a cantilevered external stair leads to a roof terrace.

Architectures Jean Nouvel

Dentsu Tower
1-8-1 Higashi-shimbashi, Minato-ku, Tokyo 105-7090

174 ◻ COM 2002

A facade of subtly graded grey glass panels and a crescent plan shape mean that this 50-storey skyscraper appears almost weightless despite a massive, earthquake-proof internal steel structure. It also gives the tower an elusive presence, constantly changing depending on the angle of view.

Renzo Piano Building Workshop

Maison Hermès
5-4-1 Ginza, Chuo-ku, Tokyo 104-0061
Tel +81 3 3289 6811

175 ☐ COM 2001

This 15-storey, slender fashion headquarters shimmers even during the day – its glass-block facades supported by floors cantilevered off a flexible steel earthquake-proof structure. The latter feature relies on visco-elastic dampers to allow for seismic movement.

Klein Dytham Architecture

Undercover Lab
Harajuku, Shibuya-ku, Tokyo

176 ▮ COM 2001

Despite a stunning cantilevered showroom, this fashion design studio is understated and composed: a glazed circulation spine and three-storey studio in imported London brick supports the showroom 'tube' and a suspended ground-floor warehouse. Its compactness makes the most of a tight, 12 metre square site.

Atsushi Kitagawara Architects

P.E.N. Club
20-3 Nihonbashi, Kabuto-cho, Chuo-ku, Tokyo 103-0026
Tel +81 3 5614 5391

177 ▮ ✆ COM 2002

The ellipse form of this club's headquarters is unusual amidst Tokyo's area-maximizing rectangular built form, yet its cylindrical shape helps resist earthquakes and its dark grey, Kawara-style tiling recalls traditional earthenware. The interior is finished in contrasting white plaster.

Akira Yoneda

White Echoes
1-46-16 Kitamachi, Nerima-ku, Tokyo 179-0081

178 ▮ RES 1998

A three-storey family house, designed as a continuous vertical, white-walled space, sits atop two floors of glass-fronted commercial space on a 3 metre wide site. A wall obscures the spiral stair connecting dwelling entrance to pavement, and a loft sits at the back of the roof garden.

EDH Endoh Design House

Natural Ellipse House
7-1 Maruyama-cho, Shibuya-ku,
Tokyo 150-0044

179 ▮ RES 2002

With references to the
modernist *Existenzminimum*,
1950s British high-tech and the
'love hotels' of Tokyo's Shibuya
district, this elliptical toroid
accommodates two residential
units. Openable cuts of glass
and curves of fibre plastic
reflect the internal forms on its
steel-ribbed exterior.

Kei'ichi Irie

C House
Arakawa-ku, Tokyo

180 ■ RES 2001

The house is a composition
of three volumes – one blue,
containing parental bedroom
and floating above the glazed
entrance; one silver, indicating
the entrance itself; and one
white, emerging from the street
elevation. At upper level, a glass
table runs the length of the
house, forming the focus of the
family living space.

Kei'ichi Irie

T House
Asagaya, Suginami-ku, Tokyo

181 ■ RES 1999

A lower-level pair of apartments
are grouped into one yellow
volume, above which the
bathroom and stair for a
projecting, upper-level house
are suspended in an intruding
cylindrical form a half-level
between the two dwelling types.
This facade 'bulge' also shelters
the street entrance to the
apartments.

Kazuyo Sejima & Associates

Small House
Minato-ku, Tokyo

182 ■ RES 2000

Restricted by zoning and light regulations, this diminutive dwelling, clad in opaque glass and galvanized steel, tapers at the top and recesses at its base, resembling an industrial flue. This is, in fact, how it responds to the local climate – drawing warm air up through its four-storey volume and discharging it at the top.

Jun Aoki

Louis Vuitton Omotesando
5-7-5 Gingumae, Shibuya-ku,
Tokyo 150-0001
Tel +81 3 3478 2211

183 □ COM 2002

With its sales and office areas and their staircases all treated as stacked luggage trunks – the object for which Vuitton became famous – the elevations of this nine-storey building comprise overlapping wire-mesh curtains. Four types of metal weave on polished steel and glass yield unlimited facade treatments.

Studio MYU Architects

House of Shadows
Musashino, Tokyo

184 ■ RES 2002

This dwelling was designed to enjoy the beauty of shadows. Water pools and shadow pictures animate a world of muted, suffused light that respond to transitions of the sky and are used to make the architecture disappear. Sliding full-height panels of glass cover the south facade, which helps the house absorb maximum heat from the winter sun.

Atsushi Kitagawara Architects

Gifu Academy of Forest Science and Culture
88 Sodai, Mino, Gifu 501-3714
Tel +81 575 35 2525

185 ✏ EDU 2001

Its timber construction based on traditional elastic connections, the fractal and curved roof forms of this study centre combine with lattice walls to resist seismic forces on its sloping forest site. Educational and residential blocks are here sited as much as 40 metres apart in height.

Kazuyo Sejima + Ryue Nishizawa/SANAA

Daycare Centre for the Elderly
2-3-211 Mutsukawa, Yokohama, Kanagawa 232-0066
Tel +81 45 716 0682

186 ✏ RES 1999

This single-storey building uses mobile partitions to divide its linear volume – and may even be used as a single large space. A variety of glazing types provides privacy for patients, and imparts a shimmering appearance by day and a soft glow at night.

Foreign Office Architects

Yokohama International Port Terminal
1-1-4 Kaigan-dori, Yokohama, Kanagawa 231-0002
Tel +81 45 211 2304

187 ☐ TRA 2002

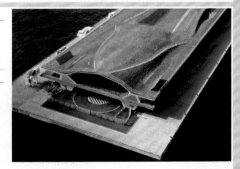

The architects envisaged this building as an extension of the city 'floor' – with its 430 metre long curving landscaped roof covering arrival and departure facilities. Elegant handrails and an ever-present sea view provide lightness and a connection to the ocean.

LEGORRETA + LEGORRETA

Private House
Zushi, Kanagawa

188 ■ RES 1998

This collection of cool stone rooms, spacious verandahs and courtyards opens only to its Pacific Ocean vista – even Legorretta's trademark vibrant Mexican colours are banished inside. Here, a blue-vaulted gallery runs at high level across the dwelling, and a red wall shields the living room from view.

Satoshi Okada Architects

Mount Fuji House
Minamitsuru-gun, Yamanashi

189 ■ RES 2000

This weekend residence on a forested and lava-strewn site gives little away, with its black-stained Japanese cedar cladding masking flush shutters and folding doors – but a white entrance ramp hints at the interior. Inside, large, airy living spaces are divided from private sleeping and *tatami* rooms by a bisecting diagonal white wall.

Kazunari Sakamoto Architectural Laboratory

Hut T 2001
248-1 Chayanodan,
Minamitsuru-gun, Yamanashi
401-0501

190 ▮ RES 2001

A pavilion for small concerts and overnight stays, this tiny house achieves a deceptive spaciousness. Excepting one timber section, the upper storey comprises sandwich panels of glass and polycarbonate, while the lower floor mixes timber and glass.

Asia

Kazuyo Sejima + Ryue
Nishizawa/SANAA

O Museum
3942-1 Izuki, Iida, Nagano
399-2434
Tel +81 265 27 4178

191 ✏ CUL 1999

A single-storey box of glass
and steel raised on square,
glass-clad columns, this
mountainside museum faces
the ruins of a castle. Its
full-height glazing is either
opaque or scored with fine
vertical white lines to allow
its character to change with
the sun's movement.

Shigeru Ban

Paper Art Museum
437 Honjuku, Nagaizumi-cho,
Shizuoka 411-0945
Tel +81 559 88 2401

192 ✏ CUL 2002

Comprising exhibition and
office volumes, separated by an
atrium and joined by bridges at
all three levels, this museum/
gallery can open its garden
facade of fibreglass-reinforced
plastic panels like traditional
Japanese awnings. The atrium
performs a similar feat through
its shutters.

Arata Isozaki & Associates

**Museum of Modern Ceramic
Art, Ceramic Park**
4-2-5 Higashi-machi, Tajimi-shi,
Gifu 507-0801
Tel +81 572 28 3100

193 ☐ CUL 2002

In a nation housing the largest
number of ceramics museums
in the world, this partly sunken
building houses an exhibition
and conference hall. Lakeside
Japanese tea rooms, a roof
plaza and an observatory for
enjoying the mountain scenery
complete the attractions.

Shuhei Endo

Springtecture B
1188 Sone, Biwa-cho, Shiga
526-0103

194   ▯ RES 2002

In this weekend house, a
continuous twist of corrugated
metal forms both roof and walls,
while sliding glass doors and
black-and-white brickwork
contrast with apparently
random angled steel columns.
As a result the accommodation
consists of a two-level zigzag
plan interspersed with garden
areas.

Shuhei Endo

Slowtecture S
688-10 Samegai, Maihara-cho,
Shiga 521-0035

195   □ CUL 2002

A corroding steel skin is
stretched over this linear
cultural centre, housing ground-
floor shops and upper-level
training facilities, and is pierced
by a protruding glass-and-steel
shard at one end. This
corrugated weatherproof skin is
intended to weather and rust,
forming a protective coating.

Tatsuo Kawanishi

Quiet House
103-1 Nishigamo Kakinoki-cho,
Kita-ku, Kyoto 603-8821
Tel +81 75 494 2255

196   ⌕ PUB 1998

Conforming to administrative
guidelines, this small cedar-clad
building splits its clinic and
pharmacy facilities into two
blocks – each with independent
entrances – which can
nevertheless function as a
single unit. All spaces in the
timber-lined interior are
designed to be comfortable.

Kiyoshi Sey Takeyama and
AMORPHE

Refraction House
Sasame-cho, Anjo, Aichi
446-0073

197 ❑ RES 2000

This zinc-and-steel-clad
dwelling houses a full-length
glass-and-steel gangway, which
leads to a mezzanine bedroom
and a square concrete tower.
This is attached to the main
house only by a glass cube –
housing a guest room and
bathroom overlooking a garden.

Toyo Ito & Associates

T Hall
1338-9 Kizuki-Minami, Taisha-
machi, Shimane 699-0711
Tel +81 853 53 6500

198 ☐ CUL 1999

Using an artificial mound-
shaped volume that sweeps
around the site perimeter, the
architect united a collection of
existing buildings and provided
a new centre for Kabuki theatre,
whose fly tower rises above the
curving glazed wall. A second
curved volume contains a new
public library.

Shuhei Endo

Rooftecture C
732 Sayooka, Taishi-cho,
Hyogo 671-1575
Tel +81 792 77 5500

199 ✏ REL 2002

This crematorium sits below
four curved surfaces that cross
in plan and section: an upright
outer wall of textured stone, an
arcing vault spanning the
entrance, a double-height roof
for the hall of remembrance,
and a narrow exit curve. This
latter element punctures the
exterior as mourners depart.

Shuhei Endo

Springtecture H
358 Tsunogame, Singu-cho,
Hyogo 679-5163

200 □ PUB 1998

Also described by the architect
as 'Halftecture', because it is
both open and closed, this
corrugated-steel public toilet
facility is a rigid spiral supported
on steel frames, with wet areas
contained in simple orthogonal
brick structures within. Spaces
are separated by battered,
translucent glass infill panels.

Fumio Toki Associates

**Kansai-kan, the National Diet
Library**
8-1-3 Seikadai, Seika-cho,
Soraku-gun, Kyoto 619-0287
Tel +81 757 74 98 1200

201 □ CUL 2002

The entrance to this extension
to the National Diet (Parliament)
Library is marked by a waterfall
and path running parallel to the
grass-covered, serrated rooflights of the reading room
below. The 20 million volume
collection is housed in climate-
controlled subterranean stacks.

Arata Isozaki & Associates

Nara Centennial Hall
7-1 Sanjomiyamae-cho, Nara-
shi, Nara 630-8121
Tel +81 742 34 0100

202 □ CUL 1998

This building contains three
halls: a main convention
chamber; a medium-sized
concert hall, appearing like a
glazed box within the elliptical
shell; and a multipurpose gallery
beneath the concert hall. The
main chamber can be adjusted,
with movable seating and stage,
into eight configurations.

Tadao Ando Architect &
Associates

Komyo-ji Temple
550 Omachi, Saijo-shi,
Ehime 793-0030
Tel +81 897 53 4583

203 ☐ REL 2000

Consisting of a large space with
three layers of interlocking
beams, this reconstruction of a
250 year old shrine appears to
float. Its laminated timber
framework is a conscious effort
to re-examine the origins of
wooden building, without
slavishly copying the original.

Tadao Ando Architect &
Associates

**Shiba Ryotaro Memorial
Museum**
3-11-18 Shimokosaka, Higashi-
Osaka-shi, Osaka 577-0803
Tel +81 6 6726 3860

204 ☐ CUL 2001

Incorporating the private library
of Shiba Ryotaro, a twentieth-
century novelist, this museum
is a crescent-shaped glazed
volume around a wall of
reinforced concrete. The books
are stacked on Japanese oak
shelves from floor to ceiling.

Shotaro Suga

Abeno House
20 Bandai 1-3, Abeno-ku,
Osaka 545-0036
Tel +81 666 26 1920

205 ✏ RES 1999

Two walls of corrugated steel
sheeting – braced by floors of
the same material – mark the
boundaries of this minuscule
residence. Inside floor toppings
of knotted timber, steel
staircases and wooden bed
bases are positioned to barely
touch the building's shell. Triple-
height spaces light the interior.

Shigeru Ban

GC Osaka Building
2-3-17 Minami Shinmachi,
Chuo-ku, Osaka 540-0024

206 ▯ COM 2000

This steel-framed office block
uses a 'flammable barrier'
design, in which its fire-resistant
timber covering doubles as the
external finish, and glazing
mullions repeat the rhythm of a
tartan particle-board facade
grid. An external escape stair
hugs a five-storey boundary
wall of foliage.

Tadao Ando Architect &
Associates

Sayamaike Historical Museum
2 Ikejirinaka, Osakasayama-shi,
Osaka 589-0007
Tel +81 72 367 8891

207 □ CUL 2001

A historical exhibition of the
adjoining irrigation pond, this
austere concrete edifice
conveys the elemental power of
water, introducing visitors, via a
switchback ramp, to a central
pool. Cascades of water diffuse
the light entering exhibition
rooms below.

Waro Kishi + K Associates/
Architects

Hu-tong House
Osaka

208 ■ RES 2002

Like traditional dwellings of the
Hakka area, where courtyards
are referred to as 'streets', this
house and studio for an artist is
surrounded by walls containing
a continuous flow of space
between three pavilions. This
strategy ensures no corridors,
and a courtyard that becomes a
stage for all domestic activities.

Shuhei Endo

Rooftecture K
4-22 Koshimizu, Nishinomiya,
Hyogo 662-0864

209 ■ COM 2000

This three-storey project stretches a continuous 'roof' skin over, around and through itself to create an interlocking puzzle of corrugated-steel sheeting, apparently held in place by large sheets of fragile glass. A rooftop conference room and first-floor offices sit atop a transparent foyer.

Tadao Ando Architect & Associates

Awaji Yumebutai
1 Yumebutai, Higashiura-cho,
Hyogo 656-2301
Tel +81 799 74 1000

210 □ COM 1999

This is a complex of multidirectional spaces housing conference hall, gardens and outdoor theatre on land cleared for the Osaka Bay project. It became a symbol for physical and spiritual rebirth when the area was further devastated in 1995, partway through design.

Katsuyasu Kishigami

Private House
8-29 Imazato-cho, Takamatsu,
Kagawa 760-0078

211 ■ RES 1999

Uncluttered spaces comprise the interior volume of this two-storey residence, whose corrugated steel-sheeting and polycarbonate-panel outer walls allow light in, preventing any oppressive sense of enclosure without compromising privacy. The house recalls the traditional paper architecture of Japan.

Hideki Yoshimatsu & Archipro
Architects

Mirasaka Ceramics Studio
563 Nika, Mirasaka, Miyoshi,
Hiroshima 729-4302
Tel +81 90 3633 6922

212　☐ CUL 2000

Designed to a tight budget, this
studio comprises a timber
frame of posts and beams at
600 millimetre intervals, infilled
with painted timber cladding
and coloured text-covered glass
panels. Plywood, lightly coated
with white preservative paint,
lines the inside walls.

Hideki Yoshimatsu & Archipro
Architects

Cemetery for the Unknown
1513-12 Haizuka Nakayama,
Mirasaka, Hiroshima 729-4303
Tel +81 824 44 2237

213　☐ REL 1998

To offset the impact of the
enormous Haizuka Dam project,
the town of Mirasaka
commissioned a cemetery for
the people whose unmarked
graves were flooded by the
works: they are represented by
1,500 vertical stainless-steel
rods.

Maki and Associates

Kaze-no-Oka Crematorium
3032-16 Aihara, Nakatsu-shi,
Oita 871-0022
Tel +81 979 22 2553

214　☐ REL 1998

Incorporating an existing
cemetery and ancient burial
mounds, this crematorium
comprises three buildings: an
octagonal brick funeral hall;
monumental concrete
crematorium spaces
surrounding a water court; and
linking spaces providing a
sense of repose and calm.

Kazuyo Sejima & Associates

Kitagata Apartments
1857 Aza-Hasegawa, Kitagata,
Gifu 501-0431

215 ▮ RES 1998

This 107-apartment block with
an unusually shallow plan uses
a single room as its basic
module. The rooms are
combined in various ways, yet
all are serviced by diagonal
escape staircases. Each
apartment has a *tatami* room
and an *engawa*, or terrace,
constituting a buffer space.

Diller + Scofidio

Slither Housing
Kitagata, Motosu-gun, Gifu

216 ▮ RES 2000

Each of these 15 interlocking
residential towers is set at a
slight angle to, and 20
centimetres lower than, its
neighbour – producing the
characteristic 'slither' in
elevation and giving each
apartment its own 'minifacade'
and balcony. The curve is
accentuated by a V-shaped
common room.

Hiroyuki Arima + Urban Fourth

Atelier and Gallery
1657-6 Tzusurayama, Keya,
Shima, Fukuoka 819-1335

217 ☐ CUL 1999

On a steep site in the Genkai
Quasi National Park, these five
interlocking volumes subtly
control artworks and visitors
with careful positioning of
screens and pivoting spatial
dampers. In contrast, the 'up-
and-over' entrance sequence
takes a vertiginous route across
the roof.

Toyo Ito & Associates

Agricultural Park
1-1 Hisashi, Yamaga, Hayami-gun, Oita 879-1312
Tel +81 97 728 7111

218 ☐ REC 2000

Designed as a series of greenhouse structures, each building has east-facing glazing and west-facing shallow-pitched roofs – all part of a development promoting agriculture. Cottages with farmland for rent, boat-hire facilities, orchards and a zoo are ranged along its axis.

Toyo Ito & Associates

Notsuharu Town Hall
1753-1 Notsuharu-machi, Oita 870-1203
Tel +81 97 588 1111

219 ☐ GOV 1998

An existing slope is incorporated into this building as a ramped meeting place, with administrative offices visible through translucent glass. Located between two major roads, it functions as a hub for the populace to pass through and conduct their business with the council.

Kisho Kurokawa Architect & Associates

Oita Stadium
1351 Yokoo, Oita 870-0126
Tel +81 97 528 7700

220 ☐ SPO 2001

One of many venues for the 2002 World Cup, this gently curving space-frame structure houses a football pitch and athletics track with retractable seating. The roof shell is retractable, but its transparent Teflon membrane allows sufficient daytime light through.

Naito Architect & Associates

Makino Museum of Plants and People
4200-6 Godaisan, Kochi,
781-8125
Tel +81 88 882 2601

221 ☐ CUL 1999

The silvery roofs of this complex on the slopes of Mount Godai are covered with stainless-steel-laminated sheets to protect them from salty ocean breezes – and have undersides of Japanese cedar-wood. These roof a corridor which connects the two sections of the museum.

Gigantes Zhenghelis Architects + Ryoji Suzuki Architects

Ashikita House of Youth
Tsurugiyama, Ashikita-machi,
Kumamoto 869-5454
Tel +81 966 82 3092

222 ▮ TOU 1999

These state-sponsored leisure amenities are sheltered below undulating protective roofs that shield gymnasium, bath-house and hotel facilities from strong sun and typhoon winds. The concrete lattice-shell roof of the dining hall is a vast tent over an uninterrupted interior space.

Jerde Partnership

River Walk Kitakyushu
1-1-1 Muromachi, Kitakyushu,
Fukuoka 803-0812
Tel +81 93 573 1500

223 ☐ COM 2003

Surrounded by the Kokura Castle gardens and the Yasaka shrine, this complex contains cultural, information and commercial zones, in a series of coloured sculptural forms. It is entered through the dome-roofed 'Energy Court' atrium, leading to the outward-canting red drum of Canyon Walk.

Asia

Japan South

Hiroshi Hara + Atelier Phi

Ito House
Chijiwa, Nagasaki

224 ■ RES 1998

In this collection of domestic pavilions on a sloping site, one cube, with a glazed living area above a services basement, houses the parents; another, with a simpler open-plan layout, the children of the family; while a triangular 'shard' forms a private study room. Living areas have mullion-free glazing, maximizing forest views.

2.7   225–248   **Southeast Asia**

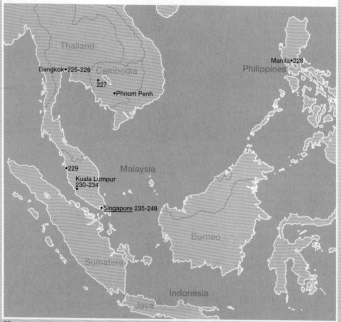

Architects 49

Prabhakorn House
23 Lardpraw Road, Bangkapi,
Bangkok 10230

225 ▯ RES 2001

This 'tree-house' concentrates
services and circulation
centrally, allowing the ground-
floor living, upper-level sleeping
and rooftop music rooms to
interact with their surroundings.
They do this via translucent or
wire-mesh sunshades or – in
the case of the living room – via
a wall that opens in a sweep.

Duangrit Bunnag Architect

V42 House
Bangkok

226 ▮ RES 2002

Consisting of five bands of
accommodation, this
townhouse packs studio/
playroom and family spaces –
both with bedrooms above –
into two parallel wings
overlooking a courtyard. Its
combination of built and open
form, connected at upper level
by bridges, also facilitates
airflow in this humid climate.

Asma Architects

Kantha Bopha Centre
Angkor Road, Slakram,
Siemréab
Tel +85 5 1281 2231

227 ▯ PUB 2002

Within a fragmented hospital
complex, this conference centre
orders its surroundings with two
large red-brick volumes, united
by a vertical grid of concrete
and bamboo beside a series of
water pools. Employee rooms
are set along a white east-west
wall, while a red north-south
wall anchors the cafeteria.

Eduardo Calma, Lor Calma
Design Associates

Pablito Calma House
Manila

228 ■ RES 2000

In a redefinition of the Filipino-
townhouse perimeter wall, this
brick facade emphasizes its
horizontal bond to lessen its
scale, windows are horizontal
slots, and the main stairwell,
clad in timber louvres, permits
privacy. Internally, the U-shaped
residence is air-conditioned, but
can also be naturally ventilated.

TR Hamzah & Yeang

Menara UMNO
128 Jalang Macalister, Bandar,
George Town, Penang 10400
Tel +60 3 226 1096

229 ✆ GOV 1998

Unlike most Penang office
buildings, this 21-storey tower
ventilates itself – using
prevailing breezes, directional
wing-walls and adjustable
balcony doors – as well as
maximizing natural light to the
extent that no desk is more than
6.5 metres away from openable
windows.

Cesar Pelli

Petronas Towers
Petronas Twin Towers, Kuala
Lumpur 50088
Tel +60 3 2051 5000

230 ☐ COM 1998

Evoking Islamic arabesques
and employing repetitive
geometries characteristic of
Muslim architecture, these
towers – planned around an
eight-point star motif – employ
a ring of super-columns outside
square concrete cores to
support their offices.

Asia

Hijjas Kasturi Associates

Telekom Malaysia Headquarters
2 Jalan 4/83A, Jalan Pantai Baru, Kuala Lumpur 50672
Tel +60 3 2240 9494

231 COM 2001

Modelled on a sprouting bamboo shoot – the corporate symbol of Malaysia – this 55-storey office tower minimizes its facades, with a tapering organic form, to reduce exposure to direct sunlight. Sky-gardens punctuate its accommodation at every third level.

TR Hamzah & Yeang

Guthrie Pavilion
2A Persiaran Tebar Layar, Section U8, Shah Alam, Selangor 40150
Tel +60 3 7847 2020

232 SPO 1998

Essentially a golf clubhouse, this building also contains a block of lettable office space, connected to the first pavilion by a slender service wing. Three steel masts support a five-canopied membrane roof with aerodynamically formed concrete-framed blocks.

Ngiom Partnership

Pat's House
181 Persiaran Perupuk, Sungai Buloh, Selangor 47000
Tel +60 3 4043 4833

233 RES 1999

Its mid-point entrance gives this white, concrete-framed dwelling a twist, raised on *piloti*, encapsulating the view over Kuala Lumpur's surrounding hills. A single-level plan integrates living, dining and kitchen areas, and outward-sloping walls largely negate any need for overhanging roofs.

Asia

Southeast Asia

Kisho Kurokawa Architect & Associates

Kuala Lumpur International Airport
Sepang, Selangor
Tel +60 3 8777 8888

234 ☐ TRA 1998

The undulating moss-green roof of this terminal complex recalls both the lines of Islamic domes and Malaysia's rainforest heritage – the latter impression enhanced by tree-like granite columns clad in wood and decorated with patterns found on the trunks of oil palms.

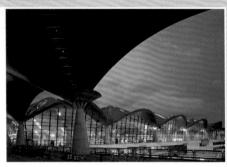

Singapore 235-246

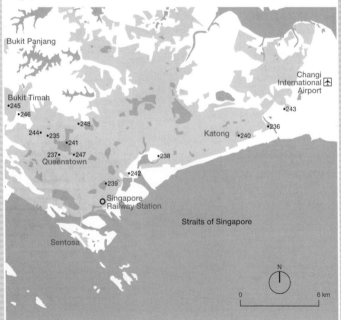

W Architects

Morley Road House
4 Morley Road, Singapore
267726

235 ▯ RES 1999

Comprising three pavilions – for living, dining and recreation – this residence forms a sequence of ever-more-private spaces linked by a lobby that extends from an entrance court, offering baffled views of the house, into a sky-lit gallery. A swimming pool pushes elements toward the boundary.

W Architects

Lem House
33 Eastwood Way, Singapore
486363

236 ▯ RES 1998

Turning its back on its neighbours with a solid wall that turns into a 2 metre roof overhang, this raised residence still allows passers-by on the adjoining canalside a view of its study and dining areas. Its large glazed elevations are fitted with aluminium-framed openings to permit natural ventilation.

Ettore Sottsass and Johanna Grawunder

Jasmine Hill
Singapore

237 ▮ RES 2000

In this luxury residential enclave, six homes cluster along site contours, employing a palette of maintenance-free finishes that includes ceramic tiling, asphalt shingles and stone. In time, the extensive landscaping will grow to dominate the built form of the development.

Kerry Hill Architects

Singapore Cricket Association Pavilion
Kallang Playing Fields,
Singapore 397639
Tel +65 6345 7111

238 ☐ SPO 1999

Stairs, tiered seating, offices, bar and players' ramp are treated as sculptural elements, sheltering below a concealed pitched roof. The oversized eaves are supported on cruciform-section composite-steel columns, which permit the resultant 'floating plane' effect.

William Lim Associates and TangGuanBee Architects

The Gallery Hotel
76 Robertson Quay, Singapore 238254
Tel +65 6849 8686

239 ✎ TOU 2000

This designer hotel is a collage of disjointed reinforced concrete forms; its river facade appears almost industrial, while other elevations of its ten-storey bedroom block are enlivened by red, blue and yellow bay windows, protruding from their aluminium-panel-clad walls.

SCDA Architects

Sennett House
39-41 Sennett Lane, Singapore 466932

240 ▮ RES 1999

Challenged to design dwellings for a mother and two children divided by a site boundary – rather than linked by a party wall – the architects provided mirror-image villas facing each other. The houses are organized into three blocks, connected by transparent bridges, with large windows.

Asia

Kerry Hill Architects

Cluny Hill House
18 Cluny Hill, Singapore 259658

241 ☐ RES 2000

Adopting the typology of a
Malayan planter's bungalow,
two blocks meet alongside a
pool, their solid bases forming
a podium, while wrap-around
first-floor glazing reflects the
sky's changing hues, below a
'floating' tiled, hipped roof.
Wisely placed lower openings
testify that the garden alone
justifies this house.

Michael Wilford & Partners in
association with DP Architects

Esplanade Theatre Complex
1 Esplanade Drive, Singapore
038981
Tel +65 6828 8222

242 ☐ CUL 2002

Designed to give 24-hour views
of Singapore as well as provide
a meeting point between
neighbouring districts, this
complex wraps its two theatres
– set on rubber footings to
isolate them from subway
vibration – in a dual glass shell.

Foster and Partners

Expo Station
1 Expo Drive, Singapore 486150

243 ☐ TRA 2001

Serving a new exhibition centre,
this interchange forms an urban
gateway with two dramatic roof
structures: a stainless-steel, 38
metre disc covering the ticket
hall; and a 200 metre ellipse
sheltering passengers. The
titanium cladding on the latter
deflects the sun's rays, creating
a microclimate four degrees
Celsius cooler than outside.

SCDA Architects

Coronation Road West House
178 Coronation Road West,
Singapore 269387

244 ◗ RES 2000

The house consists of two
volumes: a main living block
and a smaller pavilion above a
reinforced-concrete wall
connecting the two. Structural
mullions obviate the need for
columns, and all openings and
timber screens are carefully
placed to form a variable filter
to the outside.

WOHA

House at Hua Guan Avenue
Hua Guan Avenue, Bukit Timah,
Singapore

245 ◗ RES 2001

This house is dominated by
the idea of wrapping and
folding. Poolside rooms are
tucked below an overhanging
roof, and a circulation gallery is
formed from the wrapping-up of
the rear wall. Bedroom-pods,
cantilevering over the pool,
become balconies by unfolding
their timber screens.

WOHA

House at Maple Avenue
Maple Avenue, Bukit Timah,
Singapore

246 ◗ RES 2001

Bisected by a circulation void
but united by an enfolding,
curved roof, this family house
has alternating areas of glass
and screening, allowing privacy,
air and views to be controlled
to a high degree. The interiors
and landscape continue the
stretched, weightless
architectural language.

Asia

Richard Meier & Partners

Camden Medical Centre
1 Orchard Boulevard, Singapore
248649
Tel +65 6838 7383

247   ▉ ✆ PUB 1998

The 18-storey cylindrical
building's footprint was
minimized to allow greenery to
extend through and below it,
creating an outdoor lobby with
sculptural access ramp and
screened patient drop-off area.
North and south sides are
screened from the sun by an
extensively layered facade.

Bedmar & Shi

Trevose 12
17 Trevose Crescent, Singapore
298031
Tel +65 338 651

248   ✆ RES 2002

This development of 12 houses
is 'contoured': functional layers
are vertically stacked and
partitioned by walls, between
which an additional wall-plane
is inserted, creating a linear
open court. Moving from the
rear to the front, living and
bedrooms receive the best
views of the city beyond.

Greenland, Denmark

•249-250 Nuuk

Iceland

•251

Reykjavik •252-254

KHRAS Architects

Nature Institute
2 Kivioq, Nuuk 3900
Tel +299 36 12 00

249   ☐ EDU 1999

Orientated to resist an
inhospitable climate, the two
Canadian-cedar-clad wings of
this building point the lowest
end of its monopitch roof into
the prevailing north winds, and
open up to the south with a
single huge window. An
aluminium-roofed central space
gives access to the naturally
ventilated offices.

Europe

Schmidt, Hammer & Lassen

Katuaq Culture Centre
21 Imaneq, Nuuk 3900
Tel +299 323 300

250 ☐ CUL 1998

Housing a multitude of facilities, this Nordic art, cultural and conference centre takes as its inspiration the spectacular phenomenon of the Northern Lights, its undulating, gleaming, light-filtering facade following the course of the Skibshavnsvej River. The building's triangular plan also fits naturally into the town centre of Nuuk.

Studio Granda

Bifröst Business School Extension
Bifröst, 311 Borgarnes
Tel +354 433 3000

251 ☐ EDU 2002

Situated on a lava field, this extension to a business school complex unites the disparate parts, using large areas of glazing in its corrugated-copper facades. Lava removed during construction was carefully reinstated on the roof, where moss can continue to grow undisturbed.

Studio Granda

Art Museum
Tryggvagata 17, 101 Reykjavík
Tel +354 590 1201

252 ☐ CUL 2000

In a converted 1930s harbourside warehouse, a new entrance hall – off which all the galleries lead – traces Reykjavík's 'umbilical cord to the world': its historic main pier. Doors, 7 x 4 metres, open in summer, creating an interplay between midnight-sun exterior and dark, rolled-steel-lined interior.

Studio Granda

**Car Park & Public Space,
Kringlan Shopping Mall**
Kringlan 8–12, 103 Reykjavík
Tel +354 568 9200

253 □ COM 1999

Tough materials link this car park to Iceland's rugged landscape; rusticated stone is expressed in sedimentary layers and sheet-metal piling is left raw. Trees line access ramps and gargoyles have been positioned both to irrigate them and to provide spectacular frozen sculptures in winter.

Arkibúllan

Service Centre in Nautholsvik
Ylstrond, Nautholsvik,
101 Reykjavík
Tel +354 511 6630

254 □ SPO 2001

Located on an 'imported' white-sand beach – which has geothermal currents warming the water, but nevertheless becomes inhospitable in winter – this year-round bathers' facility digs its L-plan back into the hillside and throws a protective verandah over its openable waterside facade.

Svalbard, Norway
•255

•256
•282

•270
•269

Finland

•283

Sweden

•258
•259

•285

•265   257•

296•   •286   284

Norway
•260

Espoo
287-289
297

•Helsinki 290-295

266•   Oslo•261-264   •274
•268   267•   271-272

Estonia

275•   Göteborg
        273

Latvia

298•
299•   300-301
        •303-304   Helsingborg
302•   •305 310   276-278
307• 306• •318
319• 321• 317• •Malmö 279-281
                   Køpenhavn 308-309, 311-316

Denmark

320

Lithuania

Jarmund/Vigsnæs Architects

Governor's Headquarters
Longyearbyen, Spitsbergen
Tel +47 79 02 43 00

255 ☐ GOV 1998

Built in the earth's northernmost regularly inhabited settlement, this louvred building with inward-sloping walls was erected on the concrete base of a previous structure – avoiding the need for drilling into the permafrost. It must cope with viciously low temperatures and the contrast between complete darkness and 24-hour sunlight.

Stein Halvorsen & Christian Sundby

Sami Parliament Building
Kautokeinoveien 50,
9730 Karasjok
Tel +47 78 47 40 00

256 ☐ GOV 2000

The complex is rampart-like from the outside, modulating its concrete with timber shades against the low sun, but it opens up within to encircle a conical debating chamber. This timber-clad form has been built to resemble the traditional Sami tent, the lavvo.

Lund & Slaatto Arkitekter

Protective Construction for Hamar Cathedral Ruins
100 Strandvegen, Hedmark,
2300 Hamar

257 ☐ REL 1998

The ruins of this twelfth-century cathedral are enclosed in a sloping 'tent' of tempered plate glass on a trussed steel structure, whose controlled internal environment maintains temperatures above freezing. The enclosure is surrounded by a concrete base.

Europe

Slyngstad Aamlid Arkitekter

3rd District Coastal Authority Headquarters
Nørvevika, 6008 Ålesund
Tel +47 70 16 01 00

258 ✆ GOV 2000

The building presents a glazed facade to the sea and shields its other side from highway noise with a pair of slate-hung battered 'pylons'. Inside visitors find themselves bathed in the grey light typical of this coastline. Secondary spaces are arranged off a long, double-height internal corridor.

Sverre Fehn

The Ivar Aasen Centre for Language and Culture
176 Indrehovdvegen, Hovdebygda, 6160 Ørsta
Tel +47 70 04 75 70

259 ☐ CUL 2000

Dug into a hillside beneath a curving, grass-covered roof – the entrance to this building is marked by a stone sentinel, leading to glazed, triangular display areas under concrete vaults. Each year it hosts the National Festival of Literature and Music.

Arne Henriksen Arkitekter

Eidsvoll Railway Station
Holstangen, Eidsvoll, Akershus, 2080 Oslo

260 ☐ TRA 1998

The last halt on Oslo's northern commuter line, this 'cabin' uses laminated timber for just about all aspects of its construction: beams, bracing, supporting columns and the articulated canopies sheltering the island platforms. A gentle main roof is still steep enough to deal with Nordic snow loads.

Jarmund/Vigsnæs Architects

Red House
Oslo

261 ■ RES 2002

Set on the east bank of a river valley, perpendicular to the stream to maximize views, this lapped-timber-boarded and framed house has its children's areas on the lower level, while living spaces and master bedroom are on the top floor. The colour of this fire-engine-red object was chosen to match the client's temperament.

Jensen & Skodvin
Arkitektkontor

Mortensrud Church
15 Helga Vaneksvei,
Mortensrud, 1281 Oslo
Tel +47 22 62 91 70

262 □ REL 2002

This new worship space incorporates rocks and pine trees within its steel-and-glass shed, rubble walling, raw timber belltower, glass gallery and non-orthogonal steel girders. Its form is a deliberate attempt to disrupt the view of churches as reverential spaces.

Knut Hjeltnes, AS Silvarkitekter
MNAL

Private House
5a Dronninghavnveien, Bygdøy,
0277 Oslo

263 ■ RES 2002

The dining room and kitchen of this family house are both part of a large, travertine-covered terrace, while living room and library boast timber surfaces - the latter featuring a reflective pool. Five bedrooms with different views are connected by a glazed passage.

Europe

Lund Hagem Arkitekter

Double House
10 Furulundsveien, Ullern,
0282 Oslo

264 ▮ RES 1998

Each of these oak-clad
dwellings is arranged around a
central corridor – the northernmost house is at ground level,
and leads from the entrance to
a garden belvedere; the most
southerly residence is at first-
floor, and is lit by a full-length
skylight. Internal timber finishes
celebrate the wooded site.

Haga and Grov with Knut
Hjeltnes and Ivar Egge

Nordic Artists' Centre
Fjaler Community, 6963 Dale i
Sunnfjord
Tel +47 57 73 72 20

265 ☐ CUL 1998

A coastal retreat, studios form
an arc to the north of a hill,
while the houses lie on the
south side – forcing residents
to cross the hill in all weathers
to reach their workspaces.
Internally, the studios are
connected to one another, and
to a workshop, by a tunnel.

Snøhetta

Karmøy Fishing Museum
Sletten, Karmøy,
4295 Vedavägen
Tel +47 52 81 74 55

266 ☐ CUL 1998

This sculptural tube of a
building reinterprets vernacular
traditions to forge a bond with
its historic west-coast fishing
community. Wooden screens
are woven from a native coastal
bush called Einer; the interior is
open, allowing rearrangement;
and the seaward end acts as a
viewing window.

Carl-Viggo Hølmbakk

Mortuary at Asker Crematorium
143 Kirkeveien, 1384 Asker
Tel +47 66 75 40 90

267 ✆ REL 2000

Without using any of the familiar forms and symbols of sacred architecture, this brick-vaulted ceremony chamber still provides fitting surroundings for final farewells. Internally, it has floors of ground concrete, doors and window-frames of oiled pine and light-fittings of sandblasted stainless steel.

Arkitektfirma Helen & Hard

Two Houses on Sølvberget
21 Steinkargate, Rogaland, 40 4001 Stavanger

268 ▯ RES 1999

These two dwellings – linked at lower level with a viewing gallery – display different characters: one forming a tower in traditional ship-lapped wood; the other stepped-roofed, mediating with surrounding building heights. The white-painted cladding reflects light into an adjoining public square.

Åke Larsson

Icehotel
Jukkas AB, 63 Marknadsvägen, 981 91 Jukkasjärvi
Tel +46 980 66 800

269 ▢ TOU 1998

From a one-room igloo, Sweden's Icehotel has grown to a 100-bed hotel rebuilt from scratch each winter. Its cinema, suites and exhibition spaces are supported with immense pillars formed from ice rendered crystal clear by the pure, fast-flowing river water from which it is made.

Lars Sundström Arkitektkontor

Kiruna Sami School
37 Bävervägen, 981 37 Kiruna
Tel +46 980 81 772

270 ✎ EDU 2002

A school for a nomadic, non-hierarchical culture must itself face challenges in its design: the rooms are flexible and non-determined. Open copper gutters emphasize the sound of trickling water, and timber-framed windows allow occupants to follow nature's patterns.

Gulichsen Vormala Architects

Finnish Embassy
Gärdesgatan 11, Gärdet,
104 51 Stockholm
Tel +46 8 676 67 00

271 ☐ GOV 2002

This palazzo-like assemblage of white blocks opens out, through a garden, on to the Gärdet field, a historic landscaped space. In the long wall of the street facade, a tall gate leads to the central paved courtyard surrounded by offices, banqueting hall and sauna facilities.

Johan Celsing Arkitektkontor

New Art Gallery
Herserudsvägen, Lidingö,
181 34 Stockholm
Tel +46 8 446 75 90

272 ☐ CUL 1999

Externally, the building, with its signature copper-clad rooflights, adheres to the small scale of nearby villas – inside, however, the impression is of a space inserted into hilly terrain: one large room with a staircase doubling as seating for events. The gallery opens on to terraces overlooking its island site.

Studio Grön Arkitekter

Trädgår'n Restaurant
Nya Allén, 411 38 Göteborg
Tel +46 31 10 20 80

273 ☐ COM 1998

Situated in Sweden's oldest public park, this 'place for festivities and partying' incorporates a dining hall, coffee shop and performance space in a 63 metre long glazed and trellis-covered space. The building can accommodate 2,500 people, with more on a covered outdoor terrace that links it to the historic gardens.

White

Mälardalen University Library
Högskoleplan 1, 721 22 Västerås
Tel +46 21 101 344

274 ☐ EDU 2002

The library, a glazed open-plan three-storeyed hall with box skylights, is paired with a lecture hall block to form a courtyard containing pools and extensive planting. Flooded with natural light, the reading rooms feature natural materials and colours: slatted timber sun-screens, oak floors and laminated wooden boards.

Niels Bruun & Henrik Corfitsen Arkitekter

Nordic Watercolour Museum
Södra hamnen 6,
471 32 Skärhamn
Tel +46 30 460 00 80

275 ☐ CUL 2000

Designed to look like separate units – linking with five artists' units on the opposite island – this two-storey museum contains single- and double-volume interior spaces below a unifying roof. The concrete and steel structure ensures a stable indoor climate.

Europe

Henrik Jais-Nielsen Mats White Arkitekter

Private House
212a Drottninggatan, Pålsjö,
254 33 Helsingborg

276 ▮ RES 2000

Designed for a couple who wanted spaces rather than corridors, this U-shaped house gathers around a courtyard, down to which its 'shed' roof slopes, giving high-ceilinged interior spaces. The facades are of white plaster and reddish-brown Californian cedar.

Utzon & Associates Architects

Dunker's Cultural Centre
Kungsgatan 11,
252 21 Helsingborg
Tel +46 42 10 74 00

277 ☐ CUL 2002

Each part of this complex receives its own distinctive form, giving a village-like cluster and lively roofscape – the two-storey galleries are topped by pyramidal skylights, and the theatre is crowned by a billowing curve. The stepped harbourside plaza is flanked by a restaurant and concert hall.

Anders Wilhelmson

EOS Housing Scheme
Kungshultsvägen 61–113,
254 50 Helsingborg

278 ▮ RES 2002

Laid out on an organic site plan, but constructed more in a light-industrial way, these aluminium-profiled dwellings present a sole opening to their winding landscaped 'street': a front door and large square window. Inside, all the houses are open plan, and are provided with rear gardens.

Moore Ruble Yudell Architects &
Planners

Tango Ecological Housing
Salongsgatan 13+15, Boplatsen,
Västra Hamnen, Malmö

279 ◼ RES 2003

Clustered around an island
wetland space, the living rooms
of these 27 housing units
occupy triple-glazed towers,
and the roofs are covered with
grass and solar panels. All units
are connected by an 'intelligent
wall', supporting mechanical
and technical equipment.

Sandell Sandberg

Bo01 Restaurant
Fairgrounds Bo01, 211 16 Malmö

280 ☐ COM 2001

This single-storey kidney-
shaped pavilion was originally
a temporary contribution to a
housing exposition but proved
so popular that the city of
Malmö decided to keep it. The
polished metal frame is clad
entirely in striated polyurethane,
lending it a hazy transparency in
its orange-tree-grove setting.

Wingårdh Arkitektkontor

**Housing Expo Bo01
Apartment Building**
Sundspromenaden 17–27,
211 16 Malmö
Tel +46 40 31 33 00

281 ✏ RES 2001

Modelled on a medieval
settlement, these four blocks
surround a courtyard and
display variation through the
careful modulation of their
cement-rendered five-storey
bays. The whole site is served
by a network of underground
streets and car parking.

Europe

Juhani Pallasmaa

Sami Museum & Northern Lappland Nature Centre
Inarintie, 99870 Inari
Tel +358 16 665 212

282 ☐ COM 1998

Housing a roof-lit exhibition designed by the architect, this concrete-and-steel-framed building has a rolling roofscape, referencing the surrounding countryside and facilitating the removal of snow. The interior reflects the tent-like structures of the Sami, with its rolling timber ceiling.

Virta Palaste Leinonen Arkkitehdit

Main Building University of Oulu
Pentti Kaiterankatu 1,
Linnanmaa, 90570 Oulu
Tel +358 8 553 1011

283 ☐ EDU 1998

This building aligns with and · terminates an axis that cuts through the campus – its angled Great Hall, clad in blue aluminium modules, contrasting with a light-coloured concrete office wing. It provides a new focus for this thriving institution.

Teemu Tuomi

Muuraiskallio Sauna
Muuraissaari Island, Taavetti,
54500 Luumäki

284 ▮ REC 2000

Partially covered with peeled spruced trunks, this dark sauna contrasts with a relaxing area flooded with light from floor-to-ceiling insulated glazing. Timbers include red-brown birch plywood facades, internal surfaces of spruce and red alder, and red Oregon pine in the relaxation room.

Anne-Mette Krolmark & Claudia
Schultz

**Boathouse for Alvar Aalto's
Boat**
Melelammentie 2, Säynätsalo,
40900 Jyväskylä
Tel +358 14 624 809

285 ☐ CUL 1999

As the visitor approaches this
shelter, the silhouette of the
boat is visible through larch
laths – uneven in size to give an
effect of flickering light similar to
a beech forest in sunshine.
Decks on two sides allow the
visitor a closer look.

Arkkitehtityöhuon e Artto Palo
Rossi Tikka

**Sibelius Concert and
Congress Hall**
Ankkurikatu 7, 15140 Lahti
Tel +358 3 814 2800

286 ☐ CUL 2001

Part of a conversion of old
waterside industrial buildings,
this concert hall abuts the
laminated-timber structure of
the Forest Hall – a glazed
banqueting chamber. Interior
materials combine the timber
structural elements with birch
plywood wall finishes.

Arkkitehtitoimisto Lahdelma &
Mahlamäki

**Eestinmetsä Community
Service Centre**
Mäntytie 27, 02270 Espoo
Tel +358 9 816 456 96

287 ✐ PUB 1998

The radial structure of this
fibreboard-clad building –
reminiscent of a Frank Lloyd
Wright plan – houses clinics,
social services and technical
facilities in different wings,
reaching out to the rocky
landscape. No two timber-
framed windows are the same.

Europe

SARC Architects

KONE Headquarters
Keilasatama 3, 02150 Espoo

288 ▮ COM 2001

Glazed lifts form a spectacular
buffer to the south elevation of
this 18-storey glass tower,
whose two-storey entrance
vestibule and 16th-floor sky
garden act as 'breathing
spaces'. Tall strip windows
allow in controlled light, helping
to moderate thermal gain, and
finishes are of indigenous
timber throughout.

Jyrki Tasa

House Into
Soukan Rantatie 66,
02360 Espoo

289 ▮ RES 1998

This bachelor-pad contains
large reception rooms and a
sculptural plywood staircase,
suspended on ceiling-hung
steel cables, which leads to a
top-floor indoor swimming pool.
Set on a rock with sea views,
a curved east wall shelters the
building, while its west facade
opens to the evening sun.

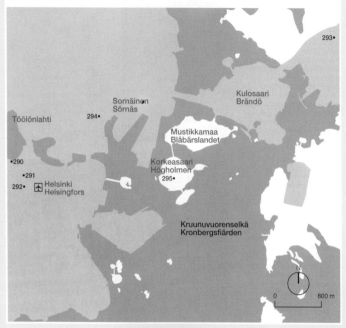

293•

Kulosaari
Brändö

Sornäinen
Sörnäs

294•

Töölönlahti

Mustikkamaa
Blåbärslandet

•290

Korkeasaari
Högholmen
295•

•291

292• ⊞ Helsinki
     Helsingfors

Kruunuvuorenselkä
Kronbergsfjärden

N

0   800 m

Niko Sirola/HUT Wood Studio
Workshop

Café Carbon
Karamzininkatu, Hakasalmi
Park, 00100 Helsinki

290 ■ COM 2000

Designed to give a frame
through which to view the city,
this temporary pavilion was a
site-assembled Glulam box,
weatherproofed with carbon
and creosote. The interior was
left as natural timber, separated
from its terraces by glass sliding
doors.

SARC Architects

Sanoma House
Töölönlahdenkatu 2,
00100 Helsinki
Tel +358 9 1201

291 ☐ COM 1999

Presenting double-glazed
facades, and punctured by
public walkways, this
newspaper headquarters opens
itself, and its workings, up to
urban surroundings that include
Helsinki's main railway station.
The steel roof over its central
Media Plaza rests on three
concrete columns.

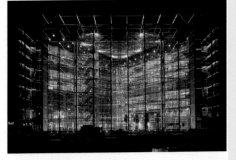

Steven Holl Architects

**Kiasma, Helsinki Museum of
Contemporary Art**
Mannerheiminaukio,
00100 Helsinki
Tel +358 9 1733 6501

292 ☐ CUL 1998

In this new gallery – named
'kiasma', or 'intertwining', in
Finnish – a gently curved wall of
glass admits the northern light,
and skylights cascade daylight
into semi-rectangular galleries.
The project aims to 'intertwine'
both city with building and art
with urban activities.

Heikkinen-Komonen Architects

Vuotalo Cultural Centre
Mosaiikkitori 2, 00980 Helsinki
Tel +358 9 310 88802

293 ☐ CUL 2000

Surrounded by a school and
shopping centre, this complex –
an 80 metre wide semicircle
mirroring a landscaped square –
was envisaged as a 'hinge',
linking neighbouring facilities.
The ground floor houses a
library, above which sits an
auditorium; and light is brought
in via large wells and a full-
height winter garden.

Heikkinen-Komonen Architects

Lume Mediacenter
Hameentie 135C,
00560 Helsinki
Tel +358 9 75631

294 □ CUL 2000

This university audiovisual department occupies a huge metal warehouse-like volume, attached to a converted factory by multiple studios, workshops and theatres united by two broad 'streets'. A long glazed gallery mediates between old and new, and provides lobby and exhibition spaces.

Ville Hara/HUT Wood Studio Workshop

Korkeasaari Lookout Tower
Korkeasaari Zoo,
00570 Helsinki
Tel +358 9 169 591

295 □ CUL 2002

This delicately transparent landmark behaves like an eggshell – so that even when the outer layer is punctured, it withstands its loads. The structure consists of 72 square battens treated with a linen-oil-based wood balm offering ultra-violet protection.

Arkkitehtisuunnitteln Huttunen & Lipasti

Villa Linnanmäki
Somerniemi, Uusimaa

296 ■ RES 2002

This house contains a ground-floor living, workroom and kitchen 'box', with a smaller box, containing a bedroom reached by narrow wooden hall stairs, perched on top. The lakeside facade is almost entirely glazed, and glows like a lantern when viewed across the water at night.

Olavi Koponen Architect

Villa Långbo
Långholmen, Kemiö
Tel +358 505 425 423

297 ☎ RES 2001

Constructed by hand on a semi-inaccessible island, this building creates a shelter below a U-shaped canopy where rough-plywood-shingle boxes of accommodation stand. A stone hearth, contrasting with the impermanence of the timber structure, serves two fireplaces – one facing inward, one out on to an external terrace.

Friis & Moltke

Ålborg South Hospital Chapel
Mølleparkvej, 9000 Ålborg
Tel +45 9932 1111

298 ☎ REL 2000

The exterior of this cool, white, rendered chapel is a hermetic triangle, containing a serene courtyard filled by a pool of water, on to which louvred openings provide views. Inside, the chapel is rectangular, with one glowing wall of semi-opaque glass and hexagonal lamps suspended from its double-height ceiling.

Nøhr & Sigsgaard Arkitektfirma

Viborg Swimming Centre
Banegårdspladsen, 8800 Viborg
Tel +45 8725 3180

299 ☐ SPO 1998

An imposing, glass-fronted double-height entrance foyer leads – via changing rooms, tanning parlour and gym – to a curved and tilted glass wall adjoining a railway line, through which the 25 metre pool's waterslides can be seen. Changing rooms have walls of opaque glass blocks.

Poulsen Architects

Future Parcel House
Skovsyrevej 8, Hornbæk,
8900 Randers

300 ▢❚ RES 2000

The project is enclosed in a stepping wall of heat-treated pine, within which a double-height 'gateway' garage – convertible into a future small apartment – leads to a courtyard sheltered by projecting upper rooms. Steel, timber and plywood lend an impression of lightness.

3XN

Kronjylland Savings Bank
Tronholmen 1, 8900 Randers
Tel +45 8912 2400

301 ✎ COM 2002

The ground floor of this bank headquarters disappears behind modernist *piloti* and only a single timber volume projects from this recessed plinth, while the main, serigraphed-glass-clad block hovers above. An atrium rises the full height of this glass block, and an ashwood art installation softens the functional environment.

Søbye & Toustrup Arkitekter

Community Centre
Evald Tangs Allé 45,
8730 Hadsten
Tel +45 87 61 27 60

302 ▢ PUB 2001

The four parts of this building – hall, library, activity wing and café – may be combined in various ways around its ramped central space; the hall can be opened to outside, forming a market or concert area. The library is a protruding box supported by steel cables and concrete beams.

Europe

Arkitekter WWH

Villa Valborg
Assens

303 ■ RES 1999

Outwardly appearing as a red Flensborg-brick 'box', the house's roof planes slope inwards, producing a more intimate scale around its central courtyard, paved in dark slate. Living and bedroom wings face each other, and a feature fireplace cuts into the western facade between large living room windows.

Dorte Bach Schmidt & Thomas Kranz

Villa in Skåde
Rensdyrvej 11, Skåde,
8270 Århus

304 ■ RES 1998

A brick volume containing service areas is flanked on one side by two cedar-clad cubes – the sauna and the pantry – and on the other by a two-storey steel-framed structure containing the living space. The partially recessed top floor accommodates a balcony.

Claus Hermansen Architects

Summer House
Engagervej 56, Dyngby,
8300 Odder

305 ■ RES 1999

Two archetypal 'house-shaped' wings are joined by a flat-roofed block and covered in expanded metal panels over which ivy is being trained to grow – eventually blanketing the building in greenery. A large living space with attic, and three tall bedrooms extending into the roof void, occupy the wings.

Wohlert Arkitekter

Kings' Jelling Historical Monument Buildings
Gormsgade 23, 7300 Jelling
Tel +45 75 87 23 50

306 ☐ CUL 2000

Two white-painted, brick rectangular buildings are placed parallel to each other, the area between containing the foyer, café and main staircase of this Viking museum. The larger of the two wings, housing permanent exhibitions, lines up with an existing church.

CF Møller Architects

Billund Airport Car Park Building
Passagerterminalen 16B, 7190 Billund
Tel +45 75 35 40 33

307 ☐ TRA 2002

The upper floors of this facility are clad with vertical louvres in extruded aluminium, covered in larch and jabota (a Brazilian hardwood), which give a side-on impression of solidity but which form a transparent front elevation. Public walkways are lit by continuous light panels.

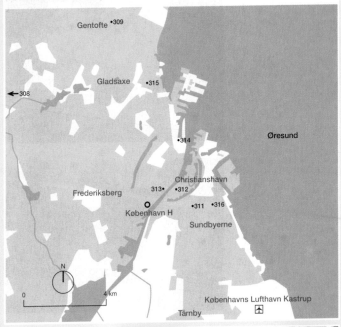

Gentofte •309

Gladsaxe •315

← 308

Øresund

•314

Christianshavn

313• •312

Frederiksberg

København H

•311 •316

Sundbyerne

N

0 4 km

Københavns Lufthavn Kastrup

Tårnby

Lundgaard & Tranberg
Arkitekter

Housing for the Elderly
Skovlunde Torv 8–12,
2740 Ballerup
Tel +45 44 77 19 77

308 ☐ RES 2001

The ground floor of this U-
shaped design houses
communal facilities, while the
upper two floors contain care
units grouped around common
access and leisure areas.
Siberian larch-framed bay
windows and timber cladding
lend the project a tactile nature.

Entasis

Kildeskovshallen, Extension to Public Baths
Adolphsvej 25, Gentofte,
2800 København
Tel +45 39 98 06 13

309 □ SPO 2002

A large yet deferential addition to an existing iconic modernist swimming centre, this hall for competitive swimming is lit by matt glass skylights, supported on two 60 metre trusses. A canvas screen, flush with the pool's sides, puts the focus on the water and the swimmers.

Henning Larsen Tegnestue

Private House
Drosselvej 1, Vejby Strand,
3210 Sjælland

310 ■ RES 2000

A house and retreat for artists, this horizontal, larch-clad box is divided internally by a central, brick, bathroom-and-kitchen core into a studio and living area. The south facade, almost entirely glazed, contrasts with a floor-level line of glazing in the plywood-clad studio, which emphasizes the forest floor.

Dorte Mandrup Arkitekter

Neighbourhood Centre
Jemtelandsgade 3, Amagerbro,
2300 København

311 □ PUB 2001

A striking new timber-and-glass hall on sloping concrete columns gives this warehouse conversion a daytime transparency and a glowing street presence by night. Internally, floor slabs were removed to create an atrium – a structural loss offset by a new external steel-and-timber frame.

Europe

Henning Larsen Tegnestue

Unibank Headquarters
Strandgade 3, Christianshavn,
1401 København

312 ■ COM 1999

Six gigantic portals of full-height
burnished copper act as
gateways to the long, thin
buildings that comprise this
complex – each mediating
between harbour and city. The
border between the front and
back of the building is
formalized by passageways of
glass connecting the boxes.

Schmidt, Hammer & Lassen

Royal Library
Søren Kierkegaards Plads 1,
1016 København
Tel +45 33 47 47 47

313 ■ ✎ CUL 1999

Nicknamed the 'Black
Diamond', the inclined granite-
clad facades appear to float on
a ribbon of raised glass that
allows views into the foyer and
panoramic vistas out to the
waterfront. Inside, the hard lines
of the black exterior are
tempered by organic, wave-like
balconies.

3XN

**FIH (Finance for Danish
Industry)**
Langelinie Allé 43,
2100 København
Tel +45 72 22 50 00

314 ✎ COM 2002

Adjoining a listed warehouse,
this office block adopts the
scale of its neighbour while
asserting its own identity: its
considerable plan-depth is
improved by recessed gardens
and entrances. A system of
adjustable aluminium shutters
is controlled by photocells.

Entasis

Auditorium at Svanemøllen Barracks
Ryvangs Allé 1, Svanemøllen,
2100 København
Tel +45 39 15 11 02

315 🖊 CUL 2002

This teaching facility uses the black slate of the barrack roofs to clad its concrete-framed elevations: a series of portals, within which glass facades and detailed fixtures subvert the masculinity of its settings. It is approached through a small square with a 'floating' roof.

Nøhr & Sigsgaard Arkitektfirma

Sundpark Kindergarten
Strandlosvej 73, Sundby-Øster,
2300 København
Tel +45 32 84 16 00

316 ▯ 🖊 EDU 1999

This larch-boarded volume leans towards the rear to accommodate a main entrance oriented to pedestrian and bicycle access, and sloping to reduce the scale on the opposing side. The infant-care rooms are laid out along a full-length corridor punctuated by niches and seating areas.

CASA Arkitekter

Amtmandsstien
Amtmandsstien 2–16,
4700 Næstved
Tel +45 55 78 66 66

317 🖊 RES 2001

Each unit planned over two levels with access via an inserted split level, this row of eight timber-clad one-bedroom houses commands panoramic views over the city. The ground floors comprise combined kitchen/dining areas with terrace access, while bedrooms and living room are above.

Europe

Søren Robert Lund Architects

**Sjællandske Newspaper
Printing Facility**
Skovsøvej 27, Skovsø,
4200 Slagelse
Tel +45 55 72 45 11

318   ∎ ✎ COM 2000

Central to this structure are the
huge printing and ventilation
halls, the deep gutter between
their roofs representing the
folding of newspapers. The
central hall is clad in folded zinc
panels; the lower volumes in
concrete and black-stained
timber.

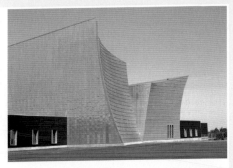

CUBO Arkitekter

**University of Southern
Denmark**
Campusvej 55, 5230 Odense

319   ∎ EDU 2003

CUBO's extension to a 1970s
landmark provides a campus
square – and the concrete over
Cor-ten, on its solar-screened
facades, lightens the original
palette. Bridges are a feature:
leading from stairs to the social
sciences faculty, and one of a
pair spanning the entrance hall
housing a restaurant.

Flemming Skude

Heaven House
Kompagnistræde 9,
4983 Hummingen, Lolland

320   ∎ RES 1999

The angled black-aluminium
walls of this dwelling cant
inwards, while accommodation
tucks beneath the sloping
facades. On the north side an
internal concrete wall stabilizes
temperatures. A central flight of
stairs climbs to an observation
platform, reminiscent of the
bridge of a yacht.

ARKOS Arkitekter

**Musholm Bay Vacation &
Recreation Centre**
Musholmvej 100, 4220 Korsør
Tel +45 70 13 77 00

321   🖋 REC 2001

In this turf-roofed residential
centre for people with muscular
dystrophy, wheelchair-
accessible single villas and
duplex units are grouped
between high, thuja-wood party
walls, resembling the
breakwaters found along this
coastline. Conical bathrooms
were decorated by 16 artists.

3.3   322-331   United Kingdom North

Europe

Sutherland Hussey Architects

An Turas
Tiree, Inner Hebrides

322 ☐ CUL 2003

A waiting area for the ferry on the westernmost island of the Inner Hebrides chain, the whitewashed entrance corridor and glass box of this shelter draw a line in the landscape. Protected from the weather, but open to the beach through a slatted floor, a traditionally felt-roofed bridge space connects the two.

Gehry Partners

Maggie's Cancer Caring Centre, Ninewells Hospital
Ninewells Hospital, Dundee
DD1 9SY
Tel +44 131 537 2457

323 ☐ ✆ PUB 2003

A therapy centre at an existing hospital, Frank Gehry's tiny first UK commission gathers dining, common-room and library facilities beneath an irregular, folded-plate roof designed to imitate the surrounding hills. A family room in a white-painted tower punctures this roofline.

Richard Murphy Architects

Dundee Contemporary Arts Centre
152 Nethergate, Dundee
DD1 4DY
Tel +44 138 290 9220

324 ☐ CUL 1999

A small entrance draws visitors into more expansive spaces beyond, where the route past gallery spaces drops to a double-height café and cinemas below. Copper, white render and intricate metalwork are mixed with existing eroded brickwork.

Munkenbeck & Marshall

Mount Stuart Visitor Centre
Mount Stuart, Isle of Bute
PA20 9LR
Tel +44 170 050 3877

325 □ CUL 2001

Conceived as a wall to be
walked on, this centre contrasts
with its setting – the Gothic
Revival Mount Stuart family
home – where visitors are
invited to enter across a moat
and up to a rooftop restaurant.
This frameless, fully-glazed
space sits atop the hardwood-
louvred box of the centre.

RMJM Architects and Tony Gee
& Partners

Falkirk Wheel
Lime Road, Tanfourhill, Falkirk,
Stirlingshire FK1 4RS
Tel +44 132 461 9888

326 □ TRA 2002

The first ever rotating boat lift,
the Wheel connects the Grand
Union and Forth and Clyde
canals with two giant steel arms
– each with lock-gated boat
'containers' – that revolve
around a hub. Both are derived
from fish-skeleton and Ferris-
wheel forms.

Benson & Forsyth

Museum of Scotland
Chambers Street, Edinburgh
EH1 1JF
Tel +44 131 247 4422

327 □ CUL 1998

This extension encloses, links
and reinforces the physical and
historical context of Edinburgh,
in addition to housing five levels
of the national collection.
Staircases and terraces give
visitors a choice of routes that
culminates in a dramatic
roofscape with spectacular city
views.

Europe

Malcolm Fraser Architects

Dance Base: National Centre for Dance
14–16 Grassmarket, Edinburgh
EH1 2JU
Tel +44 131 225 5525

328 ☐ CUL 2001

Nestling below the castle, this centre is spread between its historic medieval Grassmarket entrance; a glazed-roofed central space; and two smaller, upper studios with split-pitch and pyramidal roofs. Each has a distinct quality and captures views of the Old Town.

Page and Park Architects

The Lighthouse
11 Mitchell Lane, Glasgow
G1 3NU
Tel +44 141 221 6362

329 ☐ CUL 1999

This lively conversion houses architecture exhibition space, education and IT facilities, a children's area, café, and a Charles Rennie Mackintosh-dedicated exhibition and conference space – inserted into the Glasgow Herald Building. A water-tank tower provides a viewing balcony.

Page and Park Architects

Graham Square Housing
10, 20, 30 Graham Square,
Glasgow G31 1AN

330 ◼ RES 1999

These seven buildings – with their thin, curved elevations on the site of a historic cattle market – are known as the 'Matador' houses: their simple, brick rear elevations contrast with the flamboyant fronts. The internal layouts of these apartments are based on the traditional tenement plan.

Europe

United Kingdom North

Wilkinson Eyre Architects

Gateshead Millennium Bridge
Baltic Square, Gateshead,
Tyne and Wear
Tel +44 191 433 3000

331 ☐ INF 2001

A significant development in
swing-bridge evolution, the
whole of this crossing rotates
on hinges located at the
intersection of its arch and
walkway elements, until the
apex of each curve reaches a
common level. Echoing the form
of the Tyne Bridge, it provides a
route to the Baltic Art Factory.

3.4 332-408   United Kingdom South & Republic of Ireland

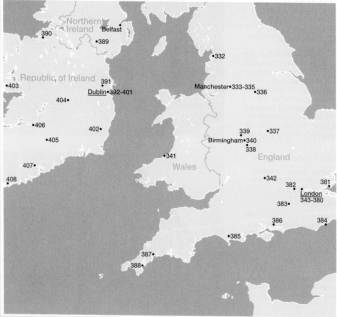

Europe

MJP Architects

Ruskin Library, University of Lancaster
Lancaster University, Bailrigg,
Lancaster LA1 4YW
Tel +44 1524 593 587

332 ☐ EDU 1998

This building recalls Ruskin's beloved Venice in its marble banding and internal expression of the archive as a freestanding treasure-chest in a moat of glass. Entrance, archive and reading room form a church-like progression of narthex, choir and sanctuary.

Michael Wilford & Partners

The Lowry Performing and Visual Arts Centre
Pier 8, Salford Quays M50 3AZ
Tel +44 870 787 5780

333 ☐ CUL 2000

This set of galleries for the work of Salford artist LS Lowry is joined by two contrasting theatre spaces in distinct metallic forms. New cladding materials – including stainless-steel shingles and extensive perforated sheet metal – give way to bold oranges and purples in the striking interior.

Arup Associates and Arup Group

City of Manchester Stadium
Sportcity, Rowsley Street,
Manchester M11 3FF
Tel +44 161 231 3200

334 ☐ SPO 2002

Built for the city's hosting of the 2002 Commonwealth Games, this stadium, with its spiralling access ramps and undulating saddle roof, is now the home of Manchester City Football Club. The roof, which provides shelter for every seat, is supported by an cable-net structure.

Daniel Libeskind

Imperial War Museum of the North
Trafford Wharf Road,
Manchester M17 1PL
Tel +44 161 836 4000

335 ☐ CUL 2002

Libeskind's highly internalized visitor experience also makes its mark externally, with three fragmented roof-shards – symbolizing the historic battlefields of earth, air and water. Within, a curving floor plane and display 'pods' double as projection screens.

Pringle Richards Sharratt

Winter Gardens and Millennium Galleries
Surrey Street and Arundel Gate,
Sheffield S1 2LH
Tel +44 114 278 2600

336 ☐ CUL 2001

The Winter Gardens rise from either end of a T-shaped, enclosed public space, their glazed elliptical timber arches rippling towards the surrounding streets. The light-filled, airy complex also contains galleries, an arcade and a public space.

Grimshaw

National Space Centre
Exploration Drive, Leicester
LE4 5NS
Tel +44 116 261 0261

337 ☐ CUL 2001

Through a low, square research and planetarium block, visitors are led on a spiralling route – reflected in a landscaped roof – to the main attraction: a rocket tower accessed by scenic lifts. Its space-age ETFE-cushion skin forms 3 metre high structural horizontal ribs on an eccentric concrete core.

Europe

Arup Associates and Arup Group

Arup Campus
Blythe Gate, Blythe Valley Park, Solihull B90 8AE

338 ■ COM 2001

This environmentally responsible and responsive office building for Arup engineers utilizes carefully oriented, layered and louvred facades; expressive rooftop ventilation cowls; exposed internal thermal mass; and individual occupancy control.

Caruso St John

Walsall Art Gallery
Gallery Square, Walsall
WS2 8LG
Tel +44 1922 654 400

339 □ CUL 1999

As much a catalyst for the regeneration of the Midlands as a home for the Garman Ryan Collection, Walsall's new gallery is a pale-terracotta-clad tower punctuated by crisply framed windows. An informal internal route weaves between grand formal halls and intricate timber-panelled rooms.

Future Systems

Selfridges Department Store
Upper Mall East, Bullring, Birmingham B5 4BP
Tel +44 870 8377 377

340 □ COM 2003

The fluidity of the aluminium-disc-covered 'bubble' exterior is matched inside with an organically shaped atrium stretching across the floor plan. The soft, curvaceous external form responds to the natural curve of the site, and signifies its department-store function without the need for signage.

Foster and Partners

The Great Glasshouse
National Botanical Garden of
Wales, Llanarthne SA32 8HG
Tel +44 1558 668 768

341 ☐ CUL 2000

Embedded into the hills of
Carmarthenshire, the world's
largest single-span glasshouse
rests its elliptical curved-glass
roof on a retaining wall that
contains public and educational
facilities. The structure spans
99 metres and comprises 24
tubular steel arches springing
from a concrete ring beam.

Dixon Jones Architects

**Said Business School,
University of Oxford**
Park End Street, Oxford
OX1 1HP
Tel +44 1865 288 800

342 ▐ ✎ EDU 2001

This modern cloister
development passes from a
covered entrance court, through
an outer quadrangle, to a
semicircular library and rooftop
amphitheatre. A double-height
limestone colonnade is
repeated in a rotated form to
border the inner cloister.

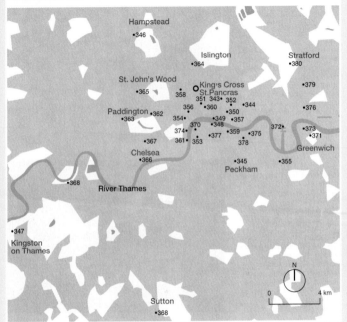

Hampstead
•346

Islington
•364

Stratford
•380

St. John's Wood
•365

○ King's Cross
St.Pancras

•379

•358
351 343 352
•344

356 •360 •350

Paddington •362
•354 •349 •357

•376

•363
374• 370 348• 359 375

372•
•373
•371

361• 353 •377 378

Greenwich

Chelsea
•366

•345
Peckham

•355

•368

River Thames

•347
Kingston
on Thames

N

0   4 km

Sutton
•368

Adjaye Associates

Dirty House
Chance Street, London E2

343 ☐ RES 2002

The dark exterior of this building conceals a series of live-work studio spaces for two artist-clients – with self-contained rooftop living spaces above double-height workspaces and a guest suite. The impenetrable street facade of this converted warehouse conceals a two-storey lightwell, doubling as entrance to the home above.

Adjaye Associates

Elektra House
Ashfield Street, London E1

344 ▮ RES 1999

A blank, resin-coated plywood street facade conceals a three-bedroom home held between two double-height lightwells – one immediately behind the street elevation, the other to the rear. The restrained interior includes an unsealed concrete ground floor, maple stairs and full-height doors throughout.

Alsop Associates

Peckham Library and Media Centre
122 Peckham Hill Street, London SE15
Tel +44 20 7525 0200

345 ☐ CUL 1999

L-shaped in section rather than plan, this iconic building houses media centre and support accommodation in its tall, vertical arm, while the library projects out over a new public square. The reading room has freestanding timber-framed pods for specialist functions.

Alison Brooks Architects

VXO House
16 Spaniard's End, London NW3

346 ▮ RES 2001

This house extension draws in the visitor – past the sculptural 'O' garage port and the 'X' of the new garden gymnasium and guest pavilion, to the 'V'-support of the new entrance hall. The fully glazed pavilion addresses both house and carport, its massive X-column supporting a sedum roof.

Europe

David Chipperfield

Knight House
Kingston-upon-Thames, Surrey

347 ■ RES 2001

This extension to an existing residence places an archetypal pitched-roof house form alongside the original, to which it is connected on both levels by a translucent fibreglass link. Living/working accommodation is arranged as two continuous rooms, the upper having a large, vertically sliding window, which transforms it into a balcony.

Foster and Partners with Anthony Caro

Millennium Bridge
South Bank, London SE1

348 ☐ INF 2002

Linking St Paul's Cathedral and the South Bank, this footbridge, with its slender, 'blade of light' form, uses a low-lying curved profile to optimize views. Eight high-tension cables, rising and falling between two Y-shaped concrete-and-steel armatures, support the metal-decked walkway.

Herzog & de Meuron

Tate Modern
Bankside, London SE1
Tel +44 20 7887 8000

349 ☐ CUL 2000

The highlight of this new 'art factory' is the sloping-floored turbine hall – its vast space housing a rolling programme of large-scale installations, overlooked by 'light boxes' adjoining the upper-gallery entrances. The top two floors constitute the only external intervention: a clerestory containing a restaurant.

Foster and Partners

Swiss Re London Headquarters
30 St Mary Axe, London EC3

350 ◼ COM 2003

Containing shops and a public plaza at its base, offices in the tower and restaurant at the top, this 40-storey skyscraper has a circular plan, widens as it rises and tapers towards its apex. Naturally ventilated, its aerodynamic form draws fresh air up through a series of spiralling lightwells.

Eric Parry Architects

30 Finsbury Square
30 Finsbury Square,
London EC2

351 ◼ COM 2002

Located close to the City, the new office building for insurance company Scottish Widows comprises a series of exposed concrete beams, Portland Stone piers and a discreet glazing system. The trabeated facade is uncluttered, its tripartite fenestration rising vertically to end in a colonnade.

William Russell Architecture and Design

House on Bacon Street
Bacon Street, London E2

352 ◼ RES 2001

Built on a small plot in Bethnal Green, this house contains a variety of spaces designed to allow for different types of occupation over time. The lower floors form a separate flat, and the main house occupies the levels above. Clad in glass and steel, the building makes a contemporary statement.

dRMM

One Centaur Street
1 Centaur Street, London SE1
Tel +44 20 7803 0777

353 ∎ ✎ RES 2003

Situated close to a railway, this residential building rises from a narrow strip that was formerly a scrap yard. Incorporating prefabricated components that can be recreated in any number of patterns, the apartment block serves as a model for a new housing typology for London brownfield sites.

Richard Rogers Partnership

Broadwick House
15–17 Broadwick Street, London W1

354 ∎ COM 2002

Occupying a quadruple-aspect site in Soho, this development provides six floors of office space above street-level retail and restaurant facilities. Set back from the main mass, the rooftop double-height office suite is topped by an arched roof, the key architectural motif of the building.

Herzog & de Meuron

Laban Centre
Creekside, London SE8
Tel +44 20 8691 8600

355 ☐ CUL 2003

This facility, which over two levels contains a dance theatre and studios, lecture hall, health facility, library, conference facilities and café bar, is located in Deptford on the South Bank of the Thames. The facade, a collaboration with London artist Michael Craig-Martin, is a skin of coloured transparent and translucent panels.

Foster and Partners

Great Court, British Museum
Great Russell Street,
London WC1
Tel +44 20 7323 8000

356 □ CUL 2000

Covering an area of 6,100
square metres and containing
information points, a bookshop
and café, the Great Court is the
largest enclosed public space in
Europe. Two broad staircases
encircle the Round Reading
Room and a glazed roof-canopy
spans the irregular gap between
its dome and the galleries.

Richard Rogers Partnership

Lloyd's Register of Shipping
71 Fenchurch Street,
London EC3

357 ■ COM 2000

The new building for the
Lloyd's Register of Shipping
dramatically rises 14 storeys
within a conservation area in
the City of London. Two slender
glazed towers, the primary
circulation zones, are joined
by two central atria which
maximize day-lighting and air-
conditioning.

Colin St John Wilson & Partners

British Library
98 Euston Road, London NW1
Tel +44 20 7412 7000

358 □ CUL 1998

Completed over a period of
almost 25 years, this building
was designed to provide a
reading room and storage
facilities. Asymmetry and
irregular articulation are used to
fulfil complex functional needs
while sympathizing with the
flamboyance of nearby St
Pancras Hotel.

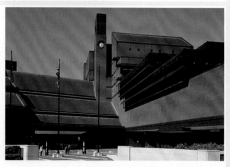

Europe

Foster and Partners

**Greater London Authority
Headquarters**
The Queen's Walk, London SE1
Tel +44 20 7983 4000

359 □ GOV 2002

Housing the chamber for the
London Assembly, the offices
of the Mayor and 500 staff, this
highly public building is situated
in an undeveloped section of
the Thames's South Bank.
Energy consumption is
minimized by using a form
based on a modified sphere.

Richard Rogers Partnership

88 Wood Street
88 Wood Street, London EC2

360 ▮ COM 1999

This building comprises three
vertical slabs of office
accommodation. The space
between each block is
articulated by glass-and-steel
lift shafts and stairs. Clad in full-
height glazed panels, the ends
of the slabs display the
concrete frame and diagonal
bracing.

Marks Barfield

Millbank Millennium Pier
Millbank, London SW1
Tel +44 20 7887 8888

361 □ TRA 2003

Situated on the Thames's
Millbank, this pier is used for
the boat service that links Tate
Britain, Tate Modern and the
Saatchi Gallery. A functional
floating sculpture formed of
faceted steel plates, at night the
pontoon is transformed by the
lights of Angela Bulloch's *Flash
& Tidal*, their sequence
determined by the tidal cycle.

John McAslan + Partners

Royal Academy of Music
Marylebone Road, London NW1
Tel +44 20 7873 7373

362 ☐ EDU 2003

This concert hall and recording
studios are housed in a
structure designed also to
function as a passage between
two historic buildings. Set
below-grade, the volume
required to achieve optimum
acoustics pushes the barrel-
vaulted roof above ground level.

John Pawson

Pawson House
2 Rosmead Road, London W11

363 ▮ RES 1999

Leaving the Victorian terrace-
house facade undisturbed,
Pawson stripped out the interior
and opened the rear elevation,
creating an architecture where
the threshold between inside
and outside all but disappears.
Glass walls and enlarged
apertures allow natural light
inside and views become part
of the landscape of the interior.

Sarah Wigglesworth Architects

9 Stock Orchard Street
9 Stock Orchard Street,
London N7
Tel +44 20 7607 9200

364 ✎ RES 2001

In a north London street
alongside a railway line, this
L-shaped experimental home
and studio includes innovative
features such as polycarbonate
and straw bale construction.
Spring-loaded gabion *piloti*
reduce vibrations from passing
trains and a sandbag facade
provides sound insulation.

Europe

Future Systems

Lord's Cricket Ground Media Centre
St John's Wood, London NW8
Tel +44 20 7289 1611

365 ⌒ SPO 1999

This facility seats 120 sports journalists in its terraced media suite, allowing uninterrupted glare-free views of the pitch. The latest advances in boat-building technology have been used to create the world's first all-aluminium semi-monocoque building.

Tony Fretton Architects

Red House
Tite Street, London SW3

366 ▮ RES 2002

Situated on Tite Street in London's Chelsea, Red House, an eclectic mix of classical and contemporary forms, presents a powerful new form of domestic monumentality. In a 6 metre high reception room, concealed lighting and a subtle mix of materials creates a gallery-like space for the owner.

John Pawson

250 Brompton Road
250 Brompton Road,
London SW3
Tel +44 20 7591 8111

367 ☐ COM 2001

The B&B Italia furniture showroom is a collaboration between Pawson, Antonio Citterio and B&B Italia. Its monumental facade of glass, stone and bronze fronts a site that stretches back more than 120 metres. Generous windows at either end and skylights bathe the interior in natural light.

Pierre d'Avoine Architects

Big House Little House
99 Mortlake High Street,
London SW14

368 ■ RES 2003

Situated in west London's
Mortlake, this house, which is
roughly the size of a typical
terraced house, is a
freestanding box clad in
Douglas fir and set on a red-
brick plinth. By placing the
building end-on to the street
and presenting a blank facade,
traffic noise is reduced.

Bill Dunster Architects

**BedZED, Beddington Zero
Energy Development**
London Road, Hackbridge,
Sutton, Surrey SM6 6BZ
Tel +44 20 8404 4880

369 □ RES 2002

Including 82 dwellings,
workshop and office space, and
community accommodation,
BedZED offers a model for a
low-energy, mixed-use
development. Three-storey
blocks and a network of streets
are designed to optimize the
use of solar power to the south.

Marks Barfield

British Airways London Eye
Westminster Bridge Road,
London SE1
Tel +44 870 5000 600

370 □ TOU 2000

Situated in front of London's
most famous skyline at 135
metres tall and bearing 32
capsules, the London Eye
provides a 30 minute view over
the capital. Its creation included
the construction of 44 33 metre-
deep piles to carry the wheel's
massive compression forces.

Europe

Alsop Architects

North Greenwich Underground Station
Blackwall Lane, London SE10
Tel +44 845 330 9880

371 ☐ TRA 1999

On the North Greenwich peninsula, this new station is generously proportioned in order to cater for a large number of visitors. The triple-height, single-volume subterranean space is divided horizontally by suspended floors and further articulated by cobalt-blue ovoid columns.

Foster and Partners

Canary Wharf Underground Station
Canary Wharf, London E14
Tel +44 845 330 9880

372 ☐ TRA 1999

Set within gardens at the base of Canary Wharf Tower, the entrances to this underground station appear as three discreet, elliptical canopies. Below are spaces of cathedral-like proportions with concrete columns that rise through the 27 metre height of the building.

Foster and Partners

North Greenwich Transport Interchange
5 Millennium Way, London SE10
Tel +44 20 8599 4470

373 ☐ TRA 1998

Positioned directly above the entrance to North Greenwich Underground Station, this public transport hub is part of the overall regeneration project. Comprising a bus terminus, a car and taxi drop-off point and a waiting room, the interchange is signalled by its dramatic curving roof.

Hopkins Architects

Westminster Underground Station
Bridge Street, London SW1
Tel +44 845 330 9880

---

374 ☐ TRA 1999

This station and the New Parliamentary Building above it are an integrated structure. The weight of the building's central courtyard is transferred through a quadruple-height subterranean box. Features include the exposed rock of retained walls.

Eva Jiricna Architects

Canada Water Bus Station
Rotherhithe, London SE16
Tel +44 20 7222 1234

---

375 ☐ TRA 1999

Situated in London's Docklands, this bus interchange provides amenities for staff and passengers while protecting nearby housing from noise and pollution. The facility is dominated by an extensive canopy, its two massive wings cantilevered from a central glass-enclosed truss and also acting as acoustic buffers.

John McAslan + Partners

Canning Town Underground Station
Silvertown Way, London E16
Tel +44 845 330 9880

---

376 ☐ TRA 1999

As well as the Jubilee Line, this complex structure houses Railtrack services and the Docklands Light Railway, and connects with the bus station at ground level. A three-level reinforced-concrete viaduct combines with lightweight steel and glass ticketing enclosures.

Europe

MJP Architects

Southwark Underground Station
68–70 Blackfriars Road,
London SE1
Tel +44 845 330 9880

377 ☐ TRA 1999

The entrance to this new underground station, located on London's South Bank, pays homage to the 1930's circular ticket halls of Pick and Holden. Below, the curved theme continues in the dramatic triple-height entrance hall lit from above.

Ian Ritchie Architects

Bermondsey Underground Station
Jamaica Road, London SE16
Tel +44 845 330 9880

378 ☐ TRA 1999

Bermondsey Station, one of 11 stations in the Jubilee Line Extension scheme, is a mixture of light, transparent glass and heavy, anchored concrete. The glass-roofed interior lets sunlight into the station, some of it seeping into the below-ground platforms.

van Heyningen and Haward Architects

West Ham Underground Station
Manor Road, London E15
Tel +44 845 330 9880

379 ☐ TRA 1999

Unlike most of the Jubilee Line Extension projects, this station is sited above ground and is constructed of traditional materials. Red brick is predominant, with robust materials, such as glass blocks, concrete beams and stainless steel, used for articulation.

Wilkinson Eyre Architects

Stratford Station Concourse and Depot
45 Gibbins Road, London E15

380 ☐ TRA 1999

The simplicity of this single-volume design belies the fact that this is an interchange for four rail lines and the terminus for the Jubilee Line Extension. The curved roof extends over the public outdoor space, unifying the concourses, bridges and stairs below.

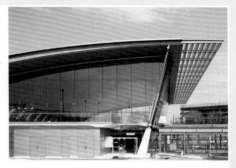

Cottrell + Vermeulen Architecture

After School Club, Westborough Primary School
Macdonald Avenue, Westcliff-on-Sea, Essex SS0 9BS
Tel +44 1702 349 249

381 ✆ EDU 2001

Europe's first permanent cardboard building, it uses 90 per cent recycled materials and is 90 per cent recyclable at the end of its anticipated 20 year life. Load-bearing composite cardboard panels and columns give it strength.

David Chipperfield

River and Rowing Museum
Mill Meadows, Henley-on-Thames, Oxfordshire RG9 1BF
Tel +44 1491 415 600

382 ☐ CUL 1998

Comprising galleries, public function areas and caretaker's accommodation, the form of this museum refers to traditional Oxfordshire barns and Henley's boathouses. Timber barns 'float' above a glazed ground floor, and oak decks, establishing another raised plane, link the pavilions.

Grimshaw

**European Institute of Health
and Medical Sciences**
University of Surrey, Guildford,
Surrey GU2 7TE
Tel +44 1483 686 700

383 ☐ ✎ EDU 1999

This new landmark building
amalgamates three healthcare
colleges and acts as a new
campus gateway in the heart of
Guildford. The six-storey prow-
like teaching and administration
block, accompanied by the
single-storey laboratory wing,
is clad in zinc and glass.

Niall McLaughlin Architects

**Bandstand, De La Warr
Pavilion**
Marina, Bexhill-on-Sea, East
Sussex TN33 9BN
Tel +44 1424 830 355

384 ☐ CUL 2000

A contemporary bandstand for
the De La Warr Pavilion
designed by Mendelsohn and
Chemayeff in 1935, its design
reflects the involvement of local
children and a craftsman. The
wings of the plywood and
fibreglass canopy help project
the sound forward.

Tony Fretton Architects

Faith House
Holton Lee Centre for Disability
in the Arts, Dorset BH16 6IN
Tel +44 1202 625 562

385 ☐ REL 2002

A non-denominational building
to encourage reflection and
contemplation, the Faith House
is situated at the highest point
of the Holton Lee estate and,
with its simple post and lintel
tectonic, has been likened to a
Greek temple. Inside are a quiet
room, glazed lobby, toilets,
assembly room and sun porch.

Edward Cullinan Architects

Downland Gridshell, Weald and Downland Open Air Museum
Singleton, Chichester, West Sussex PO18 0EU
Tel +44 1243 811 363

386 ☐ CUL 2001

The latest addition to this museum houses a store for an archive of construction artefacts and, above it, a workshop for timber repairs. The double-layer gridshell is formed from green oak sections and is clad with red cedar and polycarbonate.

Grimshaw

The Eden Project
Bodelva, St Austell, Cornwall PL24 2SG
Tel +44 1726 811 911

387 ☐ CUL 2001

Comprised of eight geodesic domes spread over 23 hectares, The Eden Project continues the tradition established by Britain's historic glasshouses. The desired internal conditions are maintained by the minimal shadows cast by the Biomes and the Ethyltetrafluorethylene skin.

Long & Kentish Architects

National Maritime Museum, Cornwall
Discovery Quay, Falmouth, Cornwall TR11 3QY
Tel +44 1326 313 388

388 ☐ CUL 2002

Straddling the sea wall of the Fal estuary in Falmouth's dockland area, this museum is a branch of the Greenwich-based National Maritime Museum. A tower stands like a lighthouse, and the timber-clad exhibition halls reflect the local vernacular of warehouse-like sheds.

Glenn Howells Architects

Market Place Theatre and Arts Centre
Market Street, Armagh, County Armagh BT61 7AT
Tel +44 28 3752 1820

389 □ CUL 2000

Built on the slope to St Patrick's Cathedral, the Market Place has transformed the social and cultural life of this previously troubled Northern Ireland city. Its low external profile allows uninterrupted views of the cathedral, and the use of stone creates an elegant, clean look.

McCullough Mulvin Architects

Model Arts and Niland Gallery
The Mall, Sligo, County Sligo
Tel +353 71 914 1405

390 □ CUL 2000

Incorporating the now-redundant Model School, this refurbishment provides galleries, performance spaces and a new pavilion to house the Niland collection of Jack B Yeats paintings. A day-lit courtyard gives the arts complex a revitalized heart and links the simple cedar-clad box to the existing stone gallery.

Grafton Architects

Meath County Council
Drumree Road, Dunshaughlin, County Meath
Tel +353 1 825 9132

391 □ GOV 2001

This modest building serves the housing estates that surround it. The projecting council chamber and two existing cedars frame a slender space above which floats a cantilevered canopy. The building's skeleton of exposed concrete is combined with timber and glass screens.

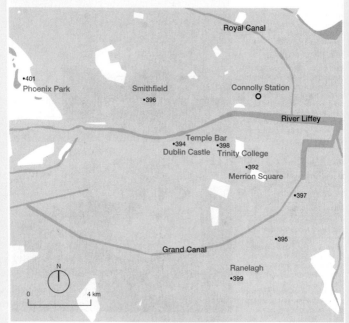

Royal Canal

•401
Phoenix Park

Smithfield
•396

Connolly Station
O

River Liffey

Temple Bar
•394 •398
Dublin Castle Trinity College

•392
Merrion Square

•397

•395

Grand Canal

Ranelagh
•399

N

0   4 km

Benson & Forsyth

**National Gallery of Ireland
Millennium Wing**
Merrion Square West, Dublin 2
Tel +353 1 661 5133

392 ☐ CUL 2002

The Millennium Wing, an
extension of the existing
National Gallery of Ireland, is
situated close to Dublin's
Parliament building. From its
modernist sculptural facade,
visitors enter through a cubic
antechamber into a quadruple-
height atrium, which connects
with the existing galleries.

Europe

Bucholz McEvoy Architects/
BDP Dublin

Fingal County Hall
Main Street, Swords, County
Dublin
Tel +353 1 890 5000

393 ☐ GOV 2000

Located on the edge of Dublin,
this local government building
is the result of an international
competition. Defining the
eastern edge of the new town
square, its atrium, with curved
glass facade, is the meeting
point of public and private.

de Blacam and Meagher

**Temple Bar Residential
Building**
Exchange Street Upper, West
End Temple Bar, Dublin 8

394 ▮ RES 2000

Part of the redevelopment of
Temple Bar in the centre of
Dublin, this building comprises
a five-storey and a nine-storey
block, with courtyard garden
and crèche, and underground
car park. The reinforced
concrete structure is clad in
brickwork and oak panelling.

de Blacam and Meagher

3 Mews Houses
84, 85, 86 Waterloo Place,
Dublin 4

395 ▮ RES 2002

Imitating existing houses on
adjacent plots and traditional
Dublin Lanes, these three
dwellings are modest in scale,
fitting on a site only 12.5 metres
wide. Each house has the same
design, including a main living
area on the first floor and a roof
terrace. Screens throughout
control privacy and daylight.

Grafton Architects

North King Street Apartments
Cnr North King Street and
Church Street, Dublin 7

396 ▯ RES 2001

Located in the centre of Dublin,
its character is a reinterpretation
of the surrounding warehouses.
The brick and timber street
facade has large sliding shutters
that provide privacy, security
and noise protection. By
contrast, the courtyard facades
are constructed from brick,
steel and glass.

Grafton Architects

The Long House
Percy Lane, Dublin 4

397 ▯ RES 2001

Located on a narrow lane in the
southern inner city, this house
is built over the entire plot in
order to maximize its narrow
and long dimensions. Internal
and external rooms are carved
out of the solid mass. A large
timber gate provides protection
and privacy from the street and,
along with the second-hand
bricks, reflect the character of
the lane.

McCullough Mulvin Architects/
Keane Murphy Duff Architecture

Ussher Library, Trinity College
Nassau Street, Dublin 2
Tel +353 1 608 1652

398 ✆ EDU 2002

Situated between the Trinity
College campus and the city,
the new library provides 750
undergraduate reader places
and space for 350,000 volumes.
Three prismatic blocks, the two
longer blocks connected by a
glazed atrium, are devoted to
reading rooms and book
conservation and storage.

Europe

O'Donnell + Tuomey Architects

Multi Denominational School
Ranelagh Road, Dublin 6
Tel +353 1 496 1722

399 ✏ EDU 1998

Built on a sloping site near the
city boundary, the materials –
brick, stone and timber – used
for this school building match
those of the surrounding
houses. A series of classrooms
are arranged off a corridor. The
street facade is tightly packed
whereas the south facade, with
a long zinc-clad canopy, is more
open.

O'Donnell + Tuomey Architects

**Centre for Research into
Infectious Diseases**
University College Dublin,
Belfield, Dublin 4
Tel +353 1 706 1627

400 ✏ EDU 2003

Providing a new landmark for
the city, this simple and
expressive building contains a
medical microbiology research
institute and laboratories. The
two wings of the building are
arranged around a landscaped
court with the north-facing
laboratories raised on columns.

Scott Tallon Walker Architects

**New Entrance Pavilion,
Dublin Zoo**
Phoenix Park, Dublin 4
Tel +353 1 474 8900

401 ☐ REC 1999

Unified by a single, flat roof
supported by ten columns, this
single-storey pavilion contains
a shop, ticket kiosks and a cash
office. The walls are clad in
Wicklow granite and clerestory
glazing allows views of the
parkland. Interior materials
include Welsh slate, stainless
steel and American white oak.

Scott Tallon Walker Architects

Tulach a'tSolais Monument
Oulart Hill, County Wexford

| 402 | ☐ CUL 1998 |

This monument (Mound of Light), a powerful symbol of enlightenment, commemorates the 1798 rebellion by the Irish against British rule. The narrow slot bisecting Oulart Hill is orientated east–west to frame the rising and setting sun. Beneath the mound and on either side of the deep passage is a double-cube chamber.

O'Donnell + Tuomey Architects

Letterfrack Furniture College
Letterfrack, Connemara,
County Galway
Tel +353 95 41047

| 403 | ✒ EDU 2001 |

This college includes workshops, a radio station, student accommodation and administrative space. Timber is used throughout, providing an economical form of construction that is in keeping with the landscape and existing building.

ABK Architects

Offaly County Council Civic Offices
Áras an Chontae, Charleville
Road, Tullamore, County Offaly
Tel +353 50 646 800

| 404 | ☐ GOV 2002 |

The new council offices stand in sharp contrast to Tullamore's other institutional buildings. Beyond the small entrance forecourt are a top-lit atrium and three-storey offices. A single-storey extension contains the café, archives, walled garden and crèche.

O'Donnell + Tuomey Architects

Galbally Social Housing
Galbally, County Limerick

405 ▮ RES 2002

Built within the planned nineteenth-century town of Galbally and sited close to the town square, this social housing development epitomizes architecture that is both contextual and contemporary. The scheme comprises six three-storey family houses and five single-storey sheltered units for the elderly.

Bucholz McEvoy Architects

Limerick County Hall, Local Government Office
Dooradoyle, Limerick, County Limerick
Tel +353 6 149 6000

406 ☐ GOV 2003

The entrance to this new County Council headquarters is from an open space of uncultivated land. An atrium in the main part of the facility, along with its timber truss *brise-soleil* and the building's structure and fabric, controls the temperature and ventilation.

(EEA) Erick van Egeraat associated architects

Crawford Art Gallery Extension
Emmet Place, Cork, County Cork
Tel +353 21 427 3377

407 ☐ CUL 2000

Within the wedge-shaped former courtyard of the gallery is a new two-storey extension. As well as providing two large temporary exhibition spaces, the extension links the old building to create a unified whole.

Gumuchdjian Associates

Think Tank Boathouse
Skibbereen, County Cork

408 ■ RES 1998

Set into the River Ilen, this film-maker's retreat comprises a single volume containing just a bookshelf, a small kitchen and a lavatory. Inspired by boathouses and Japanese pavilions, the timber roof with its generous eaves dominates and provides protection. Timber decks and a long jetty complete the idyll.

3.5   409-468   Netherlands

Europe

Space Group

Self Referential House
Prinsenstraat, Achter de
Barakken, 9711 CL Groningen

409 ◼ RES 2001

This house challenges notions
of domesticity and boundaries
between inside and outside,
public and private. With its
facade of projecting panels and
varied geometric planes, the
building establishes itself as an
autonomous unit. Occupants
can move interior walls to
determine their own spaces.

Foreign Office Architects

Blue Moon Residential Hotel
Kleine Gang and Grote Gang,
Schuiteschuiverskwartier,
Groningen

410 ◼ TOU 2001

As part of the 2001 Blue Moon
Festival, architects were invited
to design dual-function
live/work buildings. The four-
storey, corrugated steel hotel
houses a café and apartments.
The front facade is a system of
shutters that articulates the
concepts of public or private.

John Hejduk

Wall House 2
AJ Lutulistraat 17, Hoornse
Meer, 9728 WT Groningen
Tel +31 50 312 3395

411 ▢ RES 2001

Designed by Hejduk in 1973 but
only built after his death as a
tribute by Groningen city
council, the spaces of the
house are divided according to
function on either side of a
dividing wall. The stacked living
spaces have curved walls, while
the service spaces are
geometrically shaped.

Atelier Zeinstra van der Pol

Bastion Island Housing
De Wielendwinger 1–20,
8926 XJ Leeuwarden

412 ☐ RES 2000

These 20 holiday houses are arranged around a rectangular communal courtyard, projecting out on to the lake. Presenting an introspective face to the courtyard, each house points out like a boat towards the water and alternate volumes of prow and conservatory living spaces line the waterfront.

Neutelings Riedijk Architecten

Water Support Building
Harlingen

413 ■ INF 1998

The form of this building, constructed to house the offices, storage and service facilities of road and waterway service providers, is determined by its functional requirements. The structure and heights vary according to the differing activities of the interiors. The facility is clad in panels of fibre-reinforced concrete.

SeARCH/de architectengroep

Triade Centre for Art Education
Middenweg 2, Geleerdenbuurt,
1782 BG, Den Helder
Tel +31 223 537 200

414 ☐ EDU 2001

This new cultural centre is dominated by its glass-panelled facade and timber-clad roof, pierced with openings of different sizes. The building was designed around the remnants of an existing school, and the old and new spaces have been carefully integrated.

Europe

Oosterhuis.nl

Noord-Holland Pavilion
Floriade, Haarlemmermeer

415 ☐ CUL 2002

This pavilion encloses a multimedia presentation promoting North Holland. Using digital technology, each triangular structural element was individually sized and transferred to the steel manufacturer's cutting machines. Visitors enter through winged doors that rise up hydraulically.

Asymptote

Hydra-Pier
Floriade, Haarlemmermeer

416 ☐ CUL 2002

Asymptote have created a viewing pavilion for the town of Haarlemmermeer, which is set on an artificial lake resulting from land reclamation. This theme is reflected in the continually streaming water that shrouds the building, flowing into pools above a laminated glass bubble.

NIO Architects

Fluid Vehicle Bus Station
Spaarne Hospital Square,
Hoofddorp, Haarlemmermeer

417 ☐ TRA 2003

Located in the forecourt of Hoofddorp's Spaarne Hospital, this bus station functions as a turning circle for buses. A limited budget forced a review of materials and construction techniques, resulting in a structure made entirely of polystyrene foam and polyester.

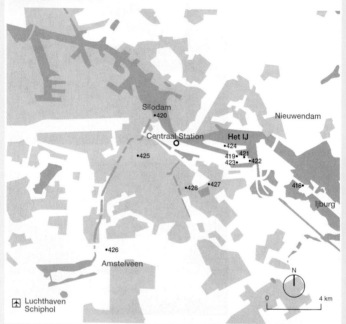

Silodam
•420

Centraal Station
○

Het IJ

Nieuwendam

•425

•424
419• 421•
423• •422

•428 •427

418•

IJburg

•426

Amstelveen

N

0   4 km

Luchthaven
Schiphol

Grimshaw

IJburg Bridges
IJburg, Amsterdam

418 □ INF 2001

Involving the creation of seven
artificial islands in the Ijmeer
lake, the two Ijburg bridges are
crucial to the infrastructure of
Amsterdam's new housing
development southeast of the
city. The sculptural steel and
concrete structures carry
roadways, tramlines, cycle
paths, pedestrian footways and
services.

Europe

de Architekten Cie

Whale Housing
Sporenburg Peninsula, Baron
GA Tindalplein, 1019 TW
Amsterdam
Tel +31 20 20 18 800

419 ☐ ✎ RES 2000

Located beside the river Ij, the
project stands out within a low-
rise development intended to
combine the density of the
inner city with a suburban feel.
Despite its scale and mass, the
Whale's interior and central
courtyard garden create a
feeling of intimacy.

MVRDV

Silodam
Silodam, 1013 AW Amsterdam

420 ☐ RES 2002

Appearing like stacks of
shipping containers on the
waterfront, this building
contains 157 apartments, as
well as offices and public
space. Different apartment
sizes and configurations are
grouped together within mini-
neighbourhoods, identified by
the graphic treatment of the
elevations.

West 8

Borneo Sporenburg
Borneo Sporenburg, 1019 WX
Amsterdam

421 ☐ RES 2000

Borneo and Sporenburg are two
huge quays in Amsterdam's
eastern docks that have been
redeveloped, comprising 2,500
dwellings designed by different
architects. West 8 stipulated
that each house incorporate a
void occupying 30–50 per cent
of the plot, resulting in a
coherent urban structure.

MAP Arquitectos

Borneo Dock Housing
Borneo Dike, Borneo Island,
1019 AV Amsterdam

422 ▮ RES 2000

Part of the Borneo Sporenburg
development, these 26 housing
units are typical of the
characteristics laid down by
West 8's masterplan. The
dwellings are low-rise but high-
density, the overall form being
a rectilinear block but with each
unit demarcated by its own
entrance.

MVRDV

**Houses on Borneo
Sporenburg, Plots 12 and 18**
Borneo Sporenburg, 1019 WX
Amsterdam

423 ▮ RES 2000

For their allocated plots on
Borneo Sporenburg, MVRDV
devised two spatially distinct
solutions. Plot 12 (shown) is
orientated along the length of
the narrow site, with four levels
of stepped internal and external
terraces. The other is turned
through 90 degrees.

Diener & Diener

**Apartment Houses KNSM,
Java Eiland**
Bogortuin 109, JAVA-KNSM
Eiland, 1019 PE Amsterdam

424 ▮ RES 2001

These two red-brick apartment
blocks link two contrasting
residential areas of the new
development in Amsterdam's
eastern harbour. The severe,
regular fenestration of the larger
building, eight storeys high, is
made more lightweight by
reflections of sky and water.

Europe

Benthem Crouwel Architekten

**Anne Frank Museum
Expansion**
Prinsengracht 267, 1016 GV
Amsterdam
Tel +31 20 55 67 105

425 ☐ CUL 1999

This museum extension
includes further exhibition and
educational facilities, and office
space for the Anne Frank
Foundation. Using similar
proportions and by integrating
modern materials, the building
echoes the design of the
traditional canalside house.

Meyer en Van Schooten
Architecten

ING Group Headquarters
Amstelveenseweg 500, 1081 KL
Amsterdam

426 ▢ COM 2002

Sited next to Amsterdam's
encircling motorway, this
headquarters building is
intended to symbolize the
banking and insurance
conglomerate's dynamism and
openness. The double-skin
facade buffers outside noise
but allows natural ventilation.

(EEA) Erick van Egeraat
associated architects

**Mauritskade Apartment
Building**
Mauritskade 66, 1093 RP
Amsterdam

427 ▢ RES 2000

Completing the corner of a
nineteenth-century city block,
this building contains ground-
floor commercial space and 12
luxury apartments above. The
narrow triangular site is
emphasized by the canted
layering of the floors.

Steven Holl Architects

Sarphatistraat Offices
Sarphatistraat 410, 1018 GW
Amsterdam

428 ◼ COM 2000

Connected to his renovation of a former canalside warehouse, Holl has constructed a pavilion for public and community events. The building is clad in perforated copper, complementing existing brick, and composed of interlocking volumes juxtaposed with coloured windows.

UN Studio

Gewild Wonen Expo 2001, Flexible Housing
Eilandenbuurt, Almere-Buiten, Almere

429 ◼ RES 2001

The 15 teams who participated in the 'Wild Living' project were asked to focus on flexibility. UN Studio's strategy was to design standard house units to which owners could add customized 'plug-in' boxes. Building laws prevented freedom of choice so the add-ons were attached in a fairly uniform manner.

Marlies Rohmer

Exhibition Houses
Tahitistraat, Almere-Buiten, 1339 PJ Almere

430 ◼ RES 2001

For 'Wild Living' Expo 2001, Rohmer presented prototype terrace houses that allow flexible living spaces. Each house has a slate-clad tower for the staircase, bathroom and kitchen, and a two-storey metallic box that can be left open or subdivided as the occupant wishes.

Europe

Claus en Kaan Architecten

Apartment Tower
Hengelostraat 101-158, 1324 GZ
Almere

431 ■ RES 2001

Located close to the centre of
Almere, a town built in the 1980s
beside an artificial lake, this
aluminum-cladded tower
contains 58 apartments of
varying room heights and
layouts. At lower levels, the
block projects out towards a
park, while at upper levels it
turns towards the lake.

René van Zuuk Architekten

**De Verbeelding Centre for the
Arts**
Verbeelding 25, 3892 HZ
Zeewolde
Tel +31 36 522 7037

432 □ CUL 2000

Sited in a park dedicated to the
preservation of art and nature,
this pavilion, its sculptural form
a response to its water-based
location, houses exhibition
spaces. The elongated form
was influenced by Richard
Serra's *Sea Level*, which can be
viewed from the end glass wall.

UN Studio

Het Valkhof Museum
Kelfkensbos 59, 6511 TB
Nijmegen
Tel +31 24 36 08 805

433 □ CUL 1999

This museum of archaeology
and modern art houses storage
and administrative functions on
the ground floor and display
spaces above. Its rectilinear
exterior gives no indication of
the unusual approach inside,
where UN Studio's interest in
human circulation is reflected in
the undulating ceiling.

Europe

Netherlands

Brookes Stacey Randall & IAA
Architecten

De Maere Textile School
Ariënsplein 2–3, 7511 JX
Enschede
Tel +31 53 484 82 60

434 ▮ ⚲ EDU 2001

This project included the
refurbishment of the existing
school and demonstration
factory, as well as a new
building to house a textile
teaching and research centre.
Existing buildings have been
adapted to new functions and
integrate old and new.

VHP stedebouwkundigen

Sound Wall Houses
Charley Tooropstraat 2–24,
1213 LH Hilversum

435 ▮ RES 2001

Backing on to a busy road,
these houses are dug into the
embankment, which forms an
acoustic barrier, and are
orientated to look over the
adjoining park. The first-floor
cantilevered storey is clad in
white panels and houses the
living space, its front tilted for
privacy.

Leidsche Rijn
•442

441

Centrum

Utrecht
Centraal ⊙ •438
Station

437•
De Uithof
•440

•439
Oudenrijn

Amsterdam-
Rijnkanaal

N

0   3 km

•436

Architectenbureau Micha de
Haas

The Aluminium Forest
Voorveste 2, 3992 DC Houten
Tel +31 30 638 5566

436   ☐ COM 2001

This aluminium information
centre is made of the material
that it is promoting. A simple
1,000 square metre box sits on
368 *piloti* of varying dimensions.
The dense distribution of the
columns enables the building to
defy expectations of the
strength of aluminium.

Bosch Architects

Ronald McDonald House
Lundlaan 4, De Uithof, 3584 EA
Utrecht
Tel +31 30 256 3333

437 ◻ ✏ PUB 1999

This building, at the Wilhelmina
Children's Hospital,
accommodates the relatives of
hospitalized children. The
formal modernist order set by
the four overhanging
rectangular floor slabs is
subverted by the informal
variety of coloured, curving
shapes sandwiched between.

Miralles & Tagliabue

City Hall
Korte Minrebroederstraat 2,
3512 GG Utrecht
Tel +31 30 28 6 1000

438 ◻ ✏ GOV 2000

Miralles has reworked Utrecht's
confusing city hall, which had
been altered and extended
through the centuries, re-
orientating the complex so that
it opens on to a new public
square. New additions have
been inserted into the existing
fabric, while elsewhere older
fragments have been exposed.

NL Architects

WOS 8, Heat Transfer Station
Rijkstraatweg 12a, 3545 NA
Utrecht
Tel +31 30 24 7 2211

439 ◻ ✏ INF 1998

Built to recycle energy from
a local power plant and to
distribute heat to thousands
of new homes, WOS 8 also
performs unexpected functions.
In order to maximize public
interaction with the facility, the
seamless polyurethane
sculptural form incorporates
an over-sized 'door spy'.

UN Studio

NMR Laboratory
Bloemberengebouw 8,
Padualaan, 3584 CH Utrecht
Tel +31 30 25 3 2652

440 ▯ ✆ COM 2000

This building houses eight high-frequency magnets for Neutron Magnetic Resonance experiments, control panels and support equipment. Because the magnets are highly sensitive and emit harmful radiation, they are kept isolated within continuous concrete surfaces that wrap around each other.

UN Studio

Möbius House
Het Gooi

441 ■ RES 1998

Designed for a family in which both parents work from home, this scheme addresses the notion of continuous change and is loosely based on the Möbius strip. Issues of shared and private spaces, their relation and access, are reflected in the overlapping fabric, where external glass walls slide into the structure.

Bosch Architects

Drinking Water Pumping Station
Leidschenrijn, Utrecht

442 ▯ INF 2003

Measuring 90 metres by 40 metres and 14 metres tall, the pumping station is a huge landmark. It is planned to make the surrounding land a park for a new residential area, so an aluminium skin conceals the workings of the building, which will also become the entrance to the proposed amenity.

Bolles+Wilson

De Brink Centre
De Markt, 7551 JC Hengelo
Tel +31 74 291 6578

443 ☐ COM 1999

This mixed-used development centred around a new 'brink' (square) off Hengelo's faceless market square has revitalized the area. A digital clock tower stands at the intersection of the squares, giving the town a new vertical focus. The new department store, a three-storey shed with folding roof, is a strong corner presence.

SeARCH/de architectengroep

Posbank Tea Pavilion
Beekhuizenseweg 1,
Veluwezoom, 6991 JM Rheden
Tel +31 26 495 3050

444 ☐ COM 2002

Located in Veluwezoom National Park, this pavilion complements its environment and acts as a model of energy-efficient architecture. Unmilled oak tree trunks and steel provide the structure and the strength to support the cantilevered space.

Behnisch, Behnisch & Partner

Institute for Forestry and Nature Research
Droevendaalssteg 3a, 6708 PB
Wageningen
Tel +31 31 747 7771

445 ☐ EDU 1998

Home of the Netherlands Forestry and Nature Research Institute (IBN), housing research laboratories, offices, educational and social facilities, this building was constructed using energy-efficient methods and materials, and is a model of sustainability.

Europe

UN Studio

City Hall and Theatre
Overtoom 1, Zenderpark,
3401 BK IJsselstein
Tel +31 30 686 1611

446 ☐ CUL 2000

Located between the new and
old parts of IJsselstein, this City
Hall and Theatre provides the
town with a new civic focus.
Built on a kite-shaped site, the
building is divided into cultural
facilities on one side and civic
functions on the other, but
unified by its cladding of
recycled glass.

Meyer en Van Schooten
Architecten

Minerva Housing Project
Dominicanenweg, 6823 PN
Arnhem

447 ■ RES 2001

This housing development
comprises six three-storey
blocks, alternately aligned at
45 or 90 degrees to the street,
propped on columns and set
into the ground at the rear.
Glass panels reveal the
insulation material and reflect
surrounding trees.

KCAP Kees Christiaanse

Hooikade Housing
Spoorbaanpad 0, Hooikade,
2627 Delft

448 ■ RES 1998

Built next to a railway line on
a former industrial site in Delft,
and spread over four blocks,
this project comprises 140
apartments designed as
affordable housing. The design
reworks the typical modernist
block, but uses timber cladding
to soften the concrete and steel,
and glazes the balconies.

UN Studio

Waste Transferral Station
Schieweg 11, 2627 BD Delft
Tel +31 15 260 2200

449 ◾ INF 2000

In articulating the entire system for delivering, processing and shipping waste, this building represents the waste management policy of the City of Delft. The dynamic and fluid form of the scheme is determined by the circulation of vehicles and waste, so that the whole complex appears as a unified machine.

Mecanoo Architecten

Technical University Library
Prometheusplein 1, 2628 ZC Delft
Tel +31 15 278 2933

450 ✎ EDU 1998

Mecanoo has created a subterranean library beneath a grassy hill. The great white protruding cone provides light for the reading room beneath and marks the library's presence. The interior also contains study areas, book storage, offices and a café.

Kruunenberg Van der Erve Architecten

Laminata, House of Glass
Koningin Emmalaan 118, 4141 EE Leerdam

451 ◾ RES 2001

Located in Leerdam, this house is a rectangular block formed of layer upon layer of laminated glass. A central courtyard, allowing light and air in, extends downwards where a concrete base houses more private rooms. The lamination creates shadowy light effects.

Europe

MVRDV

Hagen Island Housing
Hagen Island, Ypenburg,
's-Gravenhage

452 ☐▮ RES 2001

A stylized, pitched-roof house type is repeated in clusters, each dwelling appearing unique through the use of different cladding materials and surface articulation. By welding together aluminium sheet panels, interruptions between the walls and roof are removed, adding to the form's toy-like quality.

Rotterdam 453-457

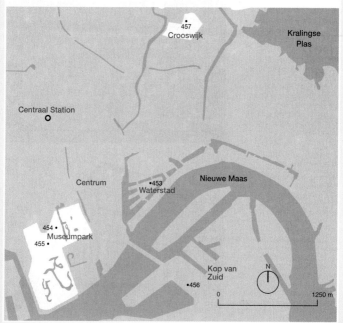

457
Crooswijk

Kralingse
Plas

Centraal Station
O

Centrum

•453
Waterstad

Nieuwe Maas

454 •
Museumpark
455 •

Kop van
Zuid

•456

N

0   1250 m

KCAP Kees Christiaanse

Academy of Architecture and Visual Arts
Wijnhaven, 3001 HA Rotterdam
Tel +31 10 241 4141

453 ☐ EDU 1998

This development, made up of simple, block-like forms, comprises the renovation of the existing polytechnic building and the construction of a new one. A vast central atrium rises from the entrance and links all the elements: staircases, a lecture theatre, work spaces, canteen and gymnasium.

Atelier Kempe Thill

Light Building
Museumpark, Rotterdam

454 ◼ CUL 2001

This building, a response to a competition to design a low-budget portable pavilion, appears at first glance to be solid but, on closer inspection, is made out of translucent beer crates. The walls allow light to penetrate the interior, creating an environment that responds to changing outdoor weather conditions.

Robbrecht and Daem

Museum Boijmans Van Beuningen
Museumpark 18–20, 3015 CX Rotterdam
Tel +31 10 441 9475

455 ☐ CUL 2003

This large-scale renovation and extension project combines contemporary insertions with a consolidated historic core. Interwoven into Van der Steur's original building are 5,000 square metres of new gallery and public areas enveloped in transparent concrete and glass.

Europe

(EEA) Erick van Egeraat
associated architects

**INHOLLAND University,
Ichthus College**
Posthumalaan 90, Kop van
Zuid, 3072 AG Rotterdam
Tel +31 10 439 9399

456 ☐ EDU 2000

Housing an experimental
business college in Rotterdam's
renovated docks, this building,
covered entirely in glass of
varying opacity, is formed of
two long parallel blocks
separated by a foyer which
rises the height of the building.

Mecanoo Architecten

St Mary of the Angels Chapel
Nieuwe Crooswijkseweg 123,
3034 PN Rotterdam
Tel +31 10 413 6308

457 ☐ REL 2001

Situated in the nineteenth-
century Roman Catholic
cemetery of St Lawrence, this
new chapel takes an irregular,
curvilinear form, its exterior
walls constructed of steel and
timber. The inside wall, fitted
between two bands of glazing,
appears to be separate from
floor and ceiling.

Marx & Steketee Architecten

**Monastery for the Brothers of
Tilburg**
Boxtelseweg 58, 5261 NE Vught
Tel +31 73 658 8000

458 ✦ REL 2000

This commission involved the
renovation and extension of the
monastery complex, creating a
new spiritual centre, domestic
and hotel accommodation,
artists' workshop and
auditorium. Soft, simple forms
and recycled materials have
muted the earlier institutional
architecture.

Claus en Kaan Architecten

Exhibition Building in the Former Concentration Camp
Lunettenlaan 600, 5260 Vught
Tel +31 73 656 6764

459 ☐ CUL 2001

A small piece of land and remnants of a crematorium have been landscaped to accommodate this pavilion, which contains exhibition spaces, an auditorium and offices. The plain rectangular form appears blank, the only interruption being bands of tiles alternating with rows of bricks.

Xaveer De Geyter Architecten

Chassé Park Apartments
Nonnenveld 100, 4811 DV Breda

460 ▮ RES 2001

Part of a masterplan that uses high-density housing in order to leave as much open parkland as possible, this group of five towers rises above a sunken inner garden from which the buildings are accessed. The facades vary according to the inside configurations and their relationship to each other.

(EEA) Erick van Egeraat associated architects

Popstage Mezz
Keizerstraat 101, 4811 HL Breda
Tel +31 76 515 6677

461 ☐ REC 2002

This new music hall, visible from Breda city centre, is part of the urban development scheme for an abandoned military campus. The double-skinned biomorphic form has an outer shell of steel and concrete covered with poured concrete and pre-oxidized copper panels.

Europe

Neutelings Riedijk Architecten/
Juliette Bekkering

Fire Station
Tramsingel 71, 4814 AC Breda

462 ▮ PUB 1999

Located on a main axis into
Breda, this landmark building is
positioned so that fire engines
have direct access to the road.
The walled, ovoid site contains
a garage, office space, sleeping
quarters, training and sports
facilities. The facade is
animated by a pattern of
horizontal and vertical bricks.

Benthem Crouwel Architekten

Popcentrum 013
Veermarktstraat 44, 5038 CV
Tilburg
Tel +31 13 460 9500

463 ☐ REC 1998

The function of this pop and
rock music venue, in the heart
of Tilburg's entertainment
district, is expressed through its
facades which are clad in black
rubber sheets with CDs placed
at each intersection. Inside,
three halls can accommodate a
mix of events and a range of
audience capacities.

(EEA) Erick van Egeraat
associated architects

Stuivesantplein Housing
Geefhuishof 1–35/1–9, 5021 GE
Tilburg

464 ▮ RES 1999

This development is composed
of two housing blocks. The
collective nature of the three-
storey block, containing 26
rented apartments, is
emphasized by its strong
horizontal grid. The lower,
terraced block contains nine
double-storey owner-occupied
houses.

Architectural Office Abel Cahen

Stedelijk Van Abbemuseum
Bilderdijklaan 10, 5611 NH
Eindhoven
Tel +31 40 238 1000

465 ☐ CUL 2002

This extension, completed after 12 years of architectural battles, has given the museum an exhibition space four times its original size. The central bevelled tower and canted geometry dominate the existing red-brick facade and bell tower that Cahen had originally wanted to demolish.

Álvaro Siza Vieira

Céramique Apartment Buildings
Toren Siza 22C–26V, Céramique Avenue, Maastricht

466 ▮ RES 2001

Part of the redevelopment of the Ceramique quarter, this landmark apartment building, standing 54 metres tall, is the highest structure in the vicinity. Clad in zinc, marble and grey stone, the two joined towers are elegant and co-exist with the surrounding housing.

Luigi Snozzi

STOA
Céramique, Maastricht

467 ▮ RES 2002

Situated overlooking the Maas river and separated from the riverbank by a park, this long building contains luxury apartments. The overwhelming horizontality of the block is mitigated by the tower-like vertical elements, and the windows, roof terraces and balconies enliven the unadorned brick facades.

Europe

Wiel Arets Architects and
Associates

Hedge House Art Gallery
Kasteel Wijlreweg 1, 6321 PP
Wijlre
Tel +31 43 45 02 616

468 ☐ CUL 2001

Built in the seventeenth-century
gardens of Wijlre Castle, this
building mixes a living room,
greenhouses, tool shed and
chicken house with gallery
space to form an integration
of art and life. Enclosed by
hedges, the exhibition becomes
part of a walk through the park.

3.6 469-482   Belgium and Luxembourg

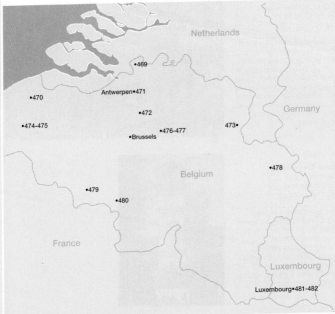

Europe

Belgium and Luxembourg

Robbrecht and Daem

Galle House Extension
Kerkplein 1, 1790 Affligem

469   ▮   RES 1999

Set within a small village, this
addition to a traditional pastor's
house in the form of a two-
storey pavilion occupies a sliver
of land in a long brick
enclosure, thus maintaining the
proportion of the existing walled
garden. The lead-clad
extension, discreetly linked to
the main building, stands as an
autonomous object.

Robbrecht and Daem

Concert Hall
't Zand 34, 8000 Brugge
Tel +32 50 47 69 99

470   □   CUL 2002

Surrounded by a skyline full of
church spires, the monolithic
form of Brugge's new red-tiled
concert hall is dominated by its
stage tower and Lantern Tower.
A large auditorium is defined by
two inclining side walls and the
chamber-music hall is arranged
as an atrium surrounded by a
spiral walkway.

Jo Crepain

Water Tower House
Elshoutlaan 23,
2930 Brasschaat

471   ▮   RES 1998

This water tower has been
refurbished to provide a seven-
storey house, encased on its
three street sides with
translucent glass planks to
provide privacy. Encasing the
base is a two-storey plinth
which contains kitchen, dining,
living and bathroom facilities.

Europe

Stéphane Beel

Roger Raveel Museum
Gildestraat 2–8,
9870 Machelen-Zulte
Tel +32 93 81 60 00

472 ☐ CUL 1999

Situated in a Flemish village on
the river Leie, this museum is
devoted to the work of Roger
Raveel who was born in
Machelen and continues to live
and work here. The linked
buildings, the museum garden
and the public park are
completely integrated within the
structure of the village.

Ettore Sottsass and Johanna
Grawunder

Mourmans House
Lanaken

473 ■ RES 2001

Sottsass is famous for his
product designs, notably those
associated with the Memphis
Group, founded in 1981. It feels
like the elements of this house
have been exploded so that
each can be treated as a
separate entity and the
landscape becomes part of
the interior.

Jo Crepain

Renson Office Building
Maalbeekstraat 8,
8790 Waregem
Tel +32 56 62 71 11

474 ✎ COM 2002

Built on a site that remained
after the completion of the
factory, this office building uses
the ventilation materials and
technology that are produced
next door. The north and south
walls have louvred air grilles,
while the west wall is glazed.
Its single level is raised on 6
metre columns.

Vincent van Duysen

Concordia Textiles Head Office
Flanders Fieldweg 37,
8790 Waregem
Tel +32 56 62 73 73

---

475 ▮ ✎ COM 2000

This addition to an existing textiles plant includes new offices and a showroom. Based on a 2.5 metre modular system, concrete, metal and glass characterize the low-rise elevation, which is punctuated by three two-storey light monitors.

Neutelings Riedijk Architecten

STUK Arts Centre
Naamse Straat 96, 3000 Leuven
Tel +32 16 320 320

---

476 ☐ CUL 2002

Working with existing buildings, ten fully independent theatres have been built round a central courtyard that links to public spaces and other facilities. Each space is its own entity, acknowledging the needs of different art forms, but the arts centre as a whole reflects a cool, contemporary aesthetic.

Rafael Moneo

Arenberg Campus Library, Catholic University of Leuven
De Croylaan 6, 3001 Heverlee
Tel +32 16 32 20 80

---

477 ☐ EDU 2002

Integrating the remains of a medieval convent with a new low-level building, this high-tech library is home to more than a million books. The design preserves the characteristics of the old buildings, such as the refectory roof, but adds a new focus at the entrance with its scalloped white facade.

Daniel Dethier & Associés

Denis-Ortmans House
81, rue Victor Close, Verviers,
4800 Liège

478 ▮ RES 2000

This house for a small family uses industrial methods and materials to create a building suited to contemporary living and is environmentally responsible. A steel-framed, glass-clad box contains a two-bedroom home. It is prefabricated and assembled on small foundations.

Pierre Hebbelink-Atelier d'Architecture

Museum of Contemporary Art
82, rue Sainte Louise,
7301 Hornu
Tel +32 65 65 21 21

479 ☐ CUL 2002

This new contemporary art museum houses a permanent collection, temporary exhibitions and performance spaces. The scheme introduces a counterpoint between the red brick of the original buildings and the black brick and white plaster of the additions.

Jo Crepain

Feyen House
Populierenstraat 9,
1600 St-Pieters-Leeuw

480 ▮ RES 2000

This family house had to be built within pre-determined constraints on plot size, building height and, more significantly, budget. It has a simple structure and uses inexpensive materials and industrially produced components. The fully glazed rear wall admits daylight, while the street side is more closed.

Europe

Belgium and Luxembourg

Paul Bretz

Combined Heat Powerplant and Office Building
23, avenue JF Kennedy,
1855 Luxembourg

481   ◼ COM 2001

This powerplant is viewed by its architect as a house for the machine. Four modules, each with its own generator, two turbines and tall chimney, are housed in separate, concrete units. The office building is a concrete frame with its entire front glazed.

Christian Bauer & Associés
Architectes

National Museum of History and Art
1 Marché-aux-Poissons,
2345 Luxembourg
Tel +35 24 79 33 01

482   ☐ CUL 2002

Within this fortified city, this museum stands on one of only three public squares. The piazza has been integrated into the overall design by the use of the same light stone as the museum's facade, in which a low slot signals the entrance.

Belgium

Germany

•484   •483

•486
•485   491-497   487
Paris   •   •
        488•   •490
        489

•498   499•

•500

•Nantes 501-502

France

Switzerland

•506   Lyon•503-504
           •505

Italy

•Bordeaux 507-509
•510

•511   512•
              •513   •514

Spain

Emmanuelle & Laurent
Beaudouin

Matisse Museum
13, place Commandant-Richez,
59360 Le Cateau-Cambresis
Tel +33 3 27 84 64 50

483 ☐ CUL 2002

This development complements
the existing eighteenth-century
building and provides an
auditorium, exhibition space
and conservation studios. The
pared-down volumes are faced
in red brick, matching the
decorative facades of the
original museum.

Atelier d'architecture Chaix & Morel et associés

Licorne Football Stadium
Stade de la Licorne, rue du Chapitre, 80016 Amiens
Tel +33 3 22 66 58 00

484 ☐ SPO 1999

Set in countryside outside Amiens, this stadium looks like a greenhouse, its tall glazed walls allowing views of the surrounding forest and the nearby cathedral. From an embankment, four large glass shells rise to nearly 26 metres above ground level.

Jakob & MacFarlane

Théâtre d'Eclat
Place Général de Gaulle, 27500 Pont-Audemer
Tel +33 2 32 41 81 31

485 ☐ CUL 2001

Based around Pont-Audemer's original theatre built by Maurice Novarina in the 1960s, this intervention encases the sandblasted skeleton of the existing structure with a skin of galvanized steel and glass panels. The interior space of the auditorium determines the folds of the continuous wall.

Bernard Tschumi Architects

Concert Hall and Exhibition Centre
Parc des Expositions, 76000 Rouen
Tel +33 2 32 91 92 92

486 ✆ CUL 2001

Visible from the motorway outside Rouen, the concert hall and the Miesian exhibition space are a bold gateway to the city. The steel skins of the concert hall wrap around each other, creating a foyer space. A restricted palette of materials allows clarity of form.

Europe

Marin + Trottin Architectes/
Périphériques Architectes

MR House
7, rue des Chênes,
77400 Pomponne

487 ▮ RES 2002

Surrounded by conventional
villas of the Paris suburbs, this
house stretches along a sloping
site, with stepped floors on two
levels. Its half-floors are clearly
articulated by horizontal,
galvanized beams. Dialogue
with the garden is achieved
through full-height windows.

Henri Ciriani

**Innovation and
Communication Centre**
Domaine de Voluceau,
78310 Le Chesnay
Tel +33 1 39 63 55 11

488 ☐ CUL 2002

Situated outside the forest of
Marly, this research institute
extension provides conference
spaces, a research facility and
centralized facilities for existing
functions. The south facade
with its pierced detailing offers
solar protection, while the north
elevation opens up to the forest.

Odile Decq & Benoit Cornette
Architectes

Motorway Control Centre
Hauts-de-Seine (A14
motorway), Nanterre

489 ▮ INF 1999

Designed for the agency that
patrols the motorways around
the western suburbs of Paris,
this facility is incorporated into
the structure of the viaduct. The
radio control room is housed in
a volume suspended from
curved steel arches that support
the roadway.

Europe

France

Bernard Tschumi Architects

School of Architecture
10–12, avenue Blaise Pascal,
77420 Champs-sur-Marne
Tel +33 1 60 95 84 00

490 ☐ EDU 1999

The result of a competition that required not only a proposal but also a reassessment of the traditional French model of architectural education, this graduate school is built around a central hall. It functions as exhibition space, café and principal circulation area.

Paris 491-497

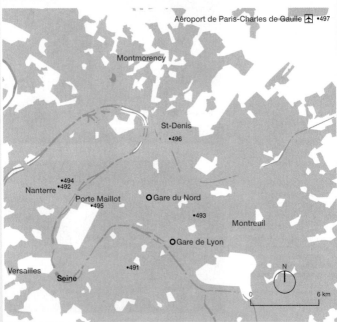

Europe

Herzog & de Meuron

Rue des Suisses Housing
19, rue des Suisses, Fond Villa
Mallebay, 75014 Paris

491 ▉ RES 2000

This apartment complex is
bordered by the rue des
Suisses and the rue Jonquoy.
Two buildings face the street
and, like the typical Paris block,
are vertical and homogeneous
in design. The courtyard
building, however, is horizontal
so that as many apartments as
possible have garden access.

Atelier d'Architecture Franck
Hammoutène

**Notre Dame de Pentecôte
Church**
Paris la Défense,
92800 Puteaux
Tel +33 1 47 75 83 25/26/27

492 □ REL 2000

Built above expressways and
surrounded by office towers,
this church is composed of a
series of planes of concrete,
aluminium, steel, glass and
granite. The visitor passes
through a low, dim hall before
entering the luminous interior.

Frédéric Borel Architecte

131, rue Pelleport
131, rue Pelleport/15, rue des
Pavillons, 75020 Paris

493 ▉ RES 1999

This housing block draws
together disparate elements to
make an excessive, dynamic
statement. The apparent tangle
of vertical planes in actual fact
reflects the interior volumes and
provides slots of private
outdoor space. 20 apartments
are arranged around a central
service core.

Pei Cobb Freed & Partners
Architects

EDF Tower
20, place de la Défense,
La Défense, 92974 Paris

494 ▮ COM 2001

Occupying a prominent site,
this 41-storey office tower
provides EDF, France's largest
electricity supplier, with offices,
a garden restaurant, a plaza
and parking beneath ground.
A monolithic sheath of stainless
steel and glass, the tower
dominates the skyline.

Christian de Portzamparc

Palais des Congrès
2, place Porte Maillot, Porte
Maillot, 75017 Paris
Tel +33 1 40 68 00 05

495 ▮ ✎ GOV 1999

Extending the existing Palais
des Congrès, this scheme
provides more exhibition space,
a new auditorium and offices,
and transforms the Louvre–La
Défense axis. The available
space was increased by
inclining the elevation and
incorporating the essential fire-
escape stairs.

Macary & Zublena

Stade de France
ZAC du Cornillon Nord, La-
Plaine-Saint-Denis, 93216 Paris
Tel +33 1 55 93 00 00

496 ☐ SPO 1998

Situated in Saint Denis, a
socially deprived area of Paris,
the stadium has become the
driving force of a new urban
culture. The cantilevered roof,
which has tinted glass at its
inner rim to counteract red and
infrared rays, appears to hover
above the stands.

Europe

Paul Andreu

Charles de Gaulle Airport, Terminal 2, Hall F
Roissy-en-France, 95713
Tel +33 1 48 62 22 80

497 ☐ TRA 1999

Terminal 2's Hall F, an innovative building, is a 400 metre long hall comprising a concrete-vaulted main building with two glass and steel arms. The lightweight, curving structures admit natural light, and spatial and visual clutter is kept to a minimum.

Emmanuelle & Laurent Beaudouin

Museum of Fine Arts
3, place Stanislas, 54000 Nancy
Tel +33 3 83 85 30 72

498 ☐ CUL 1999

This scheme doubles the size of the museum, which was founded in one of Emmanuel Héré's grand pavilions on Nancy's place Stanislas and already extended in 1936 by Jacques and Michel André. The concrete and glass planes of the new building fit comfortably with the gardens.

Zaha Hadid

Park and Ride Tram Station
Terminus Hoenheim-Nord, 67000 Strasbourg
Tel +33 3 88 60 90 90

499 ☐ TRA 2001

Part of a new initiative to reduce congestion and pollution, this tram station and car park is characterized by patterns of lines that are generated by the movement of cars, trams and pedestrians. Linearity is expressed in the ceiling strip-lights, floor markings and the lines of the parking spaces.

Santiago Calatrava

Pont de L'Europe
Orléans
Tel +33 3 38 78 75 75

500 ☐ INF 2000

Crossing the river Loire outside Orléans, this bridge is 470 metres long and carries four lanes of traffic and pedestrian and cycle paths. The graceful hybrid arch and suspension bridge comprises a steel arch deck and metal caisson, which rest on two inverted tripod piles of white concrete.

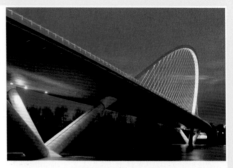

Architectures Jean Nouvel

Nantes Courthouse
Quai François Mitterand, 44000 Nantes
Tel +33 2 51 17 95 00

501 ☐ GOV 2000

Sited on the Loire's Sainte-Anne Island and part of a local regeneration scheme, this building is essentially a black perforated box of steel and glass designed on 8 x 8 metre module. The grid theme is repeated inside in the enormous mesh screens that separate the courtrooms from the vast lobby.

Odile Decq & Benoit Cornette Architectes

School of Economics and Law Library, University of Nantes
Chemin de la Censive du Tertre, 44312 Nantes

502 ■ EDU 1998

These two rectangular volumes – one housing the Economics School, the other the Law Library – are separated by a courtyard but are linked by a glass corridor. The library has a glazed facade that is protected by a screen of timber louvres.

Europe

Rue Royale Architectes

Balloon Box
Rue de la Gare,
69340 Francheville
Tel +33 78 59 02 66

503 ☐ COM 2001

Sited within a sports park, this
basketball court is a simple box
clad with rectangular laminate
panels digitally printed with an
image of climbing ivy. Raised off
the ground, its apparent
weightlessness is emphasized
at night by underlighting.
Wrapped round the box is a
glazed, polycarbonate lobby.

Dominique Perrault Architecte

Central Media Library
2–4, avenue Marcel Houël,
69200 Vénissieux
Tel +33 4 72 21 44 44

504 ☐ CUL 2001

Located between a public
square and a church, the library
is a square glass box with all its
functions on the same level.
Offices are accommodated in a
three-storey box on top of the
space. Skylights and the
perforated metal and glass
facades allow light deep into
the interior.

Lipsky & Rollet Architects

Les Grands Ateliers
Boulevard de Villefontaine,
38092 Villefontaine
Tel +33 4 74 96 88 70

505 ☐ COM 2001

These teaching workshops
provide a testing ground for the
development of prototypes in
architecture, design and
engineering. Contained beneath
a large corrugated canopy are
separate spaces: an entrance
foyer and exhibition space,
workshops, offices and
classrooms.

Europe

France

Hans Hollein

Vulcania Museum
Route de Mazayes,
63230 St Ours-les-Roches
Tel +33 8 20 82 78 28

506 ☐ CUL 2002

Situated within an extinct
volcano, this museum is mostly
underground and contains two
projection amphitheatres and
an exhibition space. A 22 metre
tall cone is clad in dark volcanic
stone and lined with a
geometric gold relief. Another
huge cone, sunk into the earth,
displays simulated magma.

OMA

Private House
Bordeaux

507 ■ RES 1998

This family house outside
Bordeaux, designed for a man
whose life is restricted by
disability, comprises three
discrete volumes stacked
vertically and partly buried into
the ground. The levels are linked
by a spiral stairway to one side
and a central open lift that faces
three storeys of bookshelves.

Richard Rogers Partnership

Bordeaux Law Courts
Place de la République,
33077 Bordeaux
Tel +33 5 56 01 34 72

508 ◧ GOV 1998

Representing the 'transparency'
of the judicial process, the
courtrooms, contained here in
seven individual cedar-clad
pods, are clearly visible behind
a 76 x 20 metre glass wall. An
internal street, bridged by glass
walkways, separates the
courtrooms from a rectangular
office block.

Europe

FLINT & Lanoire Courrian

Hangar 14
Quai des Chartrons,
33000 Bordeaux
Tel +33 5 56 11 88 88

509 ✎ CUL 1999

The facade of this exhibition building, a conversion of a wine warehouse situated in Bordeaux's historic dockyards, is clad in thick glass and articulated by steel staircases. A translucent box has been added at one end, but still the rhythm of the original building has been maintained.

Anne Lacaton & Jean Philippe Vassal

Private House
Cap-Ferret

510 ■ RES 1998

Overlooking dunes covered in birch and pine trees, this holiday home has been carefully placed among the still-growing canopy in order to minimize disturbance to the environment. Twelve 8 metre deep micro-piles support a steel frame clad in aluminium. Several large pines grow through the house.

Venturi Scott Brown and Associates

Toulouse Provincial Capitol Building
1, boulevard de la Marquette,
31090 Toulouse
Tel +33 5 34 33 30 10

511 ✎ GOV 1999

Overlooking the Canal du Midi, this building is composed of two parallel wings, one of them forming a semi-circle. The facade is clad in the local pink stone and traditional Toulouse architectural elements are appropriated and reinterpreted.

Edouard François

The Sprouting Building
Les Berges du Lez, Antigone,
34000 Montpellier

512 ∎ RES 2000

Gabions, used by engineers
as a retaining component in
embankments, form the basis
of this apartment building. The
facade is made up of steel wire
cages containing stones, which
are interspersed with plants.
Balconies protrude from the
elevation, the larger ones
supported on tripods.

Rémy Marciano

Ruffi Sports Complex
94, rue de Peyssonnel,
13003 Marseille
Tel +33 4 91 62 51 95

513 □ SPO 2001

This sports complex, encased
in pre-cast concrete slabs,
provides facilities that include
basketball and pétanque. The
building's honesty is
embellished by the roughly
patterned facades and the
glass-cased angled roofs. The
roof allows daylight through to
the interior while reducing glare.

Christian de Portzamparc

Law Courts
37, avenue Pierre Sémard,
06133 Grasse
Tel +33 4 92 60 75 00

514 ✦ GOV 1999

On a narrow, steeply sloping
site, the layout and elevated
position of the law courts
nevertheless suggest grand
scale. An elliptical rotunda is
linked by courtyards to linear
buildings. The use of concrete,
glass and metal is tempered by
regional ochre colourings.

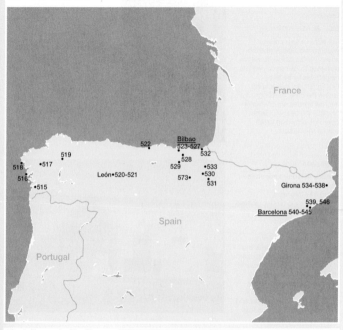

Bilbao
522
523-527
532
528
519
529
•533
518
•517
•530
516
531
•515
León•520-521
573•
Girona 534-538•

539, 546
Barcelona 540-545

France

Spain

Portugal

Alberto Noguerol + Pilar Diez

Main Library, University of Vigo
Campus Lagoas-Marcosende,
36200 Vigo
Tel +34 986 813 848

515   ☐ EDU 2000

Set into the bare hillside like
some ancient fortress, the
library is the focal point of the
university's new campus. The
building is composed of strong,
orthogonal volumes finished in
slabs of grey stone that match
the colour of the surrounding
mountains.

Europe

Spain North

David Chipperfield

House in Galicia
Galicia

516 ■ RES 2002

Set within a sequence of waterfront buildings, the form and materials of this house are designed to harmonize with its neighbours while also highlighting its individuality. Unlike the other dwellings, the internal spaces are orientated towards the sea, with large openings providing views across the harbour.

Álvaro Siza Vieira

Faculty of Communication Sciences
Praza de Mazarelos,
15703 Santiago de Compostela
Tel +34 981 58 00 11

517 ☐ EDU 2000

Part of the University of Santiago de Compostela, the Faculty is composed of a main spine with a series of adjoining volumes that form semi-enclosed patios. The library, at right-angles and raised on columns, is the conceptual and physical heart of the building.

Cesar Portela Fernandez-Jardon

Fisterra Municipal Cemetery
Cape Fisterra, A Coruña

518 ☐ REL 1999

Located on a cliff overlooking the sea, this scheme is far removed from the traditional conceptions of cemetery architecture. The simple white boxes are clustered on the sloping terrain, their interiors pared down to their essential components to convey a respectful, silent restraint.

Europe

Jorge Meijide Tomas
Arquitectos

Pilgrims' Hostel
Road to Mondoñedo,
27800 Vilalba Lugo
Tel +34 982 510 305

519 ☐ REL 2000

Each year several hundred thousand pilgrims make the journey to Santiago de Compostela, many requiring hostel accommodation. This building is constructed from slabs of local slate. The interior spaces are spare and white with highly polished stone floors.

BAAS Architects

Léon Tanatorio
Avenida de los Peregrinos,
24008 León
Tel +34 987 801 899

520 ☐ REL 2000

Surrounded by a large housing estate, this mortuary is sunk beneath a reflecting pool, the chapel light chutes the only aspect of the project visible above ground. Inside, the simplicity of unadorned rectilinear volumes lit by the skylights cut through the pool evokes a contemplative mood.

Mansilla + Tuñón Arquitectos

Concert Hall
Avenida de los Reyes Leoneses,
24008 León
Tel +34 987 244 663

521 ☐ CUL 2002

Occupying a tight site, this building asserts its presence through its sculptural, grid-like facade, its slanted, recessed openings reminiscent of traditional Iberian architecture. The open, white interior spaces contrast with the auditorium itself, which, clad in dark timber, uses subdued lighting.

Europe

Spain North

Juan Navarro Baldeweg

Altamira Museum and Research Centre
Cuevas de Altamira,
39330 Santillana Del Mar
Tel +34 942 818 005

522 ☐ CUL 2001

As a result of having to restrict the number of visitors to the Altamira caves, this complex has been designed to house a replica cave, research centre and museum. Built into a sloping site, a series of volumes rises up from the vestibule, allowing natural light inside.

Bilbao 523-527

Estudio Mariscal/Iñaki
Aurrekoetxea

Gran Hotel Domine
Alameda de Mazarredo, 61
48009 Bilbao
Tel +34 944 253 300

523 ☐ TOU 2002

Sited in front of Frank Gehry's
Guggenheim Museum in Bilbao,
this hotel pays homage to its
neighbour with a mirrored
facade. Inside, the building is
dominated by its 26 metre tall
light-flooded atrium with an
exuberant, full-height gabion
column at its centre.

Eduardo Arroyo, No.mad
Arquitectos

Primary School
Carretera Santo Domingo a
Derio, 48150 Sondika
Tel +34 944 541 400

524 ✏ EDU 1998

Positioned on the outskirts of
Bilbao, this kindergarten is
designed from the perspective
of a child, with doors and
furniture built at their own scale.
The glazed classrooms face the
sun, while the translucent glass
of the resting rooms filters light
and colour.

Santiago Calatrava

Bilbao (Sondika) Airport
48180 Loiu/Vizcaya
Tel +34 944 869 663/4

525 ☐ TRA 1999

With the growing demand for
flights to Bilbao, a recently
popular cultural destination,
Bilbao Airport has been
supplemented by a second
building. The complex consists
of a giant glazed hall of shallow
shells combined with slender
concrete beams, its soaring roof
reminiscent of an aeroplane at
the point of take-off.

Federico Soriano & Dolores
Palacios

**Euskalduna Conference
Centre and Concert Hall**
Avenida Abandoibarra, 4
48011 Bilbao
Tel +34 944 035 000

526 □ CUL 1999

Part of the regeneration of
Bilbao's docks, this building
appears like a giant, abandoned
ship. Inside, suspended bridges
connect the light-filled open
concrete floors of the offices,
service areas and foyers to the
Cor-ten steel concert hall.

Alonso, Hernández &
Asociados, Arquitectos

**Ericsson Bilbao Technology
Centre**
Parque Tecnológico, 700
48160 Derio
Tel +34 944 892 400

527 ✐ COM 2001

Each part of this technology
centre is designed to meet the
specific requirements of a
particular function, whether it
be administration, design or
sales. The simple concrete
volumes are combined to
cascade over the steep site.

Juan Carlos Osinaga – Sol
Madridejos Fernandez

Galdakao Sports Complex
48960 Galdakao
Tel +34 944 573 209

528 □ SPO 2000

Sited among residential blocks
in the small town of Galdakao,
the monolithic scale and
unadorned concrete facade of
this municipal sports complex
assert its presence. Long
stretches of skylight illuminate
the swimming pool, running
track and spectators' gallery.

Europe

Acebo + Alonso Arquitectos

M-U Housing
Lilibaso, 12A–B
20700 Urretxu

529 ■ RES 2001

Perched on top of a man-made cliff overlooking the town of Urretxu and occupying the gap between two existing buildings, this house is entirely glazed in section but blind to its neighbours, and contains a narrow internal courtyard. Raised on stilts, the lightweight steel construction appears to float above the ground.

Rafael Moneo

Bodegas Julián Chivite
Ribera 34, 31592 Cintruenigo
Tel +34 948 811 000

530 □ COM 2001

Located in a densely wooded area at the foot of the Pyrenees, the new, more functional, buildings of this bodegas harmonize with the existing neo-classical church, tower and old house. The discrete volumes, finished in hammered concrete with copper roofs, house the various stages of the winemaking process.

Alonso, Hernández & Asociados, Arquitectos

Vineyard and Wine Museum
Plaza Teobaldos 10, 31390 Olite
Tel +34 948 740 754

531 □ CUL 1999

This museum incorporates a seventeenth-century facade and recreates behind it the body of the historic building, at the same time juxtaposing a contemporary addition. The steel structure and strip metal cladding of the new building contrast with the golden stone of the old palazzo.

Rafael Moneo

Kursaal Auditorium
Avenida de Zurriola, 1
20002 Donostia-San Sebastián
Tel +34 943 003 000

532 ☐ CUL 1999

Standing on a river estuary beach, the two large boxes, which house an auditorium, congress room and exhibition hall, tilt away from each other, imitating the surrounding mountains. Within the outer skin of horizontal planes of translucent curved glass, stand volumes of warm cedar wood.

Francisco Mangado

San Juan Medical Centre
Plaza Obispo Irurita,
31011 Pamplona
Tel +34 948 198 344

533 ☐ PUB 2001

Situated to the west of Pamplona's old town, this zinc-clad and low-lying structure contrasts with the surrounding 1970s apartment blocks. Two 60 metre long wings are distributed over three floors, one below ground, and connected by a triple-height light well.

RCR Aranda Pigem Vilalta Arquitectes

Bath House, Tussols-Basil Fluvial Park
17800 Olot
Tel +34 972 279 100

534 ☐ SPO 1998

This public bathing pavilion stands on the shallow banks of a gently flowing river in the Tussols-Basil Fluvial Park. Stainless-steel boxes contain WC, shower and changing cubicles and black paving slabs stretch the length of the building.

Europe

RCR Aranda Pigem Vilalta
Arquitectes

Mirador House
Calle Om, 524
17800 Olot

535 ▮ RES 1999

Set before a wide, open
landscape, the design of this
house is determined by its
view. The strong lines of the
floor and roof slabs emphasize
the horizontality of the front
facade. The living areas are
housed in the transparent
spaces, while the service areas
are at the back.

RCR Aranda Pigem Vilalta
Arquitectes

Recreation and Culture Zone
17179 Riudaura
Tel +34 972 264 422

536 ☐ CUL 1999

Built for the inhabitants of
Riudaura, a small village
situated at the mouth of a valley,
this low-slung structure acts as
a gateway between the square
at the front and the sports
ground at the back. A minimal
palette of dark metal cladding
and frosted glass panels
characterize the exterior.

RCR Aranda Pigem Vilalta
Arquitectes

Vilartagues Secondary School
Canigó, 17220 Sant Feliu de
Guíxols
Tel +34 972 820 118

537 ☐ EDU 1999

Located on a sandy coastal
site, this building is designed to
withstand a harsh environment.
Much of the volume is sunk into
the ground, making the front
facade appear low. A courtyard
lies between two parallel wings,
offering a sheltered area for
outside activities.

RCR Aranda Pigem Vilalta
Arquitectes

**Girona University Law Faculty,
Montilivi Campus**
Campus de Montilivi,
17071 Girona
Tel +34 972 418 147

538 ☐ EDU 1999

Rising from the campus on a
pyramidal base, this law faculty
appears solid and impenetrable.
Three rectangular volumes
balance on the plinth, the wide
staircase of the longer box
continuing from the main
entrance in the pyramid.

BAAS Architects

**Tanatorio Municipal de
Terrassa**
Complejo Funerario Municipal
N-150, 08227 Terrassa
Tel +34 937 869 400

539 ☐ REL 2002

Situated in Barcelona's
suburbs, this low rectangular
volume houses a mortuary.
A church is located in the rear
double-height space and all
services are in the self-
contained sunken basement.
A narrow courtyard connects
the mortuary with the church.

Parc de Collserola

•543

Horta-Guinadó

Espluges de Llobregat
•541

•540

Les Corts

Sant Andreu

•545

Sant Martí

Ciutat Vella •542
Estació Barcelona Terme O

•544

N

Aeropuerto Barcelona-El Prat

0   4 km

Mar Mediterrània

Carlos Ferrater

Cataluña Convention Centre
Avenida Diagonal, 661–71
08028 Barcelona
Tel +34 933 644 400

540 ✆ COM 2000

This convention centre aims
to bring civic character to an
area dominated by private
developments. Its form is
monolithic with a massive
horizontal strip window opening
the facade to the exterior.
Recessed light wells sculpted
into the ceiling draw in
additional natural light.

Carlos Ferrater & Joan
Guibernau

Alonso-Planas House
Fronto, 46 Esplugues de
Llobregat, 08950 Barcelona

541 ■ RES 1998

This family house has been
built into the mountainside,
its assemblage of volumes
set perpendicular in order to
capture the views over
Barcelona and the Llobregat
plains. White concrete and dark
quartzite characterize both the
internal and external spaces.

Lluís Clotet Ballús & Ignacio
Paricio Ansuátegui

Library of the UPF
Ramon Trias Fargas, 25–7
08005 Barcelona
Tel +34 935 422 912

542 ☐ CUL 1999

The main library of the
Universidad Pompeu Fabra
occupies two interconnected
historic structures: the Jaume I
building and the Dipòsit de les
Aigües, a nineteenth-century
reservoir. The interiors have
been stripped back to the
original brickwork.

Miralles & Tagliabue

Casa la Clota
Passatge Feliu, 15–17
08035 Barcelona

543 ■ RES 1998

A new entrance extension,
its facade made of exposed
perforated bricks within a
concrete frame, joins two
existing adjacent houses to
create a single family dwelling.
A double-height library
dominates one building, while
the other contains living areas
with bedrooms above.

Miralles & Tagliabue

Diagonal Mar Park
Selva de Mar, Llull, Josep Pla,
08003 Barcelona

544 □ REC 2002

Located in a suburban area of
Barcelona, this new urban park
revitalizes its identity. Ceramic
walls reminiscent of nearby
facades articulate the site and
cast concrete elements
resembling graffiti, hung at high
levels, provide shady routes.
Sprinkler systems simulate rain
showers.

Rafael Moneo

Concert Hall and Auditorium
L'Auditori, Lepant, 150
08013 Barcelona
Tel +34 932 479 300

545 □ CUL 1999

Barcelona's new auditorium is
a resolutely individual building.
Within a rectilinear volume, its
outline defined by a concrete
grid filled with reddish stainless-
steel panels on the outside and
maple wood on the inside, are
two concert halls, a music
museum and a library.

Alonso, Hernández &
Asociados, Arquitectos

CS House
Camí Reial de Barcelona,
Sentmenat 36, 08181 Barcelona

546 ■ RES 2002

This house takes advantage
of views while concealing its
inhabitants from immediate
neighbours in what is a
predominantly residential area.
Extensive glazing reveals the
slender structural elements, and
the floor and roof planes appear
to float.

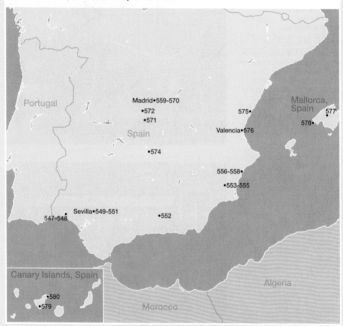

Portugal

Madrid•559-570
•572
•571

Spain

•574

Sevilla•549-551
547-548•

•552

575•

Valencia•576

556-558•
•553-555

Mallorca,
Spain

577
•

578•

Canary Islands, Spain

•580
•579

Algeria

Morocco

Cruz y Ortiz Arquitectos

**Doñana Visitor Centre of the
Marine World**
Carretera Matalascañas-
Mazagón, 21730 Almonte
Tel +34 959 50 61 28/9

547 ☐ CUL 2002

Sited among sand dunes is the
jagged form of this marine
museum, its low-slung volume
having minimal visual impact on
its landscape. A long hallway
with a faceted concrete ceiling
runs the length of the building,
with each 'tooth' forming a
separate gallery.

Europe

Ubaldo García Torrente

Camping La Torrera
Calañas, Huelva

548 ▮ REC 2001

Positioned on the banks of the Riscoso Swamp, once a mining reservoir and now a watersports centre, the site contains washing facilities, a restaurant, shops and a free camping area. The waterfront cabins are constructed of aluminium panels and sheet metal. The scheme uses raw construction materials and simple forms.

Cruz y Ortiz Arquitectos

Sevilla Olympic Stadium
Isla de la Cartuja, Sector Norte,
41092 Sevilla
Tel +34 954 48 94 00

549 ☐ SPO 1999

Sevilla's Olympic Stadium contains a hotel and offices as well as a 60,000-seat stadium and sports facilities. The site was excavated so that the track and field are below ground, thus moderating visual impact and facilitating access to seats. The exterior is characterized by its orthogonal protrusions.

Blanca Sánchez Lara

User-built houses
Avenida de las Turquillas,
Lantejuela, 41630 Sevilla

550 ▮ RES 1999

This project was designed to be simple enough for its occupants to build. The identical houses are based on two staggered volumes, enabling maximum dimensions for interior and private outdoor spaces. With no urban context, the architects were free to develop their own aesthetic.

Morales de Gilles Mariscal
Arquitectos

Herrera House
Sevilla

551 ■ RES 1999

Occupying a corner site among
Sevilla's narrow streets, this
house contrasts with the
traditional architecture of the
neighbourhood. A series of
stacked volumes are grouped
alongside a long rectangular,
double-height internal patio that
filters light into the lower levels.

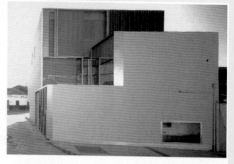

Estudio Alberto Campo Baeza

Caja General de Ahorros
Carretera de Armilla, Granada

552 □ COM 2001

The headquarters of this
savings bank emerges from
a solid podium designed to
accommodate the gradient of
the site. The deep openings on
the south-facing facades filter
the strong sunlight, while the
northerly facades are clad with
horizontal strips of glass and
travertine.

Rafael Moneo

Town Hall Extension
Plaza del Cardenal Belluga,
30001 Murcia

553 ■ GOV 1998

The extension to Murcia's town
hall stands on a corner of the
city's main square, facing the
cathedral. The facade is made
up of irregular vertical openings,
its outer stone screen shielding
the inner glazed skin. Inside,
the circulation zones determine
the layout.

Europe

Juan Carlos Osinaga, Sol Madridejos Fernández and AH&

Teaching Pavilion, Arrixaca Hospital
Carretera Murcia-Cartagena, 30120 Murcia
Tel +34 968 36 94 00

554 ☐ EDU 2001

The teaching facilities function independently from the rest of the hospital complex and this is reflected in the autonomy of the new building. The design is based on a play between solid and void, which is seen in the irregular 'castellated' facade.

Paredes Pedrosa Arquitectos

Congress Centre
Avenida Primero de Mayo, 30006 Murcia
Tel +34 968 34 10 60

555 ☐ COM 2002

Completing a group of public buildings bordering Murcia's river, the new Congress Centre is a simple concrete frame infilled with golden stone and articulated by a series of small courtyards that draw light into the depths of the scheme. Inside, the concrete structure is infilled with timber and glass.

Javier Garcia-Solera Arquitecto

Classroom Block 3, University Campus of Alicante
Campus de Sant Vincent del Raspeig 99, 03080 Alicante
Tel +34 965 90 34 00

556 ☐ EDU 2000

This university complex was built in six months on pre-existing foundations, which determined the single-storey layout. Seven rectangular modules, linked by metal decks running through internal courtyards, have transparent interior elevations.

Europe

Spain South

Alfredo Payá Benedito

Alicante University Museum
Campus de Sant Vincent del
Raspeig 99, 03080 Alicante
Tel +34 965 90 94 66

557 ☐ EDU 1998

Situated on the edge of the
university's campus, the self-
contained orange box of the
museum appears to emerge
from a surrounding shallow
pool. The complex is entered
from below the water, through
a cool, dark gallery, into a large
sunken piazza, from which the
different volumes are accessed.

Álvaro Siza Vieira

**Rectory Building, University
of Alicante**
Campus de Sant Vincent del
Raspeig 99, 03080 Alicante
Tel +34 965 90 34 00

558 ☐ EDU 1998

This new building for the
university rector turns a blank
face to the main campus and
creates its own serene
environment within. The
complex is long and low,
containing two colonnaded
courtyards that provide cool
walkways.

Abalos & Herreros

**Municipal Hall and Main
Square**
Plaza de Colmenarejo, 1
28270 Madrid
Tel +34 918 58 91 76

559 ☐ GOV 1999

This scheme for Colmenarejo,
a village on Madrid's periphery,
was designed to assert its
identity. The shed-like hall is a
semi-translucent, lightweight
structure clad in white
corrugated plastic, with a series
of pivoting doors opening on to
the square.

Europe

Abalos & Herreros

Public Library in Usera
Rafaela Ibarra 43, 28026 Madrid
Tel +34 915 60 00 68

560 ☐ CUL 2000

Standing next to Usera's town hall and rising from its half-buried ground floor as a self-contained block, this library proclaims its presence. Darker horizontal lines in the pink concrete cladding define the levels and the vertical windows are placed irregularly, so that daylight penetrates discreetly or indirectly.

Abalos & Herreros

Recycling Plant for Urban Waste
Carretera a Valencia, Rivas, 28051 Madrid
Tel +34 912 22 14 00

561 ✎ INF 2000

This plant in Valdemingomez is part of a project to repair the damage resulting from years of using this area as a large dumping ground. The ethos is reflected in the complex's construction, using recycled polycarbonate cladding and a bolted, steel structure.

Aranguren + Gallegos Arquitectos

76 Dwellings in El Encinar de los Reyes
El Encinar de los Reyes, Madrid

562 ▢ RES 1999

This residential development consists of 76 apartments in five monolithic linear volumes. The north facades are closed, resembling the large advertising hoardings of the nearby motorway, and the south facades overlook landscaped gardens.

José Ignacio Linazasoro

**Valdemaqueda Church
Restoration**
Avenida de la Iglesia,
28295 Madrid
Tel +34 918 98 49 81

563 ☐ REL 1998

The new grey granite cubic
volume simultaneously unites
and contrasts with the old door
and apse, the only remaining
fragments of the Gothic church.
Bare concrete walls and
wooden joists are juxtaposed
with Gothic columns and ribbed
vaulting.

Porras + La Casta Arquitectos

Social Housing in Coslada
Poitiers, Coslada, 1
28820 Madrid

564 ▮ RES 1999

This apparently solid volume
contains 66 apartments
surrounding a landscaped open
courtyard. The individual units
can be adapted to a variety of
functions. Each facade is
distinguished according to its
orientation by materials that
change from one surface to the
next, and irregular *brise-soleil*
create animated shadows.

Juan Carlos Osinaga – Sol
Madridejos Fernandez

Alcobendas Civic Centre
Avenida Bruselas, 19
28108 Madrid
Tel +34 914 84 16 85

565 ✒ GOV 1999

Squeezed between a main road
and a residential estate, this
civic centre houses a hall,
classrooms and library. At the
back, the stone box is solid
except for an entrance opening.
On the street, the volume has a
recessed glass front and a
extruded circulation space.

Richard Levene & Fernando
Márquez Cecilia

El Croquis Head Office
Avenida de los Reyes
Católicos 9, 28280 Madrid
Tel +34 918 96 94 10

566 ☐ COM 1998

The offices of El Croquis are
formed from two tilting prisms
sited at right-angles to each
other on Cor-ten steel planes.
While the street facade is clad
in travertine with narrow
horizontal apertures to maintain
privacy, the volumes open up to
the garden.

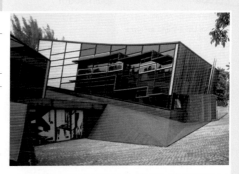

Juan Carlos Osinaga – Sol
Madridejos Fernandez

**San Fernando de Henares
Town Hall and Civic Centre**
Plaza de España, 28830 Madrid
Tel +34 916 27 67 00

567 ☐ GOV 1999

This town hall and civic centre
extends symmetrically from the
remains of an eighteenth-
century facade, with two wings
subverting its geometry, their
volumes identical except for
their pattern of windows. At the
centre is an elevated void faced
with translucent onyx.

Mansilla + Tuñón Arquitectos

Swimming Centre
Paseo de los Pinos,
28830 Madrid
Tel +34 916 71 99 11

568 ☐ SPO 1998

Part of a municipal sports
complex in northeast Madrid,
this building is organized
linearly with an entrance
followed by changing rooms,
instruction pool and main pool.
A lightweight glazed box rests
on a lattice of prefabricated
concrete girders that filters light.

Mansilla + Tuñón Arquitectos

Regional Library and Archives of Madrid
Ramirez de Prado, 3
28045 Madrid
Tel +34 917 20 88 67

569 ☐ CUL 2002

New additions fill the spaces between the buildings of a former brewery to create a library and archives complex. The archives are housed in a new building encased in a translucent double skin that allows natural light to enter without damaging the contents.

Rafael Moneo

Maternity and Children's Hospital
Calle O'Donnell y Calle de Maiquez, 28007 Madrid
Tel +34 915 86 80 00

570 ☐ PUB 2003

Part of the Gregorio Marañón Hospital, their main entrance opening on to an extremely busy street, these maternity and children's units present a defensive facade to the outside world. The aluminium-panel and glass cladding keeps the building remote.

Lapeña & Torres

La Granja Escalator
La Granja, 45001 Toledo

571 ☐ INF 2000

Cut into Toledo's massive city walls, this 36 metre tall, six-stage external escalator links a new 400-space underground car park to the hilltop. Founded on piles 30 metres deep, the ochre-coloured concrete planes retain the structure and form shelter and viewing platforms. The journey ends with the structure's belvedere.

Europe

Estudio Alberto Campo Baeza

De Blas House
Sevilla la Nueva

572 ■ RES 2000

Set into a hill outside Madrid, the house concept has been reduced to an elemental, abstract form. The solid concrete base has limited square openings and is pierced on its top surface by the staircase and the swimming pool. A metal structure supports frameless glazing to create a completely transparent box.

Santiago Calatrava

Bodegas Ysios
Camino de La Hoya,
01399 Laguardia
Tel +34 945 600 640

573 □ COM 2002

Commissioned to create a distinctive bodegas in the hills of the Sierra, Calatrava has designed a 250 metre long curvaceous building that houses the entire wine-making process. Crowned by a monumental entrance, the aluminium roof emulates the mountain landscape.

Juan Carlos Osinaga – Sol Madridejos Fernandez

Chapel
Valleaceron, 13480 Almadanejos

574 ▯ REL 2000

Placed among rocky hills of a private property, the chapel is scaleless in a landscape free of human intervention. Its profile changes dramatically from each viewing angle, glazed panels cut into the form appearing from a distance like shadows. The multi-faceted interior is unadorned.

Mansilla + Tuñón Arquitectos

Museo de Bellas Artes
Avenida de los Hermanos Bou,
12003 Castellón de la Plana
Tel +34 964 72 75 00

575 ☐ CUL 2001

Wrapped around an old cloister, the new building for the Museo de Bellas Artes forms a U-shape of silver-grey boxes. The east wing houses exhibitions and is organized on five levels around double-height spaces. The long low building on the west side accommodates restoration facilities.

Foster and Partners

Congress Centre
Avenida Cortes Valencianas, 60
46015 Valencia
Tel +34 963 17 94 00

576 ☐ COM 1998

Positioned close to Valencia's airport, this centre is a recognizable landmark, with arched glass facades and a single-pitched roof that rises towards the sky with a generous overhang. The roof construction allows air flow and full-height *brise-soleil* moderate the light.

Estudio Alberto Campo Baeza

Balearic Innovation Centre
Inca, Mallorca

577 ■ COM 1998

Standing on a triangular site within a business park, this scheme for high-tech offices focuses on an enclosed garden surrounded by quiet work spaces. Within a stone wall, frameless glass rooms topped by long flat roofs form the perimeter. The courtyard has a sunken theatre and is planted with orange trees.

Europe

Daniel Libeskind

Studio Weil
Camí de Sant Carles, 20
07157 Port d'Andratx, Mallorca
Tel +34 971 67 16 47

---
578 ☐ CUL 2003

Libeskind worked closely
with the painter and sculptor
Barbara Weil to create a studio,
consisting of a gallery,
workshop and storage spaces.
Studio Weil is introspective and
takes the form of an arc
intersected by two staircases.
Slashes of window cut through
the facades.

AMP Arquitectos

**South Tenerife Convention
Centre**
Avenida de Los Pueblos,
38660 Adeje-Tenerife
Tel +39 922 24 51 49

---
579 ✆ COM 2003

Trapped within the curve of a
motorway in a harsh terrain of
Chasna rock, this scheme is
designed to merge with the
landscape. Services that require
functional independence are
housed in artificial rock
formations leaving flexible
in-between spaces.

AMP Arquitectos

**Presidency and State
Government Building**
C/Bravo Murillo,
38003 Santa Cruz de Tenerife
Tel +39 922 24 51 49

---
580 ✆ GOV 1999

Standing on Santa Cruz's main
square, among eighteenth-
century architecture, this
government building seems
elemental and ancient, its
deeply recessed openings
appearing to have been carved
out of the structure. The interior
opens to a courtyard.

José Bernardo Távora
Arquitecto

Private House
Barcelos

581 ■ RES 1998

This holiday home stands on
stilts overlooking a wide
panorama. The concrete frame,
with roof and floor plates
cantilevered along the south
side to form a long verandah,
is filled with sandstone and is
blind on all sides except the
shaded verandah on to which
all rooms face.

Europe

Álvaro Siza Vieira

Casa David Vieira de Castro
Famalicão

582 ■ RES 1998

Siza integrated existing
foundations and walls that had
been built for an abandoned
sanatorium into his designs for
this family house and its
external landscaping. The
building appears fragmented
and reconstructed. Its
architectural form is maintained
by using fine roofing and
unobtrusive window frames.

Aires Mateus e Associados

**Student Housing, Polo II of
the University of Coimbra**
Villa Franca Pinhal de Marrocos,
3030 Coimbra
Tel +351 23 970 1514

583 ❒ ✆ EDU 1999

Set on a triangular site, this
student housing block is built
into the slope, its low wing
imitating the gradient of the
adjacent road. A five-storey
block presents a warm-toned
timber-clad facade with opening
shutters to the inner triangular
courtyard.

João Luís Carrilho da Graça

**Presidential Documentation
and Information Centre**
Praça Afonso de Albuquerque -
Palácio de Belém, 1349 Lisboa
Tel +351 21 361 4600

584 ✆ GOV 2002

The Belém Palace houses the
Presidential Documentation
and Information Centre in a
protected environment of
gardens and villas, all hidden
from external views. The L-
shaped scheme is composed
of a partly buried wing and
'floating' wall.

Álvaro Siza Vieira

**Serralves Foundation,
Museum of Contemporary Art**
João de Castro Street 210,
4150-417 Porto
Tel +351 22 615 6500

585 ☐ CUL 1999

This low, white building, the
first major museum in the north
of Portugal, is designed to
minimize its impact on the
surrounding grounds of the
Serralves country house. The
galleries are distributed downhill
in two wings that enclose a
central courtyard.

Eduardo Souto de Moura

Cinema House
Rua do arquitecto Viana de
Lima, 4150 Porto

586 ▮ CUL 2002

Commissioned by the city
to celebrate the work of the
filmmaker Manoel de Oliveira,
this building contains a library,
archive and small auditorium.
The two extruded windows
recall a double-lens camera
and direct the view to avoid
unsightly apartment blocks.

Santiago Calatrava

Oriente Station
Lote 1.07.15, Avenida D. João,
1090-096 Lisboa
Tel +351 891 8225

587 ☐ TRA 1998

Initially for World Expo 98 and in
the long term as a main terminal
for Lisboa's east side, Oriente
Station connects trains, buses
and the underground. Railway
tracks, beneath a gothic
canopy, pass the bus station's
elliptical roofs. Below ground,
among concrete rib-like arches,
is access to the underground.

Europe

Raj Rewal

Ismaili Centre
Rua Abranches Ferrao,
1600-001 Lisboa
Tel +351 217 2290

588 □ CUL 2000

This centre caters for Lisboa's
community of Ismaili Muslims,
one of the largest in Europe,
providing religious, educational
and social services. The
functions of the building are
structured round a series of
three courtyards. Stone and
steel create a contemporary
version of lattices.

Aires Mateus e Associados

**Rectory of the New University
of Lisbon**
Campus de Campolide,
1099-085 Lisboa
Tel +351 21 793 2579

589 □ EDU 2003

At the heart of the university
campus, the main body of the
Rectory is housed in a narrow,
nine-storey monolithic structure
of white limestone. A recessed,
glazed facade is complemented
by the facade overlooking the
plaza, which is decorated with
horizontal strip windows.

Gonçalo Byrne

Maritime Control Tower
Terrapleno de Algés, Doca de
Pedrouços, 1495-165 Lisboa
Tel +351 21 302 5400

590 ▯ ✦ TRA 2002

Positioned at the end of a
breakwater, this leaning tower
signals the entrance to Lisboa's
new harbour. Above a stone
plinth housing the entrance and
boathouses are five copper-clad
floors containing offices. By
night, the tower becomes a
lighthouse.

Denmark

Netherlands

•595

Hamburg•591-593

•594

Poland

•596 •597-598 •618

Berlin•619-636

•637

•600

Germany

•638-639

•599

601

Dortmund•602-603

604-606• 607

610-611

•612 •613 •609

•617

Köln
614-616

•608

•640

•641

642• •643

Dresden•644-647

Antonio Citterio and Partners

Edel Music Headquarters
Neumühlen 17, 22763 Hamburg
Tel +49 40 890 850

591 ✏ COM 2002

Overlooking the river Elbe, this
record company headquarters
is reminiscent of the modernist
tradition, with glass the primary
material on three of the
building's facades. A sunken
garage is topped by a ground
floor containing reception, bar,
restaurant and auditorium, with
three levels of offices above.

Miralles & Tagliabue

Jugendmusikschule
Mittelweg 42, 20148 Hamburg
Tel +49 40 2988 2237

592 ☐ EDU 2000

The assembly of volumes of this music school is designed to connect with the surrounding trees and landscape. For functional and acoustic reasons, the public area is located on a separate floor from the classrooms and offices. An entrance hall connects all programmes and leads to the first-floor auditorium.

Foster and Partners

Multimedia Centre
Rothenbaumchaussee 78, 20148 Hamburg

593 ▮ CUL 1999

Linked to an existing media centre by a new triple-height Media Circus, this scheme creates offices and studios, together with shops and restaurants. The five office levels focus on an atrium. A freestanding louvred roof and a second skin of glass louvres provide solar protection.

Professor OM Ungers

Bremen University IT and Media Technology Centre
Bibliothekstrasse 1, 28359 Bremen
Tel +49 421 218-1

594 ▮ ✎ EDU 2002

Standing on the curve of a busy road opposite Bremen's airport, this centre is intended to be accessible to local companies. Two parallel quarter-circle buildings accommodate teaching and research facilities, and start-up services for former students.

Atelier Kempe Thill

Rostock IGA Pavilion
IGA Park Rostock,
Mecklenburg-Vorpommern,
Rostock

595 □ CUL 2003

With this pavilion, an entry in
Rotterdam's International
Garden Exhibition IGA 2003, the
architects sought to display the
poetry inherent in the rigorously
logical model of Dutch farming.
Walls of ivy are grown on Smart
Screens, generally used in
industrial glasshouses.

Prof Josef P Kleihues

**Gymnasium Dionysianum
Rheine**
Anton-Führer-Strasse 2,
48431 Rheine, Westfalen
Tel +49 5971 91 43 990

596 ✆ SPO 2002

An addition to Germany's oldest
educational foundation, this
new building is set around three
sides of a courtyard. The
facade's lower part, with its
stripes of stone, contrasts with
the concrete render of the
upper storeys. Interior space is
clearly divided.

Gigon/Guyer

**Archaeological Museum and
Park**
Venner Strasse 69,
49565 Bramsche-Kalkriese
Tel +49 5468 92040

597 □ CUL 2002

These buildings act as signs,
references and aids with which
to imagine the 'Battle of Varus'
between the Teutons and the
Romans which is thought to
have taken place here in 9 AD.
Pavilions called 'Seeing',
'Hearing' and 'Questioning' are
used interactively.

Europe

Daniel Libeskind

Felix Nussbaum Museum
Lotter Strasse 2,
49078 Osnabrück
Tel +49 541 323 2207

598 ☐ CUL 1998

Commissioned to design a museum to house the work of Felix Nussbaum, Libeskind produced spaces that are as much intended to heighten a sensation of discomfort, as they are to function as a gallery. Unusable spaces punctuate the route and slashed walls provide disorientating views.

Bolles+Wilson

Headquarters Borkener Volksbank
Butenwall 57, 46325 Borken
Tel +49 286 180 060

599 ☐ COM 2000

The brickwork and glazed volumes of the Volksbank building 'knit' together in a stepped pattern, distinguishing a functional change, from open banking at the front to more discrete offices at the rear. Inside, the ATM hall is open 24 hours a day.

Léon Wohlhage Wernik Architekten

Residential Building
Münsterland

600 ■ RES 2000

Bordered by a stream and trees to the south, and residential buildings to the north, this family house presents a closed face to its neighbours. The living areas of this simple concrete box open on to two atria, whose spaces provide views through openings cut into the walls.

Jourda & Perraudin Architects

Mont-Cenis Academy
Mont-Cenis-Strasse 285,
44627 Herne
Tel +49 2323 96 760

601 ☐ EDU 1999

The Mont-Cenis Academy combines a variety of civic, educational and recreational functions within an ecologically aware, sustainable design. Inside the single volume of a timber and glass shed, two separate wings are connected by walkways either side of a central axis.

Mario Botta

Dortmund Municipal Library
Königswall 18, 44137 Dortmund
Tel +49 231 501 1999

602 ☐ CUL 1999

Located opposite the main railway station, the main building of this municipal library is a long, narrow block clad in red stone and pierced by tall slit windows. From this protrudes a steel-framed and fully glazed, semicircular, upturned cone, which houses the reading rooms.

ArchiFactory.de

Ebeling House
Kuntzestrasse 71,
44225 Dortmund

603 ◼ RES 2001

Located in a southern suburb of Dortmund, this extension to a 1940s family house is situated along the street front. No extraneous details disrupt the homogeneity of the timber shell. The interior spaces, distributed around a double-height living area, appear to have been carved out of the solid mass.

Herzog & de Meuron

Küppersmühle Museum, Grothe Collection
Philosophenweg 55,
47051 Duisburg
Tel +49 203 30 19 48 11

604 ☐ CUL 1999

This historic, monolithic building was renovated to accommodate a museum housing post-war German art. The removal of ceilings, walling up windows and cutting full-height slits into the brickwork – were made to create enclosed gallery spaces with optimal viewing conditions.

Ingenhoven, Overdiek & Partner

Emscher Park Housing Scheme
Hansegracht 9–15;
Speichergracht 10–14,
47051 Duisburg

605 ❚ RES 2000

This housing scheme, situated within Duisburg's harbour, is composed of parallel blocks separated by shallow canals. With an exposed concrete grid on one side and a flatter facade on the other, the blocks provide various layouts.

Zvi Hecker

Jewish Cultural Centre
Springwell 16, 47051 Duisburg
Tel +49 203 298 1242

606 ☐ CUL 1999

With a new synagogue at its core, this Jewish Cultural Centre documents the history of Duisburg's Jewish community. Like pages of a book, spaces radiate from a central 'spine'. Five portal frames reach into the park and, by imprinting in plan five letters of the Hebrew alphabet, represent chapters.

Propeller Z

Meteorit Exhibition Centre
Grillostrasse 1, 45141 Essen
Tel +49 201 32067 500

607 ☐ CUL 1998

This exhibition complex, commissioned by energy company RWE to showcase their technology, comprises an aluminium hull containing public facilities, a glazed entrance structure and an underground exhibition space. A system of bridges, landings and stairs leads visitors down to a depth of 12 metres.

Peter Kulka

House of Silence
Klosterberg 11,
59851 Meschede
Tel +49 2912 995 0

608 ✏ REL 2001

Set into a hillside, the House of Silence at the Benedictine Abbey of Königsmünster is a concrete cube with 20 guest rooms for visitors on retreats. A narrow, windowless block contains the staircase and a simple chapel. Linking bridges lead to the communal rooms and guest rooms.

Schneider + Schumacher

Erco P3 Warehouse
Brockhauser Weg 80–82,
58507 Lüdenscheid
Tel +49 2351 551 0

609 ☐ ✏ COM 2001

This warehouse and distribution facility for Erco, an innovative lighting company, is a large glazed box, partly sunk into the hillside, capable of storing up to 7,000 pallet-based goods. The internal steel racking system and translucent glass panels on the long facades form the main structure.

Europe

Alsop Architects

Colorium
Speditionsstrasse,
40221 Düsseldorf

610   COM 2001

Part of Düsseldorf's waterfront,
this 17-storey office block
occupies a long, narrow site.
His plans for a taller tower
constrained by planning
restrictions, Alsop radicalized
the facade, using coloured
glass panels to transform the
standard orthogonal structure.
A crimson plant installation
projects from its summit.

Gehry Partners

The New Zollhof
Neuer Zollhof 1–3,
40221 Düsseldorf

611   RES 1999

This residential scheme, known
as 'Father, Child and Mother', is
sited in the Zollhafen (Customs
Dock) area of Düsseldorf's
harbour. The organic structures
are composed of 355 different
prefabricated concrete
components and clad in white
plaster, reflective steel and
terracotta.

Oliver Kruse

Children Island Hombroich
Kapellener Strasse 75,
41472 Neuss
Tel +49 2181 812 262

612   PUB 1999

Set on the museum island of
Hombroich, founded in the
1980s around an eclectic art
collection, this nursery is
constructed entirely of Douglas
fir components. Standard-sized
plywood panels articulate the
rhythm of the framework, which
is constructed from glue-
laminated beams and columns.

Murphy/Jahn

HV Bayer Headquarters
Kaiser-Wilhelm-Allee, Gebäude
W11, 51368 Leverkusen

613 ◼ COM 2002

Part of a collection of buildings
in the Bayer Park, this new
headquarters houses offices
and conference facilities. A
semi-elliptical building is linked
to a pergola by a glazed atrium,
to which all four floors are
linked. The facade's twin-shell
system of glazing maximizes
natural light and ventilation.

Georg Giebeler/4000
architekten

Fogtec Building
Schanzenstrasse 19, Mülheim,
51063 Köln

614 ◼ COM 2001

This building for Fogtec, a
manufacturer of fire
extinguishing systems, stands
on a thin strip of land on a
commercial estate. A simple
warehouse structure is
enlivened by the adjoining
narrow building with bull-nose
entrance and cantilevered rear.

Professor OM Ungers

Wallraf-Richartz Museum
Martinstrasse 39, 50667 Köln
Tel +49 221 221 27694

615 ☐ CUL 2001

This museum, sited between
the historic Gürzenich and the
Rathausplatz, is composed of
two volumes linked by a
common circulation zone, the
smaller volume integrated into
the existing urban arrangement
and the larger, a cubic block,
housing all the exhibition areas.
On the northeast, panoramic
windows provide city views.

Europe

Grimshaw

Igus Headquarters & Factory
Spicher Strasse 1a, 51147 Köln
Tel +49 2203 9649 0

616 ☐ ✆ COM 2001

The design company Igus
wanted a factory and
headquarters building that
could be totally flexible. Each
factory block has at its centre
a landscaped courtyard from
which rises a steel mast with
rods supporting the roof. This
leaves the interior empty of
columns. Moveable pods
contain offices and services.

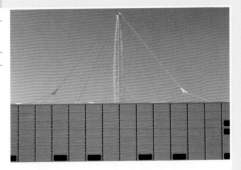

Eisenman Architects and JC
Decaux

Bus Stop
Am Elisenbrunnen, Friedrich-
Wilhelm-Platz, 52062 Aachen

617 ☐ TRA 1998

Located in the centre of
Aachen, the insertion of this
futuristic-looking structure has
caused controversy. The folded
steel sculptural form is as much
a children's climbing frame as a
functional object, but it provides
shelter while allowing views out
with minimal obstruction.

Behnisch, Behnisch & Partner

**North German Regional
Clearing Bank**
Am Friedrichswall 10,
30159 Hannover
Tel +49 511 361 4025

618 ☐ ✆ COM 2002

Occupying an entire block
between Hannover's commercial
district and a residential suburb,
shops and cafés occupy the
lower floors, while the bank
occupies the floors above. By
fragmenting the mass of the
complex, a variety of spaces
can be accommodated.

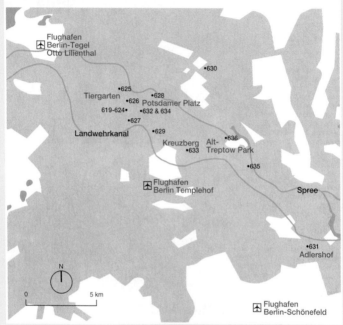

Flughafen
Berlin-Tegel
Otto Lilienthal

•630

•625
Tiergarten   •628
    •626   Potsdamer Platz
619–624•   •632 & 634

•627
Landwehrkanal

•629
    Kreuzberg   Alt-   •636
      •633   Treptow Park

Flughafen
Berlin Templehof

Spree

•631
Adlershof

N

0   5 km

Flughafen
Berlin-Schönefeld

•635

Berger + Parkkinen Architekten

Embassies of the Nordic Countries
Rauchstrasse 1, 10787 Berlin
Tel +49 30 50 50 0

619 ☐ GOV 1999

Raising questions about individuality, the five Nordic countries decided to build their embassies on a single site. This apparent tension is reflected in the solid forms and voids of the masterplan. At the entrance is the Felleshus (House for All), containing an auditorium, restaurant and consular offices.

Europe

Palmar Kristmundsson

Embassy of Iceland
Rauchstrasse 1, 10787 Berlin
Tel +49 30 50 50 4000

620 ✏ GOV 1999

The smallest of the Nordic
embassies, Iceland's slender
volume occupies the northwest
corner of the site. The ribbed
concrete of the entrance echoes
the corrugated metal common
to many Icelandic vernacular
buildings, while the smooth
facade is made from liparit,
a rare Icelandic stone.

3XN

Royal Danish Embassy
Rauchstrasse 1, 10787 Berlin
Tel +49 30 50 50 2000

621 ✏ GOV 1999

Behind the perforated rain-
screen cladding of Berlin's
Danish Embassy lie two
buildings on either side of a
curving internal street,
connected by aerial walkways.
The interior facade of the
rectilinear volume bears the
same exterior steel cladding,
while the curving volume is clad
in softer ash slats.

Snøhetta

Royal Norwegian Embassy
Rauchstrasse 1, 10787 Berlin
Tel +49 30 50 50 50

622 ☐ GOV 1999

The Norwegian embassy
building asserts its identity with
a strong vertical facade that
integrates a monumental
southern wall of Norwegian
granite, reminiscent of Norway's
mountains and tall forests. The
theme is continued in the
flanking full-height glazing and
louvred screens, which are
intended to suggest glaciers.

VIIVA Arkkitehtuuri

Embassy of Finland
Rauchstrasse 1, 10787 Berlin
Tel +49 30 50 50 30

623 GOV 1999

The Finnish embassy in Berlin is characterized by subtle modulations and attention to detail. What is ostensibly a trapezoidal box is clad with horizontal aspen strips that act as a *brise-soleil* over a triple-glazed wall. Occupants control the adjustable louvres and shutters so that the face of the embassy alters continuously.

Wingårdh Arkitektkontor

Embassy of Sweden
Rauchstrasse 1, 10787 Berlin
Tel +49 30 50 50 60

624 GOV 1999

The identity of the Swedish embassy is expressed through the range and treatment of materials. The white limestone and black diorite of the south and west elevations, and the birch cladding of the central staircase and full-height foyer, all originate in Sweden. The design evokes a sense of warmth and openness.

Diener & Diener

Swiss Embassy
Otto-von-Bismarck-Allee 4a, 10557 Berlin
Tel +49 30 390 400 00

625 GOV 2000

This intervention extends the Swiss Embassy, a fragment of what was once a grand palace, with a monolithic concrete block, which creates a contemporary dialogue between old and new. The minimally articulated front facade of the new volume maintains a sense of proportion.

Europe

Foster and Partners

The Reichstag
Platz der Republik 1,
11011 Berlin
Tel +49 30 227 37 453

626 ☐ GOV 1999

The monumental masonry shell
and formal entrance of the
Reichstag were restored, while
the intervention transformed the
interior into a place of light and
transparency. A glazed cupola
set above the debating
chamber houses a public
observation platform accessed
via helical ramps.

Giorgio Grassi

Parkkolonnaden
Köthener Strasse 2 e 3–4,
10963 Berlin

627 ☐ COM 2001

Grassi's masterplan for
Postdamer Platz, one of the
largest projects in the 1990s,
comprises five buildings
designed by various architects.
Regular fenestration and the
uniform construction materials
of brick and light sandstone
ensure that the huge scheme
is viewed as a cohesive whole.

Gehry Partners

DZ Bank Building
Pariser Platz 3, 10117 Berlin

628 ☐ COM 2001

Gehry was constrained by
planning requirements that
determined the external
massing and stipulated the
use of limestone facades. The
front adheres to these rules,
while the rear walls undulate
with projecting windows. Within
a huge glass-vaulted atrium sits
a steel-clad sculptural form
housing a conference chamber.

Sauerbruch Hutton Architects

GSW Headquarters
Lochstrasse 22, 10969 Berlin

629 □ COM 1999

This commercial office development is an assemblage of discrete and fragmented elements, designed to create flexible, user-friendly workspaces. A curving, high-rise slab rises between two low-level blocks that contain public mixed-use activities. The double skin and roof wing produces efficient ventilation.

Dominique Perrault Architecte

Olympic Cycle Stadium and Swimming Pool
Landsberger Allee, 10407 Berlin
Tel +49 30 827 083 101

630 ✎ SPO 1999

Situated in the city's Prenzlauer Berg district, this scheme forms part of Berlin's failed bid to host the 2000 Olympic Games. The two volumes, surrounded by steeply sloping banks, are submerged in a 10 hectare plateau. The flat roofs are fine-mesh steel mats mounted on steel frames.

Sauerbruch Hutton Architects

Photonics Centre
Carl-Scheele-Strasse 16, 12489 Berlin

631 ▯ COM 1998

Sited in Berlin's new City of Science and Technology, these curvaceous buildings with contrasting colour programmes house an organization that conducts research into optics. The spaces in the larger building are distributed around a sky-lit atrium, integrating structure and services.

Architekten Kollhoff und
Timmerman

**Daimler Chrysler Skyscraper,
Potsdamer Platz**
Potsdamer Platz 1, 10785 Berlin
Tel +49 30 2529 4372

632 ☐ COM 2000

The 27-storey, 101 metre tall
Daimler Chrysler building in
Potsdamer Platz draws
inspiration from Chicago's early
skyscrapers. Fitting a tight
corner site, the brick-clad
building is triangular in plan
with its end elevation only four
bays wide.

Daniel Libeskind

Jewish Museum
Lindenstrasse 9–14,
10969 Berlin
Tel +49 30 259 93 410

633 ☐ CUL 1998

Replacing the formal facades
of Berlin's Lindenstrasse, this
urban void represents notions
of absence, memory and loss.
With its deep-cut riveted zinc
walls, the building's material
and compositional strength suit
its urban scale. Inside, public
spaces are arranged around a
cavernous route.

Renzo Piano Building Workshop
/Christoph Kohlbecker

Potsdamer Platz
Marlene-Dietrich-Platz,
10875 Berlin

634 ☐ COM 2000

Piano's masterplan for a 7.5
hectare site within Potsdamer
Platz, a focus for urban renewal,
includes offices, housing,
cultural amenities, shops and
restaurants. The complex is
based on the traditional Berlin
block and integrates square
and water.

Axel Schultes Architekten &
Charlotte Frank

**Crematorium
Baumschulenweg**
Kiefholzstrasse 222,
12437 Berlin
Tel +49 30 617 54 52

635 ☐ REL 1998

With its rectangular plan and
plain, monumental forms, this
building is deceptively simple.
In fact, subtle relationships
between masses and voids are
highlighted by the animated
play of light across all surfaces
of the shuttered concrete.

Architekten Schweger Partner

Treptowers/Allianz Berlin
An den Treptowers, 12435 Berlin
Tel +49 30 53830

636 ☐ COM 1998

Situated close to the old city
centre, this office and workshop
complex integrates Ernst
Ziesel's listed AEG
administration building (1927–8)
and factory hall (1937). A tower
forms a dominant landmark,
and linear blocks arranged
around courtyards, based on
the Kreuzberg model, overlook
the river.

Barkow Leibinger Architekten

Biosphere and Flower Pavilion
Georg-Herrman-Allee 99,
14469 Potsdam
Tel +49 331 275 58 88

637 ☐ CUL 2001

Situated near Potsdam's
Sanssouci Palace, the design
of this giant greenhouse is
based on the defensive earthen
berms made here by the
occupying Soviet Army. The
structure is sunk into a series
of berms clad in oak logs, turf,
slate and poured concrete.

Europe

Auer + Weber Architekten

University Library
Universitätsplatz 2,
39106 Magdeburg
Tel +49 391 671 2925

638 ☐ EDU 2003

Part of a larger scheme to create a new square surrounded by key university buildings, the design of this library seeks to reinforce the link between campus and city. The form is dominated by long diagonal edges which lead through the building and connect the structure with its surroundings.

Sauerbruch Hutton Architects

Experimental Factory
Sandtorstrasse 23,
39106 Magdeburg
Tel +49 391 54486 19200

639 ☐ COM 2001

This research institute for the development of production processes contains a five-storey laboratory unit, a single-storey hall for large-scale experiments and a testing space for electromagnetic fields. A continuous striped roof envelops the building.

Von Gerkan Marg & Partner

Christus Pavilion, Monastery of Volkenroda
Amtshof 3,
99998 Koerner-Volkenroda
Tel +49 36025 559 80

640 ☐ REL 2000

Originally built to represent the Catholic and Protestant Churches at the Hannover Expo 2000, this pavilion was re-erected as a church in a cloister of a Cistercian monastery. The grid of the cloister is panelled and glazed in various natural and artificial materials.

Europe

Germany North

Michael Wilford & Partners and Wilford Schupp Architekten

Braun Headquarters
Werksanlagen Pfieffewiesen, 34212 Melsungen

641 ▯ COM 2001

This latest addition to the Braun Headquarters, designed by Wilford, houses offices. Accessed by a bridge from the existing administration block, the volumes relate to office functions. The various cladding materials emphasize the disparity between the volumes.

Weinmiller Architects

Federal Labour Court
Hugo-Preuss-Platz 1, 99113 Erfurt
Tel +49 361 26 36 0

642 ✎ GOV 1999

Built as part of a relocation of major federal institutions to the east, this exposed concrete and natural stone structure dominates its surroundings. As well as containing the court and administrative offices, the monolithic block houses Germany's largest labour law library.

Marcel Kalberer

Vegetal Building
Im Pappelwald beim Sportplatz, 99518 Auerstedt
Tel +49 36461 92886

643 ☐ CUL 2000

Located between Weimar and Naumburg, this building was erected by 300 volunteers, directed by the architect and assisted by artists of the building group Sanfte Strukturen. The willows, which were planted, bound and woven into a large dome, will continue to grow, covering the structure.

Europe

Auer + Weber Architekten

Officers' Mess and Refectory
Marienallee/Stauffenbergallee,
01099 Dresden
Tel +49 3528 435 550

644 ♪ GOV 1998

This pavilion contains dining
and club rooms and follows the
orthogonal structure of the
original barracks. Large sliding
doors in the fully glazed facades
give access to the park and the
long facades are fitted with
adjustable sunscreens. The
grid-like structure supports a
roof of ribbed laminated sheets.

Coop Himmelb(l)au

UFA Cinema Centre
Prager Strasse 1,
01069 Dresden
Tel +49 351 482 50

645 ☐ REC 1998

Located on a city centre site,
the two interconnected parts
house eight cinema screens,
four below ground. The
crystalline volume contains the
foyer, within which suspends
the café in a double inverted
cone. Metal bridges and stairs
carve angles through the
spaces.

Ortner & Ortner

Saxon Federal Library
Zellescher Weg 18,
01054 Dresden
Tel +49 351 4677 123

646 ☐ CUL 2003

Sited in a Dresden suburb, this
library combines the holdings
of the libraries of Dresden and
Saxony, and Dresden's
Technical University. Much of
the scheme is underground with
a monumental, sky-lit, 200-seat
reading room at its centre.
Above ground are two
rectangular, stone blocks.

Germany North

Wandel Hoefer Lorch + Hirsch

Dresden Synagogue
Hasenberg 1, 01067 Dresden

647 ▬ REL 2001

Built next to the site of the previous synagogue, which was designed by Gottfried Semper and destroyed on Kristallnacht in 1938, this building is a curvilinear stone structure, the bevelled shape resulting from the gradual layering of the 41 levels of coursing. Opposite stands the lower volume of the community hall.

3.12 648-668   Germany South

Frankfurt am Main•648-650

Czech Republic

•651

•653
•652

•655
•654
Stuttgart•656-657

Germany

•658

•659   •660

München•663-668

•661

•662

Switzerland

Austria

Italy

Grimshaw

Frankfurt Messehalle H3
Ludwig-Erhard-Anlage 1,
60327 Frankfurt am Main
Tel +61 8 8981 6868

648 □ COM 2001

One of Franfurt's Messehalle,
H3 is the largest column-free
interior space in Europe,
providing 3,715 square metres
of exhibition space over two
floors. The roof is composed of
five flexed arches constructed
from a network of welded steel
tubes. Natural light is brought in
through clerestory glazing.

Auer + Weber Architekten

Prisma Building
Hahnstrasse 55,
60323 Frankfurt am Main
Tel +49 7147 2214

649 ✏ COM 2001

The design of this huge office
building is based on a concept
of low-energy ventilation. A
wedge-shaped form is
contained within a glass shell,
creating a passive thermal
environment. The atrium,
crossed by angled walkways,
provides dramatic perspectives
from different floors.

plus+

Freie Waldorfschule
Friedleberstrasse 52,
60433 Frankfurt am Main
Tel +49 69 95 29 42 131

650 ✏ EDU 1998

The design for this extension,
containing six classrooms and
rooms for dance, music and
craft, emerged from workshops
held between the architects,
children, teachers and parents.
The curved addition wraps
around the existing building and
construction is exposed,
revealing how it works.

Brückner & Brückner Architects

Art Depot
Veitshöchheimer Strasse 5,
97080 Würzburg
Tel +49 931 322 250

651 ☐ CUL 2002

Set along the harbourside, this art gallery is a conversion of a former grain silo. The wings have been extended with boxes composed of slender horizontal stone slabs that are set at angles that subtly shift over the height of the building. Inside the elongated void, freestanding galleries were inserted.

Günther Domenig

Documentation Centre, Nürnberg Kongresshalle
Bayernstrasse 110,
90471 Nürnberg
Tel +49 911 231 5666

652 ☐ GOV 2001

The largest Nazi building in Germany to survive the war, this glass and steel intervention contains a documentation centre, an exhibition space and meeting and teaching rooms. The new structure inhabits the existing fabric but never comes into contact with it.

Kauffmann Theilig & Partner, Freie Architekten

Stripes
Adi-Dassler-Strasse,
91074 Herzogenaurach

653 ▮ COM 1999

Part of Adidas-Salomon's corporate headquarters, this restaurant is sited in woodlands by a lake, set apart from the main building to give workers a proper change of scene. Spread on different levels, the building has a glass roof, supported by slender joists.

Europe

Barkow Leibinger Architekten

Laser Machine Tool Factory
Johann-Maus-Strasse 2,
71254 Ditzingen
Tel +49 715 630 30

654 ▯ ✎ COM 2000

Located near Stuttgart, this
addition comprises production
and administrative facilities for
a manufacturer of machinery.
The buildings are sunk into the
sloping site, the undulating roof,
with diamond-shaped
openings, merging with the
landscape. The structure is of
zinc and pre-cast concrete.

Bottega + Ehrhardt Architekten

House S
Bismarckstrasse 18,
71634 Ludwigsburg

655 ▯ RES 2002

This house, containing three
apartments, presents a faceless
facade, with its sloping roof
undifferentiated from its walls
and a single, horizontal window.
By contrast, the rear facade is
fully glazed across its three
levels, flooding the interiors with
light, and the roof is cut away to
form a terrace.

Rainer Scholl

Berufsschulzentrum
Heilbronner Strasse 157,
70191 Stuttgart
Tel +49 711 2569 280

656 ▯ ✎ EDU 2000

This U-shaped building,
surrounding a multi-purpose
square and completed on its
fourth side by a neo-classical
building, houses school
classrooms. Solar panels on the
south facade generate enough
energy to heat the water and
the swimming pool. Dark green
glazing provides shade.

Werner Sobek

Sobek House
Stuttgart

657 ■ RES 2000

Designed to provide a home and energy-efficient environment for the architect himself, this four-storey glass box is set on a deep hillside overlooking Stuttgart. The modular steel frame is clad in triple-glazed panels. Water-cooled ceiling panels absorb solar radiation in summer, and store and radiate heat in winter.

J Mayer H Architekten

Scharnhauser Park Town Hall
Gerhard-Koch-Strasse 1,
73760 Ostfildern
Tel +49 711 3404 238

658 ▯ ✆ GOV 2002

Built for Scharnhauser, a new town near Stuttgart, this town hall contains a meeting chamber, wedding room, library, gym and offices. A projecting roof, from which rainwater streams in jets, signals the entrance, its underneath brightly lit. Each floor is independent from the other.

Sauerbruch Hutton Architects

Pharmaceutical Research Laboratories
Birkendorfer Strasse 65,
88397 Biberach an der Riss

659 ▯ COM 2002

Part of a scientific research campus, this seven-storey rectilinear building contains laboratories which are distributed along parallel zones according to their functions' tolerance of light. An atrium brings natural ventilation and daylight deep into the building.

Europe

Allmann Sattler Wappner
Architekten

Südwestmetall Reutlingen
Schulstrasse 23,
72764 Reutlingen
Tel +49 71 213 3310

660 ▮ ✆ COM 2002

This office complex houses the
Südwestmetall metalworking
and electrical manufacturing
company. Three saddle-roofed
buildings relate in form to the
surrounding villas but, with their
stainless-steel surfaces, stand
out. The ground and facades
feature ornamental metalwork.

Zaha Hadid

Landscape Formation One
Rathause, Schillerstrasse 1,
79576 Weil am Rhein
Tel +49 7621 704 103

661 ✆ CUL 1999

This event and exhibition space
emerges from the landscape
and the seamless flow of ramps
that create linked areas. The
exhibition hall and café stretch
out along the structure. A
performance space is sited
alongside the café and an
environmental research centre
extends into the exhibition hall.

Behnisch, Behnisch & Partner

**Museum of Fantasy,
Buchheim Collection**
Am Hirschgarten 1,
82347 Bernried
Tel +49 8158 997 060

662 ☐ CUL 2001

Sited on the sloping edge of the
Starnberger See, this building
was commissioned by Lathar-
Gunther Buchheim, author of
Das Boot (The Boat), to put on
public display his collection of
art and folk objects. The linear
building reaches out towards
the lake, ending with a pier.

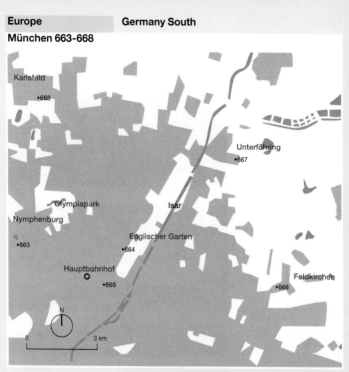

Karlsfeld

•668

Unterföhring

•667

Olympiapark

Isar

Nymphenburg

Englischer Garten

•663

•664

Hauptbahnhof

•665

Feldkirchen

•666

N

0   3 km

Allmann Sattler Wappner
Architekten

Church of the Sacred Heart
Lachnerstrasse 8,
80634 München
Tel +49 89 130 6750

663 ☐ REL 2000

This elegant church comprises
two boxes, one placed inside
the other. The nave is clad with
vertical maple louvres set close
to each other at the entrance
and becoming more widely
spaced down the nave. The
outer glass skin is gradually
less transparent.

Europe

Baumschlager & Eberle

Münchener Rück Headquarters
Königinstrasse 107,
80791 München

664 ■ COM 2001

Set in the business city of München, this office building is composed of two wings wrapped around two internal courtyards. The glass facade is composed of slanted panes that former an outer skin, part of a sophisticated passive energy environment.

Herzog & de Meuron

Fünf Höfe
Am Eisbach 3, 80538 München

665 □ CUL 2003

Situated in the city's old town, the Fünf Höfe (Five Courtyards) project, a labyrinth of shops, offices, exhibition spaces and apartments, integrates commerce with art and culture. In addition to masterminding the overall scheme, the architects designed a new Kunsthalle, making it larger than the gallery it replaces.

Meck Architekten/Stephan Köppel

Mortuary and Cemetery
Strasse am Mitterfeld 68,
81829 München

666 □ REL 2000

Located in a park opposite the old graveyard, this mortuary and cemetery stands as an austere composition of stone, concrete, rusting steel and oak. A canopy floats above the linear structure that comprises a chapel, mourning rooms and courtyards.

BRT Architekten

Swiss Re Office Building
Dieselstrasse 11,
85774 München
Tel +49 89 38440

667 ■ ✂ COM 2001

This office complex is
surrounded by a hanging hedge
of vines. Common areas – foyer,
meeting rooms, library and
dining areas – are housed in a
square, two-storey base.
Above, supported on concrete
stilts and connected by
walkways, are 16 office units
radiating from four hubs.

Meck Architekten/Stephan
Köppel

Kammerl Residence
Ignatius-Blenninger-Strasse 11,
80995 München

668 ■ RES 1998

Surrounded by blocks of flats,
an angular spiralling wall
protects this two-storey, L-
shaped house and its courtyard.
The outer walls are of roughly
finished vertical strips of larch
while, in contrast, the sheltered
courtyard elevations are clad in
red wood panels.

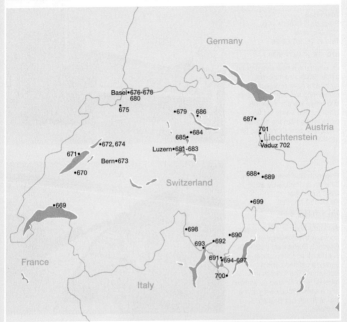

Germany

Basel •676-678
680
•675
•679 •686
•687
•701
Liechtenstein
Vaduz 702
Austria
•672, 674
•685 •684
Luzern•681-683
671•
Bern•673
•670
•688 •689
Switzerland
•699
•669
•698
•690
693• •692
691•694-697
700•
France
Italy

Bernard Tschumi Architects/
Luca Merlini

**Interface Flon Railway and
Bus Station**
Place de l'Europe, Flon,
Lausanne
Tel +41 21 613 73 73

669 ☐ TRA 2001

This first phase of Lausanne's
new transport infrastructure
comprises regional train and
bus stations, lifts, an enclosed
bridge and new traffic hub.
The different transport lines are
anchored around a central node
of glazed rectilinear structures.

Devanthéry & Lamunière
Architectes

Town Hall
Place de l'Hôtel de ville,
1530 Payerne
Tel +41 26 662 66 26

670 ▉ ✎ GOV 1999

By wrapping a new skin around
a late-1960s structure, the
architects have succeeded in
reinventing this town hall's civic
and urban identity. A simple
glass curtain wall is set 50
centimetres from the original
walls, with operable panels for
ventilation.

Mario Botta

Friedrich Dürrenmatt Centre
Chemin du Pertuis-du-Sault 74,
2000 Neuchâtel
Tel +41 32 720 206

671 ☐ CUL 2000

Set into a hillside, this museum
contains the drawings of
Friedrich Dürrenmatt (1921–90).
His house accommodates his
library, a cafeteria and a
bookshop. The fortress-like
exterior is dominated by a tower
and a semi-circular wall, at the
top of which is a viewing
platform.

Meili Peter Architekten

**Swiss School of Engineering
for the Wood Industry**
Solothurnstrasse 102, 2504 Biel
Tel +41 32 344 02 02

672 ☐ EDU 1999

Most of this building is
constructed from wood. The
teaching accommodation, with
workshops beneath, is entered
via grand porticoes. Two vertical
circulation spaces combined
with a horizontal space running
the length of the volume give
good access throughout, an
essential precaution against fire.

Graber Pulver Architekten

Vocational Training Centre
Felsenaustrasse 17, 3004 Bern
Tel +41 31 337 37 37

673 ✎ EDU 2001

This entrance block for a school for trade apprentices accommodates laboratories, offices and a computer suite. The volume of the rectilinear box appear to have been carved away to form recesses and openings that illuminate the interior. Interior spaces form different configurations depending on their functions.

Diener & Diener

Centre PasquArt
Seevorstadt 71–5, 2502 Biel
Tel +41 32 322 55 86

674 ☐ CUL 1999

Adding a new wing to the existing nineteenth-century building, the centre now comprises a contemporary art laboratory. The new building sits alongside the old, its ground-floor glazing responding to the solid sandstone base of its neighbour, and the almost closed elevation countering the conventional fenestration.

Herzog & de Meuron

Ricola Marketing Building
Baselstrasse 31, 4242 Laufen
Tel +41 61 765 41 21

675 ☐ ✎ COM 1998

This two-storey, fully glazed office building is almost part of the landscape, its roof planted with ivy and Virginia creeper, which climb along projecting rafters. The interior is a light open space, with a wide stairway that can also be used as raked seating. Coloured curtains modulate the quality of light.

Herzog & de Meuron

**Roche Pharma Research
Institute Building 92 & 41**
Grenzacherstrasse 124,
4070 Basel
Tel +41 61 688 1111

676 ▯ ✆ COM 2000

This nine-storey building
contains offices, laboratories,
auditorium, café and five-storey
library, accommodated behind
a neutral screen of completely
flat glazing. Adjustable external
screens, however, animate the
facade with their irregularly
faceted contours.

Herzog & de Meuron

Central Signal Tower
Münchensteinerbrücke, Basel

677 ▯ COM 1998

This signal tower, outside
Basel's main train station, is
a concrete core wrapped in
copper strips symbolizing the
electronics housed inside. Its
twisting shape allows maximum
usable space within a restricted
footprint. Except for slight
variations in the cladding over
the windows, there is little hint
of its being an office building.

Herzog & de Meuron

Schaulager
Ruchfeldstrasse 19, 4142 Basel
Tel +41 61 335 32 32

678 ☐ CUL 2002

The Schaulager or Viewing
Warehouse is part museum,
part warehouse, part research
centre, housing the collection
of the Emanuel Hoffmann
Foundation, which represents
over 150 twentieth-century
artists. Spread over three
storeys, the building provides
optimal climatic conditions
for storage.

Europe

Gmür-Vacchini Architekten

Three Houses
Schöntalstrasse 43,45,47,
5712 Beinwil am See

679 ■ RES 1999

Set on a grassy mountain slope overlooking the lake below, these three identical houses, commissioned by three female friends, set up a regular geometrical rhythm of parallels and opposites. The materials palette is restricted to exposed concrete and glass so as not to detract from the scheme's unity.

Gmür-Vacchini Architekten

Hospital of the Canton and the University of Basel
Spitalstrasse 21, 4031 Basel
Tel +41 61 265 25 25

680 ■ ✆ PUB 2003

The existing building was constructed between 1939 and 1945 and has been modernized to bring it up to date with medical advances. The project includes a new building for the operating theatre and gynaecology unit, in which colour, glass and natural light have created less clinical interiors.

Architectures Jean Nouvel

Culture and Congress Centre
Europaplatz 1, 6005 Luzern
Tel +41 41 226 77 77

681 □ CUL 1999

This centre contains a concert hall, an art museum and public foyers. The structure is dominated by a vast cantilevered copper-clad roof which highlights the dramatic Alpine setting. Inside, the different activities are housed in discrete, ship-like volumes reminiscent of the shipyard that formerly occupied the site.

Diener & Diener

Migros School and Shopping Centre
Schweizerhof Quai,
6002 Luzern
Tel +41 41 410 04 10

682 □ EDU 2000

Located between Luzern's old city and the Schweizerhof Quay, this new shopping centre updates the traditional typology of the market hall as an urban public space. Shops are housed in the lower part of the building, with adult education in the glazed gallery above.

Architectures Jean Nouvel

Hotel
Sempacherstrasse 14,
6002 Luzern
Tel +41 41 226 86 90

683 □ TOU 2000

The renovation of this building is based on the close relationship that hotels have always had with film and on the notion of temporary encounters. The ceiling of each of the 25 rooms is decorated with a recent film-still and objects are chosen for their resonance with the scene depicted.

Barkow Leibinger Architekten

Production and Office Facility
Ruessenstrasse 8, 6340 Baar
Tel +41 41 417 696 666

684 ■▮ ✎ COM 2002

Set into gently sloping farmland on the edge of an industrial park, this new building for a high-tech laser manufacturing company houses production facilities and office space. A series of volumes project from one another, diminishing in scale from the copper-clad, two-storey production hall at the top of the site.

Europe

Bétrix & Consolascio
Architekten

Sports Centre
Hertistrasse 17, 6300 Zug
Tel +41 1 910 9000

685 📞 SPO 2001

Located outside Zug among
sports fields and temporary
pavilions, the flat facades of
this sports centre appear blank
except for their display of a
spectrum of colour. Clad with
amethyst-toned glass sheets,
the elevations change colour
according to the angle of view,
and different effects of light.

Peter Märkli

Hürzeler House
Rankstrasse 38,
8703 Erlenbach

686 ◼ RES 1998

The pre-cast concrete planes
of this house are organized so
that, apart from the street
elevation, walls neither fully
contain nor reveal the interior
spaces. On the garden facade,
narrow balconies run the length
of the volume, occasionally
screened from view by squares
of dusky-red concrete.

Gigon/Guyer

Liner Museum
Unterrainstrasse 5,
9050 Appenzell
Tel +41 71 788 18 00

687 ☐ CUL 1998

Located on the edge of
Appenzell, this museum houses
work by father and son portrait
and landscape painters Carl
Walter Liner and Carl August
Liner. Cladding a wooden
structure, the exterior stainless-
steel panels are dazzling. The
galleries, lit by clerestories in the
sawtooth roof, diminish in size.

Bearth & Deplazes Architekten

House Willimann
Sevgein

688 ■ RES 1998

Located on the edge of the
village of Sevgein, this tall,
timber-clad building responds
to its sloping site with stepped
levels arranged around a central
stairway. As a result of its
wedge-shaped plan, the
angular volume appears to
change shape and size
according to the viewing point.

Valerio Olgiati

School
Schulhaus Paspels,
7417 Paspels
Tel +41 81 655 15 07

689 ✆ EDU 1998

Linked to the existing school by
an underground passage, this
solitary monolith rises up from
the meadows, its entrance
marked by a simple cantilevered
roof slab. Inside, all angles
deviate from the square, making
everything slightly dislocated.
The effect is intensified by the
use of concrete for all surfaces.

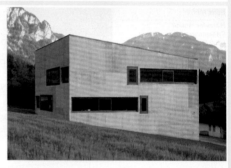

Aurelio Galfetti

Centro Civico Comunale
Gorduno, Bellinzona

690 ▯ GOV 1998

Creating a new urban space
that links the different parts of
the town, Gorduno's Centro
Civico Comunale functions as
an elementary school as well as
a town hall. The volumes of the
interiors are expressed in the
elevations via the reinforced
concrete modular structure and
the floor-to-ceiling glazing.

Europe

Luca Gazzaniga

Guglielmini House
Pregassona

691 ■ RES 1998

Built into a deeply sloping site with panoramic views over Lake Lugano, this house comprises a set of rectangular volumes with extensive glazing in carefully selected positions. The living and dining areas are arranged on either side of a courtyard, with the service areas set into the side of the hill.

Michele Arnaboldi Architetto

Ferretti Arnaboldi House
Locarno

692 ■ RES 1999

This house, sunk into a sloping terrain, is spread over three floors. The hard lines of the ground-floor concrete base are broken by a diagonal stair that crosses its face. A cantilevered roof volume, clad with timber, marks the entrance. The first-floor, glazed, living area opens on to a broad terrace.

Raffaele Cavadini

Oratorio di Porta
Porta, 6614 Brissago
Tel +41 91 75 423 27

693 □ REL 1998

This new oratory, built for the mountain village of Porta, is based on the traditional pattern, with an external portico and internal space of equal sizes. A rectangular concrete frame, in the shape of the cross on each elevation, is infilled to delineate the two volumes. The exterior is faced in stone.

Aurelio Galfetti

Multipurpose Hall, University of Lugano
Via Giuseppe Buffi 13,
6900 Lugano
Tel +41 91 912 46 11

694 ▮ ⌁ EDU 2001

An extension to Lugano's university campus, this hall can accommodate 500 people for lectures, exhibitions and other university events. To limit the visual impact on surrounding parkland, the hall is submerged underground. Daylight is admitted via a fully glazed foyer.

Giraudi & Wettstein Architetti

Laboratory, University of Lugano
Via Giuseppe Buffi 13,
6900 Lugano
Tel +41 91 912 46 46

695 ▮ ⌁ EDU 2002

Facing the library, this building defines a large green space within the university campus. The transparent skin of the facade opens the internal spaces to the park. The rear facade overlooks Lake Lugano and features narrow, vertical windows.

Michele and Giorgio Tognola Architetti

Library, University of Lugano
Via Giuseppe Buffi 13,
6900 Lugano
Tel +41 91 913 85 00

696 ▯ EDU 2002

Part of a masterplan to provide five new buildings for Lugano's university, the library is a screen-like extension to an existing U-shaped building. The new building comprises a grid of concrete slabs, creating glazed reading booths with steel screens.

Europe

Bruno Fioretti Marquez + Martini

Lecture Halls, University of Lugano
Via Giuseppe Buffi 13,
6900 Lugano
Tel +41 91 912 46 46

697 ☐ EDU 2002

The programme for this building was determined by its function and the large number of people using the theatres. The interiors are equipped with advanced audio-visual systems, acoustic isolation and air conditioning. Large, sliding windows reveal open spaces.

Roberto Briccola

Single Family House
6684 Campo Vallemaggia
Tel +41 19 1754 2327

698 ☐ RES 1998

This small weekend house, perched on concrete stilts to accommodate the gradient, is reminiscent of traditional granary buildings. The pine structure is infilled with triple-ply boards, clad with larch. Living areas, with a view of the mountains, are on the ground floor, with two bedrooms and a shower room above.

Barkow Leibinger Architekten

Start-up Offices
Ausserfeld, 7214 Grüsch
Tel +41 81 307 6161

699 ☐▮✎ COM 2001

Boxes rotated on top of each other form the basis of the design for these start-up offices. The same principle is applied to the top of the building as roof terraces, and to the bottom as cantilevers for protection against the weather. This block connects to an existing factory by underground tunnel.

Architetto Ugo Früh

Meier-Ratsiatos House
Via Vacallo 10E, 6834 Morbio
Inferiore
Tel +41 91 682 4955

700 ▮ ✎ RES 2002

Located in a residential area
close to the Italian border, this
house is a vertical volume cut
through by a horizontal block.
On approach, the building
appears as a tower cut into a
valley. From the rear, however,
the orientation is horizontal,
with the living areas opening
on to the garden.

Baumschlager & Eberle

Flatz House
Saxgasse 16, Schaan

701 ▮ RES 2002

Built from concrete blocks
and set against a mountainous
backdrop, this modernist family
home overlooks the small town
of Schaan. The simply designed
floors are stacked on top of
each other with the upper floor
being a cantilevered horizontal
slab. The position of the
windows articulates the division
of internal spaces.

Morger & Degelo

Leichtenstein Kunstmuseum
Städtle 32, 9490 Vaduz
Tel +423 235 03 00

702 ▢ CUL 2000

Smooth, light stone links
museum facade and piazza in
a restructuring of this open
space within the dense urban
fabric of Vaduz. A low slot
marks the entrance to the
museum building, leading into
an unexpectedly large atrium.
Generous windows at ground
level allow passers-by to
glimpse exhibitions.

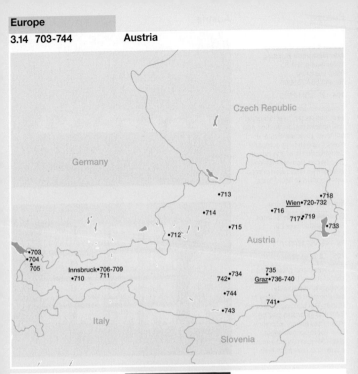

Czech Republic

Germany

•713

•714

Wien •720-732 •718
•716
717 •719
•715   •733

Austria

•703
•704
705

Innsbruck •706-709
•710   711

•734   735
742•   Graz •736-740

•744
•741
•743

Italy

Slovenia

Baumschlager & Eberle

**BTV Commercial and
Residential Building**
Unterlinden 23, 6922 Wolfurt

703 ▢ COM 1998

Banking, housing and a medical
practice are contained within
this freestanding entity located
next to a busy road. Timber
strips, alternately jutting and
receding, cover the eye-
catching glazed facade. There
are no interior load-bearing
elements, creating an open and
egalitarian working space.

Dietrich Untertrifaller Architects

Walch's Event Catering Administration Building
Millenniumspark 8,
6890 Lustenau
Tel +43 557 785850

704 🖊 COM 2000

Conceived and built in only one year, this rectangular industrial unit houses the production and administrative facilities of an event management company. Construction is of chipboard-clad timber elements covered in a net-like fabric skin printed with puddles of liquid metal.

Baumschlager & Eberle

Ecological Middle School
Neue Landstrasse 29,
6841 Mäder
Tel +43 552 364007 11

705 ▯ EDU 1998

This timber and glass middle school meets the brief for the ecological community development of the village of Mäder. The building's compact form and extensive glazing maximizes energy efficiency. Four floors contain seven classrooms arranged around a spacious relaxation area.

Holz Box Tirol

MiniBox
Colingasse 3, 6020 Innsbruck
Tel +43 512 561478 0

706 🖊 RES 1998

Perched on an elevator tower in downtown Innsbruck, the Minibox is a tiny, two-storey temporary living space, with sleeping for up to four, kitchen/dining area, a bathroom and views to the mountains. Constructed from timber clad with formwork sheets, it can be quickly assembled.

Europe

Zaha Hadid

Bergisel Ski-jump
Bergiselweg 3, 6020 Innsbruck
Tel +43 512 589259

707 □ SPO 2002

This intriguing Olympic-
standard ski-jump consists of
a bridge, tower and complex of
terrace, café and athletes' area,
with the jump twisting down
from the apex. Fluorescent
lighting transforms the dramatic
structure at night. The project
celebrates collaboration
between architecture and
structural engineering.

Baumschlager & Eberle

Wohnen am Lohbach Housing
Franz Baumann Weg,
6020 Innsbruck

708 ▮ RES 2000

This compact and sophisticated
social housing complex
accommodates over 1,000
people in 298 apartments. In a
rural environment on the edge
of Innsbruck, the irregular
positioning of the six blocks
creates an urban feel. Each
section of the facade can be
independently closed off.

Dominique Perrault Architecte

Innsbruck Town Hall Gallery
Maria Theresien Strasse 18,
6020 Innsbruck
Tel +43 512 583301

709 □ GOV 2002

The grid-like panelled facade
of the Town Hall Gallery, which
houses mixed public and
commercial services, echoes
the fenestration of surrounding
buildings and provides a new
city landmark. A glass
circulation tower provides a
focal point and a reflective
glazed wall opens onto a plaza.

Rainer Köberl & Astrid Tschapeller

MPreis Supermarket
St Margarethenstrasse 624,
6473 Wenns
Tel +43 5414 87 075

710 ☐ COM 2001

One of a series of architecturally unique supermarket branches, MPreis in Wenns is a horizontal slab suspended over a parking area, and presents a glass facade to approaching shoppers. Windows cut in the concrete side walls offer glimpses of the landscape.

Dominique Perrault Architecte

MPreis Supermarket
Bahnhofstrasse 23,
6112 Wattens
Tel +43 5224 55 8850

711 ☐ COM 2000

The simple design of the MPreis supermarket in Wattens foregrounds the surrounding landscape, incorporating voids planted with pine trees. Interior shelves step down to retain views out to the mountains. The triple-layered exterior glazing pays homage to a world-renowned glassworks nearby.

Peter Ebner & Franziska Ullmann

Showroom F+T
Esterweg 8, 5300 Hallwang
Tel +43 662 66 01 05-0

712 ☐ COM 2003

A folded strip of concrete forms the roof, rear wall and flooring of this showroom for an industrial window manufacturer. Irregular glazing sections promoting the client's products make up three walls, while a load-bearing red concrete plinth pierces and divides the interior.

Europe

Pauhof Architects

House P
Türkstetten 10,
4201 Gramastetten
Tel +43 664 262 8962

713 □ RES 2000

The plain exterior of P House, its long white wall facing the road, gives way to diversity inside, where the surrounding rural landscape is separated from the living area only by a glass wall. The bedroom area is contained in an elevated box and clad on the outside in aluminium sheets.

Najjar & Najjar Architekten

Semperit F&E Building
Triester Bundesstrasse 26,
2632 Wimpassing
Tel +43 2630 31 00

714 ✆ COM 2000

The sleek, curved aluminium envelope of Semperit's research and development centre reflects the company's innovative profile in the plastics and rubber industry. The laboratories on the ground floor are entirely glazed and arranged around a central hall. A slanted cut-off end looks towards the busy road.

Riepl Riepl Architekten

St Franziskus Church
Werner-von-Siemens-Strasse,
4400 Steyr
Tel +43 7252 75481

715 □ REL 2001

With its simple ground plan and concrete planes, the Catholic church is located in an outer urban area of Steyr. Inside, varying room heights produce spatial hierarchies and changing atmospheres. A glass cube substitutes for the conventional church tower and contains a dramatic light installation.

Adolf Krischanitz

Domestic and Atelier Building
Steinaweg

716 ■ RES 1998

Two staggered identical rectangular volumes with studio to the front and living space to the rear recline against a prehistoric rock face in this combined work/living house designed by the architect for himself and his wife. A narrow deck runs along the rear facade. Timber construction throughout kept costs down.

Riegler Riewe Architects

BiSoP Teacher Training School for Social Professions
Elisabethstrassse 14–16,
2500 Baden
Tel +43 225 248 2820

717 ✆ EDU 1998

This rectangular block housing classrooms and administrative areas is the main element in the BiSoP Institute. The climate control facade has a green glass skin perforated with windows. Inside, the corridors broaden to the south, creating student common-rooms.

ARTEC Architekten

Zita Kern Space
Pysdorf 1, 2281 Raasdorf

718 ▯ RES 1998

Despite its alien appearance, the inherent simplicity of this aluminium extension, which comprises a generous study, bathroom and exterior terrace, meshes with the existing brick stableblock. The contrast stresses the division of manual and intellectual labour. Plywood and rubber are used inside for floors, walls and ceiling.

pool Architektur

'trum' Locksmith's Hall and Bar
Theodor Körnerstrasse 55,
2521 Trumau
Tel +43 676 533 4455

719 ☐ COM 2000

A monolithic block in the middle of nowhere combines the quirky double function of production facility and popular bar. Ramps at the entrance continue inside as tilted planes. The suspended steel-frame construction is covered with rusty steel plates on the outside.

Wien 720-732

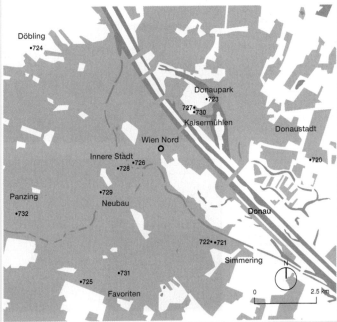

Henke and Schreieck
Architekten

AHS Secondary School
Heustadelgasse 4, 1220 Wien
Tel +43 1 285 81 12 11

720 ✦ EDU 2002

A partially roofed courtyard lies at the heart of the AHS school complex, where spatial quality and transparency inform the plain organizational structure. Wide circulation spaces allow access on all sides. Classrooms with floor to ceiling glass walls are on the upper floor, with staff offices and refectory below.

Rüdiger Lainer

Gasometer Urban Entertainment Centre
Guglgasse 43, 1030 Wien

721 ☐ REC 2001

Part of a regeneration project, the centre combines cinema, shopping and leisure in decorative and animated interior spaces. A new edge to this well-worn formula is created by an interweaving of functions, layers and platforms. Winding ribbons of material define internal and external spaces.

Coop Himmelb(l)au

Apartment Building Gasometer B
Guglgasse 12, 1110 Wien

722 ▮ RES 2000

One element in an urban mega-project of post-industrial regeneration, Gasometer B, a shield-like new building, reclines against a former gas tank to provide popular apartments. A large, airy courtyard now brings light into the gasometer. A caged fire escape follows the oblique angle of the building.

Europe

Coop Himmelb(l)au

SEG Apartment Tower
Wagramerstrasse 45, 1220 Wien

723 ◗ RES 1998

A spectacular 25-storey
housing tower with glass
facades on three sides and a
lack of supporting walls
provides open and airy
apartments. The design was
informed by wind and weather
considerations. It appears as a
cube from the north, and with
a tapering, tilted glass volume
attached from the south.

the next ENTERprise

Private Underground Pool
Wien

724 ◼ SPO 2001

Like an iceberg, only the apex
of this domestic pool complex
projects above ground level;
a 20 metre ramped corridor
connects pool and house
underground. Subdued lighting
and subtle blue-grey colours
create a cave-like atmosphere.
Glazed walls allow glimpses of
the outside world.

Massimiliano Fuksas

Twin Towers
Wienerbergstrasse 11,
1100 Wien
Tel +43 1 607 45 66 37

725 ◻ COM 2001

Providing Wien with a new
landmark, the Twin Towers ,
only 5 metres apart and at an
angle of 59 degrees, appear
first to merge and then separate
as the visitor approaches the
city. The structural fabric of the
towers is highly visible through
the non-reflective glass
facades.

Hans Hollein

Media Tower
Taborstrasse 1–3, 1020 Wien

726 ☐ COM 2001

Situated in the Donaukanal area close to Wien city centre, this 80 metre media tower inclines towards the street. Representing Austria's major media group, the building displays exuberance while remaining fairly conventional. Exposed, load-bearing columns punctuate the light and airy interior.

Hans Hollein

Public Primary School
Leonard Bernstein-Strasse 2, 1220 Wien

727 ☐ EDU 1999

Located in a re-urbanized area of Wien, linking the Danube to the city centre, the main building of the complex is a light volume capped with a floating, gently curved roof. Open corridors run down either side on the upper storey, giving a sense of transparency unusual in a school structure.

Jabornegg & Pálffy with Rachel Whiteread

Museum Judenplatz
Judenplatz 8, 1010 Wien
Tel +43 1 535 04 31

728 ☐ CUL 2000

Consisting of a redesigned Judenplatz, a Holocaust memorial represented by Rachel Whiteread's negative cast of a library and a museum incorporating medieval ruins, this project is dedicated to Memory. This minimal approach offers a dignified frame for the experience of history.

Europe

Ortner & Ortner

**Museum of Modern Art
Ludwig Foundation**
Museumsplatz 1, 1070 Wien
Tel +43 1 525 00

729 □ CUL 2001

One element within a cultural complex, this modern art gallery is an autonomous art object, presenting an almost impenetrable basalt facade punctuated by narrow incisions. Entrance is via an elevated terrace. Inside, the shallow barrel-vaulted roof is sliced along its length to let in light.

Heinz Tesar

Church Donaucity
Donaucitystrasse 2, 1220 Wien
Tel +43 1 263 0952

730 □ REL 2000

Sitting among high-rise office buildings, the dark stainless steel walls of this cube-shaped sacred space are drilled with circular apertures, inviting the visitor to come in and look out. Inside, monochrome birch cladding surfaces create a contrastingly warm and light atmosphere and direct the gaze to the openings.

Delugan-Meissl

**Paltramplatz Residential
Building**
Paltramplatz 7, 1100 Wien

731 ■ RES 2002

The central element in each of the 22 apartments in this housing block is a glazed balcony, with dramatic shading cast by the pierced overhanging roof. The supporting concrete structure allows a multiplicity of floor shapes, and therefore individual configurations of space within each flat.

BKK-3

MISS Sargfabrik
Missindorfstrasse 10, 1140 Wien

732 ▮ RES 2000

Making no attempt to blend in, MISS Sargfabrik represents a radical approach to residential building design, with each of the 39 flats opening onto a street-like communal loggia with a green courtyard. Varying room heights allow maximum density and unorthodox room divisions. Communal facilities include pool, library and disco.

Lichtblau Wagner Architekten

Podersdorf Parish Centre
Seestrasse 67, 7141 Podersdorf
Tel +43 2 177 2313

733 ✎ REL 2002

A contemporary religious building rather than a church, the Parish Centre has a glass facade inscribed with Bible quotations and thoughts about the topic of family. Natural light sources and white walls create an atmosphere of simplicity and purity inside, particularly in the mass room which is almost scaleless.

Tschapeller/Schöffauer Architekten

District Commissioner's Office
Bahnhofviertel 7, 8850 Murau
Tel +43 3 532 2101 0

734 ▮ ✎ GOV 2002

Built on a former industrial riverside site up against a hill, these council offices interact with their multi-level terrain. Much of the workings of the building are subterranean, but are accessed via a vast glazed foyer, topped by a monolithic cantilevered slab.

Weichlbauer/Ortis

Residential DNA
Koloniegasse 11A/11B,
8101 Gratkorn

735　◧ RES 2001

Sited among more conventional residential neighbours, this housing unit is based on computer-generated patterns, intuitively interpreted. Elements are simple and restricted, and regularly arranged. There is one format for windows and doors, with parking bays sheltered by cantilevered balconies.

Graz 736-740

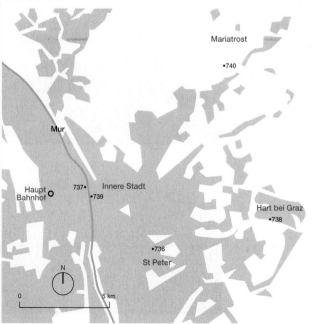

Mariatrost

•740

Mur

Haupt O
Bahnhof

737•　Innere Stadt
•739

Hart bei Graz
•738

•736
St Peter

N

0　　　　　5 km

Bernhard Hafner

Laboratory Hall LBS6
Hans Brandstettergasse 8,
8010 Graz
Tel +43 316 47 12 44

736 ✏ EDU 2001

The new workshop for the state vocational school in Graz was designed from the inside out around an open cylindrical core. The main structure is exposed as a steel grid with layers of glass cladding; staircases, bridges and rooms are constructed in different materials and various colours.

Peter Cook and Colin Fournier

Kunsthaus
Lendkai 1, 8020 Graz
Tel +43 316 8017 9200

737 ☐ CUL 2003

The new landmark home for contemporary art in Graz is a glowing blue pillow constructed from acrylic glass and dotted with nozzles that serve as windows. The biomorphic pod contains two exhibition spaces to be used as multi-disciplinary venues. Its facade of opaque tiles transforms into a low-resolution media screen.

Architekt Michael Haberz

House RB
Teichweg 11,
8075 Graz-Umgebung
Tel +43 316 49 38 00

738 ✏ RES 1998

The idea behind this house on a steep slope was to create an open two-storey hall containing boxes and spaces for domestic and work functions. The design uses bridge construction techniques and prefabricated concrete elements. Living spaces face the southwest, with other rooms looking northeast.

Europe

Acconci Studio

Mur Island
Across from Mariahilferplatz,
8010 Graz
Tel +43 316 807 50

739 ☐ CUL 2003

Vito Acconci's idea was to bring the previously neglected River Mur into the public sphere with this shell-like installation, which accommodates an open-air theatre, children's playground and café. Created to celebrate Graz as European Culture Capital 2003, the project proved technically challenging.

Pentaplan

Deep House
Teichhofweg 7–57, 8010 Graz

740 ❚ RES 1998

This dense housing unit contains 24 three-storey atrium apartments with a common core space. Privacy is maintained despite the urban concentration. Each apartment is top-lit through its atrium and accessible via both car park and garden, and can thereby be divided into working and living spaces.

Wolfgang Feyferlik and Susi Fritzer

Spielfeld Border Control
Bundesstrasse, 8471 Spielfeld
Tel +43 345 3221 0301

741 ❚ ✎ GOV 2000

Located on Austria's border with Slovenia, this bank of customs offices is made from a horizontal steel truss supported on concrete slabs at one end and a single column two-thirds of the way along. Prefabricated timber sections enclose the truss, which in turn are covered by a tensioned textile facade.

Markus Pernthaler

Bell Tower
Judenburg, 8750 Oberweg

742 ❚ REL 1998

Set among dense pine forests, Markus Pernthaler's campanile rises in a clearing beside a lake, its three large bells visible and their sound audible through spiralling larch slats. Standing on a massive concrete base which houses the electronic controls, the steel structure is topped with an glass pane displaying the cross.

Morphosis

Hypo Alpe-Adria Centre
Alpen-Adria-Platz 1,
9020 Klagenfurt
Tel +43 502 020

743 ❚ ✎ COM 2001

This multi-use complex on the outskirts of Klagenfurt provides low-density housing, commercial space, an event centre and a kindergarten. The urban focus is to the south under a large domed roof along a busy street, with houses located on the spacious and green northern side.

Marte Marte Architekten

Holiday Home
Furx 40, 6832 Zwischenwasser

744 ❚ RES 2001

Built in an area renowned for its progressive architecture, this simple yet radical timber holiday home responds to the beauty and mood of the landscape. Larch, concrete and glass are used modestly in a design reminiscent of a hay barn. Sliding elements allow the house to be closed up when uninhabited.

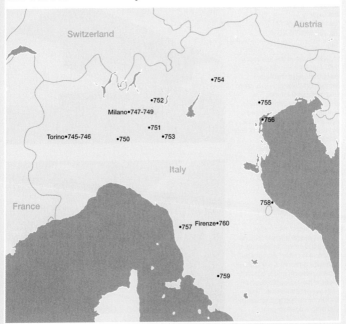

Claudio Silvestrin Architects

Museum of Contemporary Art
Via Modene 16, 10141 Torino
Tel +39 011 1983 1600

745 □ CUL 2002

Occupying the site of a former factory in a Torino suburb, this minimalist art museum clothes its cavernous volume in an immaculate, soft limestone skin. The long, pure facade is scored by vertical cuts allowing light to slice through internal spaces and punctuated by timber doors cut out in rhythmic sequence.

Renzo Piano Building Workshop

**Giovanni and Marella Agnelli
Art Gallery**
Via Nizza 230, 10126 Torino
Tel +39 01 1006 2008

746 ☐ CUL 2002

Hovering above the landmark
1917 Fiat Factory, the new
gallery displays the Agnelli
family's art collection in a calm
and minimalist interior. The
body is a partly cantilevered
wedge-shaped box, with no
apparent openings in its steel
skin. The roof is made of 16,000
glass fins.

Tadao Ando Architect &
Associates

Armani Teatro
Via Bergognone 59,
20144 Milano

747 ■ CUL 2001

This minimalist theatre for
fashion shows and exhibitions
is inserted within an existing
structure in outer Milano. The
entrance perforates the factory
facade, leading into a gigantic
foyer, a curved concrete shell
with illuminated desks. The
simply furnished interior looks
out onto a shallow pool.

Gregotti Associati International

**Redevelopment of Pirelli
Bicocca Area**
Bounded by Via Sarca, Via
Chiese, Via Sesto San Giovanni,
Via Figini Biocca, 20126 Milano

748 ☐ COM 2003

The Pirelli Bicocca industrial
site has been transformed into
a mixed urban quarter of large
perforated facades arranged
around public squares. The
masterplan retained the original
north–south grid of the factory
and the scale of its blocks.

Gregotti Associati International

Arcimboldi Opera Theatre
Viale dell'Innovazione,
20126 Milano
Tel +39 02 7200 3744

749 ☐ CUL 2003

Within the regenerated Pirelli Bicocca neighbourhood, this huge opera theatre stands out in its light-rendering and dynamic form. A contrasting rich interior can accommodate 2,300 spectators on two levels within walls of wood stained a deep red under a spectacular wavy plastered ceiling.

Antonio Monestiroli

Cemetery
Via della Folconia,
27058 Voghera
Tel +39 03 8333 6452

750 ☐ REL 2003

This fifth extension to the 200-year-old cemetery outside Voghera uses symmetry and contrasting red brick and white stone to create a formal and solemn atmosphere. Memorial plaques are arranged in a regular grid on the brick facades, while pools of water add to the sense of reflection.

Renzo Piano Building Workshop

Lodi Bank Headquarters
Via Polenghi Lombardo 13,
26900 Lodi
Tel +39 03 7159 51

751 ☐ ✐ COM 2001

The site of a dairy products factory has been transformed into an imposing and formal complex for the Lodi Bank. The building presents a fortress-like facade perforated by screened openings, softened with strips of terracotta cladding. Cylindrical storage blocks populate the central piazza.

Studio Archea

Villa Leffe
Vicolo Conti 3, Leffe,
24026 Bergamo

752 ▮ RES 1998

Filling a small site in a historical centre, this five-storey town house presents a jagged stone facade pitted with light slots. Behind a full-height metal screen on another elevation is a glazed wall bounding a courtyard. By day the house appears impenetrable, by night it glows with points of light.

Studio Architetti Associati
Arnaboldi & Partners

Casalpusterlengo Town Hall
Piazza del Popolo 22,
Casalpusterlengo, 26841 Lodi
Tel +39 03 7792 331

753 ☐ GOV 2002

A glass and steel extension to an elegant old town hall provides three floors of offices and echoes its neighbour with its strong verticality and restrained use of materials. The glass walls provide a metaphor for the desire for transparency in civic processes.

Mario Botta

MART – Museum of Modern and Contemporary Art
Corso Bettini 43, Rovereto,
38068 Trento
Tel +39 04 6443 8887

754 ☐ CUL 2002

Slotted in behind two existing civic buildings, this museum has no front; entry is via an anonymous alley which leads into a circular courtyard dramatically domed with glass and steel. A minimalist exhibition space on the top floor is lit entirely through skylights.

Europe

Tadao Ando Architect &
Associates

**Fabrica – Benetton
Communication Research
Centre**
Via Ferrarezza, 31050 Catena di
Villorba, Treviso
Tel +39 04 2251 6228

755 ✆ COM 2000

A freestanding colonnade joins
this extension to an existing
Palladian style villa; an elliptical
sunken courtyard, itself
colonnaded, forms the central
element of the new building,
which spirals underground.

Cino Zucchi

Building D
Giudecca 402, Giudecca Island,
30133 Venezia

756 ▯ RES 2000

Reminiscent in scale of a
Venetian palazzo, a social
housing block in a former
industrial area makes a simple
response to its rich context.
Its four floors, each with four
apartments, centre on a wedge-
shaped courtyard. Grey
rendering is punctured with
varied fenestration.

Massimo Carmassi

San Michele Complex
Via Degli Orafi, 56127 Pisa

757 ▢ REL 2002

This project comprises two
restored sides of a medieval
square and a new third side in
traditional brick construction
with recessed openings which
faces an existing thirteenth-
century church. The modern
element houses shops and
dwellings, and uses glass and
steel structures faced with
masonry.

Von Gerkan Marg & Partner

Rimini Exhibition Centre
Via Emilia 155, 47900 Rimini
Tel +39 0541 744 240

758 ☐ CUL 2001

This vast modern exhibition centre pays homage to the classical traditions of Emilia-Romagna with a symmetrical layout and domed rotunda. Four light-towers announce the central entrance, which leads through a large foyer and colonnaded walkways into the 12 exhibition halls. Timber vaulting decorates the ceilings.

Stefano Boeri

ENEL Bagnore 3 Geothermal Power Station
Santafiore di Grosseto, Monte Amiata

759 ◼ INF 2001

A Cor-ten steel skin dramatically envelops the fragmented parts of this addition to an existing power station set against a mountain backdrop, giving it a sculptural quality and creating a local landmark. The pitch of the roof, made up of 17 wrapping ribs, continues the slope of the mountains behind.

Mauro Galantino

Ugnano Housing Estate
Ugnano, 50100 Firenze

760 ◼ RES 2000

Raised on a plinth as flood protection, this estate just outside Firenze is composed of rectilinear planes and volumes finished with white render. Housing units are modular and without obvious repetition or overwhelming volumes. Paths converge in a public square and connect this new urban fragment to the historic city.

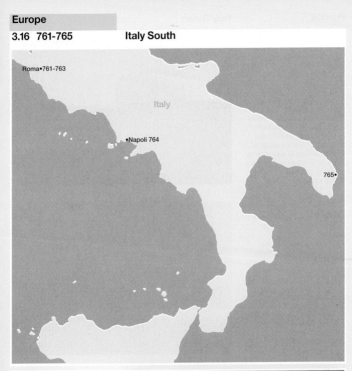

Roma•761-763

Italy

•Napoli 764

765•

Alessandro Anselmi

Fiumicino Town Hall
Via Portuense, 2498 Fiumicino

761 ⬛ GOV 2002

Located at the entrance to the city centre and facing a canal, this municipal complex forms a reinforced concrete hill with administrative, political and retail functions and a public plaza arranged underneath. The smooth brick covering layer is supported on invisible pillars and hides the main aluminium and glass structure below.

Renzo Piano Building Workshop

Parco della Musica Auditoria
Via le Pietro de Coubertin 14,
00196 Roma
Tel +39 0680 692 181

762 ☐ CUL 2002

Three concert halls with curved
outlines surround an
amphitheatre in a symmetrical
arrangement in this auditorium
complex just outside Roma.
The timber halls are wrapped in
traditional Roman lead roofing
and their rich baroque interiors
use local travertine, brick and
cherry wood.

Garofalo Miura Architetti

**Santa Maria Josefa Parish
Church and Community
Centre**
Via Padre Angelo Cerbara,
Ponte di Nona, 00010 Roma
Tel +39 06 614 0433

763 ☐ REL 2002

In fragmented suburban
surroundings, the caustic red
of the community centre pinions
the modest and neutral church
building. Subdued and formal
green marble and cherry wood
decorate the church interior.

Gae Aulenti

**Museo Subway Station,
Napoli Underground Line 1**
Piazza Cavour, 80137 Napoli
Tel +39 081 227 2111

764 ☐ TRA 2001

The low red volumes of the two
Museo station entrances, set in
a slightly convex, plain paved
square, mimic the architecture
of the surrounding Spanish
quarter. Glass walls lead the
traveller underground onto
escalators that disappear
beneath a white neon artwork
stretching along an entire wall.

Europe

MCA Mario Cucinella Architects

Maritime Services Building
Port Area of Otranto, 73028
Otranto

765 ◼ TRA 2002

This prow-shaped harbour
building straddles the fortified
city and the Mediterranean
waters. A generous staircase
climbing onto the building's
roof and connecting to a piazza
forms its urban facade. The
bright coloured surfaces of the
interior design are articulated
along a glazed skylight.

3.17 766-771   Estonia and Lithuania

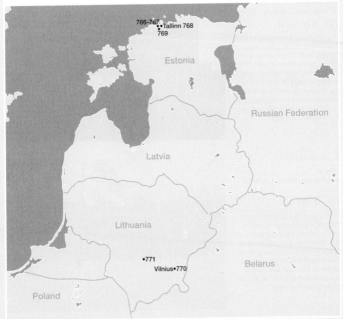

Architectural Bureau Kolde Grupp

Semi-Detached House
Lucca 2e, Tabasalu 76901

766 ◨ RES 2002

An access stair within a steel structure of cantilevered trusses supports this reinforced concrete and timber house in an unexpected response to a challenging site. Setting the house beside but not on the cliff made room for a sunny back garden on the narrow cliff top and an access road beneath.

Martin Aunin

Orro House
9 Pääsukese, Tabasalu 76901

767 ◨ RES 2002

A grass ramp leading up to this two-storey house disguises a garage and storage area below, blending the timber-clad structure with its pasture-land setting outside Tallinn. Sliding panel doors allow the first-floor living spaces to be opened up. A rectangular skylight box runs the length of the roof.

3+1 Architects

Villa V
8 Hommiku, Nõmme, Tallinn 10922

768 ◨ RES 2000

The largely transparent ground floor of this private two-storey family house, set in a generous garden in a suburb of Tallinn, is partly embedded in the ground. The simple horizontal volumes of the timber-clad upper floor contrast with the slender trunks of surrounding trees.

Europe

Indrek Näkk

Neiser Factory
6 Seljaku, Saue, Laagri 76401
Tel +372 6518 910

___
769 ☐ COM 2002

A furniture factory crouches in the steeply sloping contours of the landscape outside Tallinn. The concrete-panelled southern end contains the production facilities and sits 1 metre below ground; the lighter timber-and-glass construction at the northern end contains the showroom.

3+1 Architects

Estonian Embassy
Mickevicius 4a, Zverynas, Vilnius 8119

___
770 ▮ GOV 1998

Rigid geometry and actual and metaphorical richness characterize the Estonian Embassy near to downtown Vilnius, with its blue-flecked limestone facade punctuated by a formal window grid. A glass-and-steel curtain wall faces the rear, while high quality materials continue inside.

Architectural Bureau Vilius ir partneriai

Villa on Lake Kalviai
Kalviai Village, Kaisadorys 5628

___
771 ▮ RES 2001

Unmilled timber logs, combined with rational modern lines, allow this unobtrusive single-storey villa on the shores of Lake Kalviai to blend with its environment. Living areas screened by louvred walls reach down to the lake; private rooms are housed in an elongated volume to the rear.

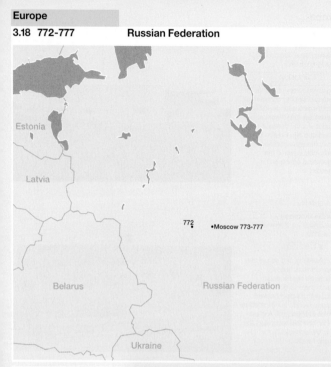

772

•Moscow 773-777

Estonia

Latvia

Belarus

Russian Federation

Ukraine

Architectural Bureau A-B

Goryachev House
Ozerninskoye Reservoir, Ruza

772   ■ RES 1998

Located beside a wide reservoir, this contemporary interpretation of the Russian dacha or holiday home is semi-octagonal in plan, with a spectacular cantilevered single-pitched roof. The placement of openings tracks the path of the sun. The log cabin motif continues throughout the design.

Europe

Alexander Brodsky

95° Restaurant
Bukhta Radosti, Pirogovo
Reservoir, Moscow

773 ☐ COM 2000

Named after the angle of the
supporting columns, this tilting
restaurant constructed largely
from reclaimed Cor-ten steel,
corrugated iron and timber sits
high on an old pier beside a
reservoir. Transparency is
achieved with a glazed entrance
facade and skylight running the
length of the roof.

Architectural Bureau A-B

Stolnik Building
Maly Levshinsky side-street 5,
Moscow 119034
Tel +7 95 967 66 04

774 ☐ ✎ RES 2003

Art Deco banding and rounded
corners combine with Stalinist
monumentality in this bold V-
shaped corner block housing
luxury apartments. The natural
stone facade is topped with an
aluminium cornice designed for
climbing plants. Inside, the
apartments are finished with
stone, ceramics and wood.

ABK Architects

British Embassy
Smolenskaya Naberezhnaya 10,
Moscow 121099
Tel +7 95 956 72 00

775 ☐ ✎ GOV 2000

Three residential pavilions and
one public office pavilion linked
at roof level make up the British
Embassy on the Smolenskaya
Embankment of the Moscow
River. The fourth pavilion
projects eastwards and bisects
the site, creating a garden
space and asserting its
significance by its height.

Europe

Sergey Kisselev and Partners

**Sports and Amusement
Centre with Aquapark**
Ulitsa Golubinskaya, Yasanevo
District, Moscow

776 ▐ SPO 2002

Five floors of leisure facilities,
two below ground, comprise
this sports centre. Its design
mediates between forest on
one side and linear urban
environment on the other. Blue
glass, brown stone and red
brick are used throughout.

Project Meganom Architectural
Studio

Private House
Moscow

777 ■ RES 2001

Located on a sloping plot in a
settlement of out-of-town
houses, but turning its main
facade away to face the forest,
this house narrows from front
to back in a stepped series of
diminishing prisms. Rustic
stone is contrasted with
contemporary flush American
pine and glass.

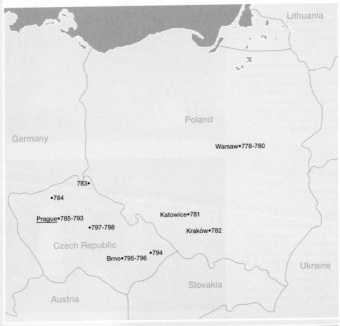

Autorska Pracownia
Architektury Kurylowicz &
Associates

Eko Park Expo Pavilion
Chodkiewicza Street, Mokotów,
Warsaw

778 ☐ CUL 2001

Originally a temporary structure
in downtown Warsaw, this
pavilion was saved by its
simplicity and now provides
permanent exhibition space.
The galvanized steel skeleton is
clad with white polycarbonate
panels.

Autorska Pracownia
Architektury Kurylowicz &
Associates

Polish Airlines Headquarters
17 Stycznia 39, Warsaw 00-906
Tel +48 0801 300 952

779 □ COM 2002

The seamless glass facade of
the LOT headquarters, located
next to Warsaw airport, reflects
the company's cutting-edge
image. The rectangular building,
with its inner skin of frosted
glazing, houses two dramatic
seven-storey atriums.

JEMS Architekci

Agora Headquarters
8/10 Czerska, Mokotów,
Warsaw 00-842
Tel +48 22 555 60 00

780 ✆ COM 2002

The sheer mass of this media
office block is undermined by
its deep-skinned facade of
changing layers of glass and
timber shading systems. A non-
hierarchical internal structure is
achieved with fully glazed walls,
a multi-directional circulation
space and uniform rhythms of
columns throughout.

Promes Architekci

Broken House
4 Granica Wesolej, Giszowiec,
Katowice 41-400, Silesia

781 ▐ RES 2002

A sloped and grassed plywood-
clad platform twists around
white rectangular blocks to
create Broken House, located in
a forest reserve near Katowice.
Internally, the twisting motif is
repeated in a circulation ramp
that winds around living room
and bedrooms, finally emerging
on the roof deck.

Europe

Romuald Loegler

Gateway to the City of the Deceased Funeral Chapel
48 Powstanców, Pradnik
Czernony, Kraków 31-422
Tel +48 12 410 6550

782 ☐ REL 1998

Standing at the edge of the old cemetery just outside Krakow, this chapel presents a glazed facade lightly encased in apparently floating rendered masonry. Light enters the long, narrow and slightly arched building through a gap in the roof.

Ivan Kroupa Architects

Snowboard Cottage
Herlikovice, Krkonose
Mountains

783 ■ RES 2001

A dark, secretive family house nestles at the foot of a ski-run, its single-pitch snow defence roof rising up on the south elevation to twice the height of the north side. Inside, where warmth and comfort are the prime considerations, light-coloured timber is used to clad the continuous space.

Emil Prikryl

Benedikt Rejt Gallery
Pivovarská 29, Louny,
440 01 Ústí
Tel +420 415 652 367

784 ☐ CUL 1998

The reinvention of this seventeenth-century former brewery as art gallery focused on the interior, with exterior work limited to cleaning up the shell and installing bold signage. Inside, spaces were opened up and waxed concrete screed floors, inlaid with steel strips, were introduced.

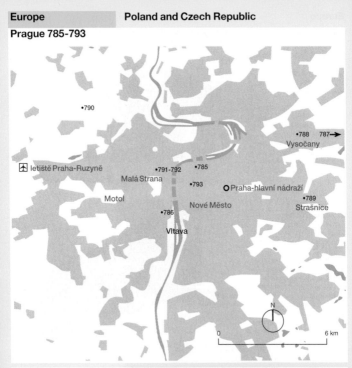

Ietiště Praha-Ruzyně

Malá Strana

Motol

•790

•788   787→
Vysočany

•791-792   •785

•793   ⊙ Praha-hlavní nádraží

Nové Město

•789
Strašnice

•786

Vltava

N

0   6 km

Eva Jiricna Architects

Hotel Josef
Rybná 20, 110 00 Prague 1
Tel +420 221 700 111

785 ☐ TOU 2002

Only one of a few new-build
insertions in historic central
Prague, this hotel continues the
roof line of the neighbouring
nineteenth-century police
station; the plain white facade
is articulated by lightweight
perforated awnings over
windows. Inside is a white lobby
featuring a signature Jiricna
spiral staircase.

Europe

D3A Fiala Prouza Zima

Novy Smíchov Shopping Centre
Plzenska 8, 150 00 Prague 5

786 ☐ COM 2001

Part of an ambitious renovation scheme over several city blocks in the Smichov district of Prague, the new shopping centre addresses two streets from its corner location with a series of glass and titanium volumes. Much of the bulk of the complex is hidden beneath a gently sloping grass hill.

DUM Architekti

Stajner House
Uzka 674, Praha-Vychod, 250 92 Sestajovice

787 ☐ RES 2001

This elegant house with its dramatic cantilever uses elemental materials and forms that belie its restricted budget. Protected against the cold with a thermal insulation facade system, the interior is lit by large openings at ground level and narrow ribbon windows above.

DUM Architekti

Kolbenova Metro Station
Kolbenova 40, Vysocany, 190 00 Prague 9
Tel +420 296 191 817

788 ☐ TRA 2001

This new concourse for an existing station on Prague's metro system provides an inviting exterior. Light floods in through a surface facade that combines metal mesh, distorted glazing and fibreboard panels. Inside, a polished stainless steel wall intensifies the light and reflects the street outside.

D3A Fiala Prouza Zima

MUZO Centre
V Olsinách 80/626,
100 00 Prague 10
Tel +420 267 197 509

789 ▯ ⟋ COM 2000

Large expanses of glazing and
operable metal-mesh blinds
create an ever-changing facade
and allow views out to the
surrounding green spaces from
this high-tech office building.
Inside in the lobby, egg-shaped
organic forms add a playful note
to the practicality of a secure
and efficient building.

D3A Fiala Prouza Zima

House in Nebusice
Nebusice, Prague

790 ▮ RES 2001

A partially sunken ground floor
leading up to first-floor living
spaces is a response to the
steeply sloping site of this
private, calm house in
Nebusice. Entrance is via a
steel-framed canopy and
concrete block wall. A full-
length glass wall with sliding
elements connects the living
area with the garden.

Josef Pleskot Atelier

**Pathway through the Deer
Moat**
Prague Castle, Hradcany,
Prague 1
Tel +420 224 373 368

791 ▢ REC 2002

This underground tunnel
provides pedestrian access
from the Vltava River to the
grounds of Prague Castle.
Egyptian style entrances with
rectangular portals and inclined
retaining walls lead into a high
oval brick vault, with a stream
running below the floor.

Europe

Eva Jiricna Architects

Prague Castle Orangery
Prague Castle Gardens,
Hradcany, Prague 1
Tel +420 224 373 368

792 ■ ✆ CUL 1998

A stainless-steel exoskeleton
leans against a sixteenth-
century wall in this iconic late
twentieth-century addition to
Prague Castle. The repeating
shell design of the new building
is constructed from stainless-
steel mesh and toughened
laminate glass. The internal
space is column-free.

DaM & Omnicrom-K

Palace Euro
Václavské námisti 2, Nové
Mesto, 110 00 Prague 1

793 □ COM 2002

This commercial, retail and
administrative block stands on
a triangular site, completing the
lower western side of Prague's
Wenceslas Square. Its curved,
transparent glass exterior
responds to its Formalist
neighbours. A contrasting cubic
volume is clothed in vertical
gold blinds.

Archteam

Private House
Pozárniku 301, Vázany,
767 01 Kromeríz
Tel +420 776 172 662

794 □ RES 2000

A family house in a semi-rural
part of Kromeríz reveals its
construction and celebrates its
basic materials, all unfinished
except for the red panels on the
short facades. The open-plan
two-storey interior uses wooden
furniture to articulate the space.
A suspended canopy marks the
entrance.

313

Kuba Pilar Architects

**Faculty of Arts Library,
Masaryk University**
Arna Nováka 1, 660 88 Brno
Tel +420 54 949 4179

795 ☐ EDU 2001

A formally simple volume
signals this university building's
presence in Brno, its striking
filigree oak facade appearing
monolithic from a distance but
resolving into a human-scale
slatted curtain at closer
quarters. The library
accommodates 400 readers
and 275,000 books.

Jaromir Walter

Villa Tisnov
Tisnov, 666 01 Brno

796 ■ RES 2000

Within a mixed residential and
industrial suburban area of
Brno, the geometrically pure
volume and monochrome
timber cladding of this two-
storey house set it apart from its
conservative neighbours. The
entrance is at the centre of the
long facade, with living spaces
to one side and swimming pool
to the other.

Ivan Kroupa Architects

Private House
Lesni 320, Mukarov,
Stredocesky Kraj

797 ■ RES 2000

Two windowless facades to the
north and south of this family
house prevent visual contact
with neighbouring buildings,
while glazed facades to east
and west allow uninterrupted
views of the forest. Within an
otherwise open-plan interior,
stairs, storage and services are
arranged along the solid walls.

Europe

Ivan Kroupa Architects

Garden House
Mukarov, Stredocesky Kraj

798 ■ RES 2000

The architect describes this project as a garden that has acquired a house. Taking only weeks to build, the timber structure clad with steel panels folds around a glazed corridor and windowless service structure. The house is raised on a concrete plinth to accommodate the sloping terrain and winter snowfalls.

3.20 799-809   Slovakia, Hungary and Romania

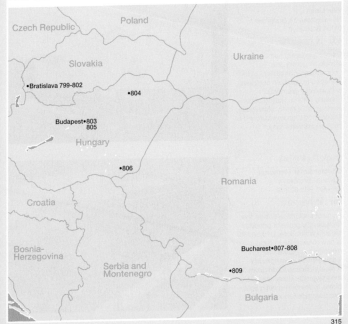

Prof Dr Justus Dahinden

Church of St Francis
Minorites Monastery
Nameestie sv Frantiska 4,
Karlova Ves, 84104 Bratislava
Tel +421 2 654 268 60

799 ✆ REL 2002

This church sits on a circular
plaza near the University of
Bratislava. Three cylindrical
chapels open through arched
incisions off a central liturgical
space. A continuous skylight
around the top of the cone
allows daylight to wash over
the interior.

Ján Bahna, AA Atelier
Architektúry

Villa Linea
Novosvetská 51, Bratislava 1,
81104 Bratislava

800 ▮ RES 2002

Combining family home and
private art gallery, the
geometrical arrangement of this
T-shaped house both contrasts
with and complements its
forested setting. Glazed upper
levels sit on a heavy stone base.
Accommodation flows around a
central glass staircase.

Studio For & Prodis

Chatam Sofer Memorial
Zizkoval, Bratislava
Tel +421 903 821432

801 ✆ REL 2002

A site of pilgrimage beside the
Danube, the grave of orthodox
rabbi Chatam Sofer (1762–1836)
is now marked by a black
reinforced concrete prism
leading into a viewing room.
A steel staircase leads down to
the grave site. Illuminated glass
plates in the ceiling bring light
into this underground space.

Europe

KSA

Family House
54 Nova Street, Stupava,
90031 Bratislava

802 ❚ RES 2000

Opaque glass panel cladding
lends an industrial appearance
to this family house on a steeply
sloping site. Raw light-bathed
interior spaces open up to the
landscape through large
windows with white roller blinds
providing shade when
necessary. Movable interior
walls make living areas flexible.

Torok and Balazs Architectural
Design Studio

Matáv Headquarters
55 Krisztina krt. 1,
Budapest 1013
Tel +36 14 5740 00

803 ✐ COM 1999

This project involved the radical
interior refurbishment of an
authoritarian 1950s office block.
Light pours into a glass-roofed
central courtyard, now the hub
of the complex, and a sinuous
timber path, punctuated by
steel columns, rises around the
space.

István Ferencz

Ecclesiastic Education Centre
5 Fényi Gyula tér, Miskolc 3535
Tel +36 46 56 0458

804 ☐ REL 2000

A complex of ten ecclesiastical
buildings, anchored to its
sloping site by the campanile,
fans out to embrace the town
of Miskolc. Traditional brick
construction incorporates
contemporary materials; here
the skin of the gable-ended
church splits to reveal a timber
and glass facade.

(EEA) Erick van Egeraat
associated architects

Liget Office Building
84 a Dózsa György út,
Budapest 1068

805 ◼ COM 2001

Renovation of this listed 1949
modernist block in Budapest
was restricted to preserve its
original character. A new glass
facade lies behind rendered
columns, an enclosed gallery
interrupts the regularity of the
facade and a top-floor terrace
is protected by a slanting roof.

Imre Makovecz

Cultural Centre
4 Posta Utca, Makó,
Csongrád 6900
Tel +36 62 21 20 44

806 ☐ CUL 2000

Traditional local styles and
materials were used to
transform a dilapidated existing
cultural centre into this stunning
new auditorium. The slate and
timber roof of the central space
is flanked by bulbous, partially
glazed towers. References to
the natural world continue
inside with tree-like columns.

Starh ACD/Florian Stanciu

Sorin Budai House
Carol Knappe Street 11,
1 Bucharest

807 ◼ RES 1998

On a narrow plot in a residential
area of Bucharest, this simple
family house is essentially a
rectangle with one long curved
wall, punctuated by a blue
entrance box. Changes of floor
level rather than solid walls
demarcate changes of function,
with sand-coloured travertine
providing a sense of unity.

Europe

Dorin Stefan Architect

**Banca Comerciala Romana,
Ghencea Branch**
Boulevard Ghencea 158,
6 Bucharest
Tel +40 21 413 10 49

808 ☐ COM 1998

The foreground line of poplar
trees provided the inspiration
for this elegant reworking of an
existing building. A bright and
spacious atrium behind a glass
wall welcomes the bank's
clients, while the rear facade
acknowledges the surrounding
architecture.

Dorin Stefan Architect

Mountain House
Main Street, comuna Moeciu,
Pestera
Tel +40 21 322 3700

809 ☐ RES 2001

In the foothills of the Carpathian
Mountains, this house perches
precariously on its steep site.
A red metal-clad volume is
pierced right through by a
timber truss that becomes a
covered terrace. Bedrooms are
arranged below the main level,
with brightly painted shutters.

Austria

•810-811

Hungary

Ljubljana•812-817

Slovenia

Romania

Croatia

•819

•Belgrade

Bosnia-Herzegovina

•820

Serbia and Montenegro

•Split

Italy

Dubrovnik
818

Njiric & Njiric Arhitekti

Baumaxx Hypermarket
Tabor, Maribor
Tel +386 23 20 73 20

810 ☐ COM 1999

This U-shaped hypermarket is
clad on three sides with
concrete panels finished with
red and silver traffic reflectors;
at night the reflectors transform
the building into a glowing shell.
The canopy of a covered
walkway is suspended from the
east facade, beneath a grass-
covered roof.

Europe

Njiric & Njiric Arhitekti

McDonald's Drive-in
Ptujska cesta, Maribor
Tel +386 24 26 03 66

811 □ COM 2000

Despite sporting the largest
Golden Arches in central
Europe, the exterior of this
McDonald's Drive-in is unique.
A wire-mesh structure sits on
top of the building. Plans to
house a basketball court here
failed to clear corporate
approval, and the functionless
cage has adopted the status
of conceptual art.

Ljubljana 812-817

OFIS

Housing Block
Bergantova ulica 10,
1000 Ljubljana

812   ▢ RES 2000

Each of three long blocks are
arranged over three levels in a
housing scheme on a redundant
industrial area. A central kitchen
and bathroom core within each
apartment allows a circular
route between living room and
bedroom behind the modulated
facade of alternating set-back
balconies and roof overhangs.

Sadar Vuga Arhitekti

**Slovenian National Gallery
Atrium**
Puharjeva ulica 9,
1000 Ljubljana
Tel +386 1 241 54 34

813   □ CUL 1998

A glazed link sits lightly
between two existing elements
of Slovenia's National Gallery,
taking no account of either
building. An entrance stairway
incorporating strip lighting leads
into an expansive main space.
A black-painted steel frame
supports the roof and facade.

Sadar Vuga Arhitekti

**Chamber of Commerce and
Industry**
Dimiceva ulica 13,
1000 Ljubljana
Tel +386 1 589 80 00

814   ☎ GOV 2000

A spectacular south facade has
made this mixed-function
government building, divided
between offices to the north
and public areas to the south,
into something of an icon in
Ljubljana. A series of projecting
steel-framed boxes cantilever
over a new public plaza below.

Europe

A Biro

Smartinka Multipurpose Building
Jarska ulica 10b, 1000 Ljubljana

815 ◼ COM 2002

The three main elements of this building are clearly expressed in the massing, with shops at the bottom, transparent office floors and more private apartment facades. Located in a rapidly changing area of Ljubljana, the top-floor apartments enjoy views out to the city's castle and the Kanmik Alps.

Alessio Princic

Union Brewery Facade
Celovska cesta, 1000 Ljubljana
Tel +386 01 471 72 17

816 ◼ ✎ COM 1999

The brief was to soften an enormous concrete building that the city council deemed degrading to its surroundings, particularly the Tivoli Gardens opposite. The solution is a massive membrane of 680 glass panels. Satinated on the outside and silk-screened on the inside, the facade becomes a projection screen by night.

Andrej Kalamar

Lev Office Building
Vosnjakova ulica 2,
1000 Ljubljana
Tel +386 1 300 07 00

817 ☐ COM 2002

This office building presents its corrugated metal and etched glass outer curve to a bleak intersection in Ljubljana's city centre, while its inner curve creates a new urban space. The visible parts, housing offices and shops, represent only one-third of the whole; parking levels are hidden underground.

Nenad Fabijanic

Public Lavatory
Old Port of Dubrovnik,
20000 Dubrovnik

818 ☐ PUB 2002

Part of the Dubrovnik
reconstruction project, the
site for this public lavatory
demanded a long, narrow
building. Nestling between
ancient city walls and the
Austro-Hungarian port authority
building, its local sandy
limestone facade contrasts with
the surrounding rough stone.

3LHD

Memorial Bridge
Mrtvi Kanal, Delta, 51000 Rijeka
Tel +385 51 209524

819 ☐ INF 2001

This Memorial Bridge in the
Croatian port of Rijeka provides
pedestrian access across a
canal between a city park and
the historic centre, and it
remembers those Croatians lost
in the Balkan conflicts. The
relationship between the vertical
sentinal slabs and horizontal
bridge sections creates a
powerful presence.

Prof Spasoje Krunic

Memorial Centre
Mount Ravna Gora, Mionica,
14000 Valjero

820 ☐ REL 2000

A monument to anti-fascism
and to Serbian history, this
memorial centre with auditorium
and library on the slopes of
Mount Ravna Gora responds to
local tradition in its materials
and compelling simplicity. The
steel roof appears to hover and
the freestanding wall protects
the facade and creates an
environment of contemplation.

Bulgaria

Macedonia

Istanbul 834

Thessaloniki
821-823

Greece

833

Turkey

Athina 824-829

Paros 831 Mykonos 830

Thira 832

Cyprus 836

Anastassios Kotsiopoulos

House in Ano Poli
1 Lysia, Timotheou & Kassianis,
54635 Thessaloniki
Tel +30 2310 231 612

821 ✆ RES 1998

A series of facade treatments
and use of sympathetic
materials break down the
impact of this house in a
protected area of Thessaloniki.
The projecting timber screened
volume with two pitched roofs
refers to ancient Greek
architectural forms. Natural light
falls through a central skylight.

Katerina Tsigarida Architects

New Helexpo Gates
154 Egnatia Street,
546 36 Thessaloniki
Tel +30 2310 292 008

822 ☐ CUL 1999

Three modernist gates form the entrance to Greece's biggest exhibition facility, the Helexpo site. Standing within a new public space, each gateway building has a layered exterior facade of steel framing, glazing and perforated copper panels. A solid barrier by day, lighting reveals the interior by night.

Sakellaridou, Papanikolaou, Pollani & Associates Architects

Harbour Offices and Shopping Centre
43 26th of October,
54627 Thessaloniki
Tel +30 2310 566 563

823 ✆ COM 2002

Located in Thessaloniki's fast developing harbour area, this luxury eight-storey complex arranges retail, parking and office levels around a full-height atrium with ground-floor public plaza. Glass and steel 'trees' announce the public entrance.

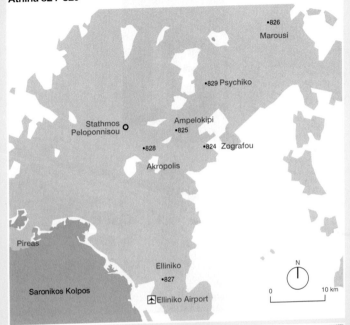

Stathmos
Peloponnisou O

•826
Marousi

•829 Psychiko

Ampelokipi
•825

•828   •824 Zografou

Akropolis

Pireas

Elliniko
•827

Saronikos Kolpos

N

0   10 km

✈ Elliniko Airport

Dimitris Biris

**Zografou Open Air Theatre,
National Technical University
of Athens**
Zografou Campus, Iroon
Polytexneiou 9, 157 80 Athina
Tel +30 210 772 1000

824 ☐ EDU 2001

The light timber and steel
structural system of this low-
cost outdoor theatre opposes
the massive concrete buildings
of the Zografou campus. The
informality of its scaffolding-like
skeleton is extended to the
seating and circulation design.

Dimitris Issaias–Tassis
Papaioannou

Office Building
28 Sinopis and Avlidos,
Ampelokipi, 115 27 Athina
Tel +30 210 779 5118

825 ☐ COM 1999

A six-storey office building on
a corner site in a dense area of
the city widens the street area
available to pedestrians without
sacrificing interior floor space;
steel box overhangs attached
to each facade create covered
entrances. Louvred timber
screens shade interior spaces.

Yannis Aesopos

Poly/mono-Katoikia
10 Parnithos, Marousi,
151 23 Athina

826 ▮ RES 2002

This project in a suburb
combines a semi-independent
two-storey single house at the
base with three separate
apartments on three floors
above. An anchored stair tower
and miniature *piloti* support the
apartments. A pebble garden
fills the void between the two
elements.

ISV Architects & Associates

Private House
23 Odos No 3, Elliniko,
167 00 Athina

827 ▮ RES 2001

Geometric whiteness combined
with porous sand-coloured
Cretan stone and an L-shaped
courtyard swimming pool create
a studied play of light and
shade around this opulent
family house. The kitchen,
conceived as the social core of
the house, occupies one arm of
the L-shaped plan.

Europe

Sakellaridou, Papanikolaou,
Pollani & Associates Architects

**National Bank of Greece
Headquarters**
82–4 Aeolou Street,
102 32 Athina
Tel +30 210 334 2035

828   ✆   COM 2001

With a view of the Acropolis at
the end of the street, the new
National Bank headquarters
proclaims its modernity in a
geometrical sandstone and
granite volume. Archaeological
remains found on site are
preserved beneath glass floors.

Zoe Samourkas

Private House
Athina

829   ■   RES 1999

Each of the three floors of this
suburban family house has an
independently constructed
concrete frame; horizontal
spaces between the levels give
an illusion of a floating structure
and allow views to the park
from the interior. A central blade
wall holds the main staircase
and is topped with a skylight to
bring in natural light.

Michalis Manidakis

Private House
Mykonos

830   ■   RES 1998

The exterior of a massive
holiday house overlooking
Parnormos Bay draws on
traditional cubic Greek island
architecture; the interior recalls
an ancient Roman villa with a
peristyle on two sides of a
layered courtyard garden.
Climatic and ecological
measures protect the interior
from the wind and heat.

Gmür-Vacchini Architects

Two Houses by the Sea
Paros

831 ■ RES 1998

In a characteristically dry, rocky and almost treeless Cycladic landscape, this deceptively simple house for two is arranged as two pavilions separated by a three-sided protected courtyard. A long white wall supporting a platform for outdoor activities extends away from the two square living boxes.

Agnes Couvelas-Panagiotatou

Summer House
Kaparies, Akrotiri,
84700 Santorini

832 ❑ RES 1998

Traditional construction techniques and authentic materials are combined with a new formal language to create a summer house that responds to the volcanic landscape and architectural vernacular of the Greek islands. A deep, three-dimensional facade protects against north winds.

Mimarlar Tasarim

B2 House
Buyukhusun Village, Ayvacik,
Canakkale

833 ❑ RES 2000

The materials used in this two-storey house create a tension between manufactured and natural: shuttered concrete against rough masonry, aluminium with reeds. Shutters cover the facade with the view; full retractable glazing behind allows the entire house to be opened to the landscape.

GAD Architecture

Chameleon Exhibition Centre
Park Orman, Maslak,
80630 Istanbul

834 □ CUL 2001

The glass and steel form of this exhibition and training centre was defined by the mature trees that dominate its site within Park Orman, a leisure destination for the urban population of Istanbul. The fully glazed building is staggered across its sloping site.

Arda Inceoglu and Deniz Aslan

Pamukkale Tennis Club
Karakurt Yolu, 20200 Denizli
Tel +258 221 8084/5/6

835 □ SPO 1999

Two contrasting buildings, arranged perpendicular to each other, define the central outdoor space of this linear complex. The first comprises independent stone pavilions linked by a metal-roofed internal street. The second, shown here, is a concrete and timber structure containing the restaurant.

Margarita Danou & Sevina Floridou-Zesimou

Oroklini Coastal Promenade
Dhekelia Avenue, 7041 Voroklini
Tel +35 7 24 644744

836 □ REC 2002

A threshold between a resort development and the coastal edge, this promenade bounded by the sea and an artificial lake provides leisure activities for the public. A series of platforms, canopies and lighting unified by a path accommodates changing facilities, a kiosk and places to sit along the way.

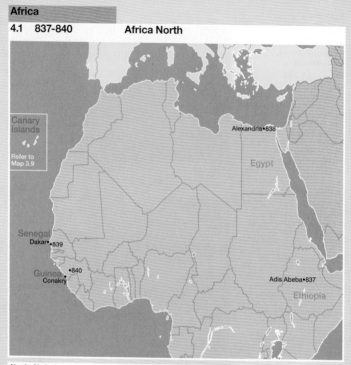

Ahadu Abaineh

Tree House
Adis Abeba

837 ■ RES 2002

Four live trees form the corners
of this double-storey
experimental house in Adis
Abeba; untreated poles create
structural frames for roofs and
doors. Mud walls can be
remoulded to accommodate the
growth of the trees and family.
A corrugated metal roof
channels rainwater to the trees
and protects the fragile walls.

Africa

Snøhetta

Alexandria Library
El Shatby, Alexandria 21526
Tel +203 483 0334

838 □ CUL 2002

Central to the grand design of
Alexandria's new library is a
monumental inclined silver disc
that covers the circular, stepped
reading room. A grove of
columns grows out of the
cascading interior landscape,
supporting clerestories that light
and animate the reading rooms.
World texts are inscribed on the
southern wall.

Hollmén-Reuter-Sandman
Architects

Women's Centre
Gouye Aldiana, Rufisque Nord,
Rufisque
Tel +221 836 90 40

839 □ PUB 2001

A strong perimeter wall
characteristic of traditional West
African settlements bounds this
women's centre and merges
with the buildings that turn
inwards on to a communal
court. Facilities include laundry
room, workshops and reception
centre for rural immigrants.

Heikkinen-Komonen Architects

**Kahere Eila Poultry Farming
School**
Koliagbe, Kindia

840 □ EDU 2000

Three elegant buildings
gathered around a central
courtyard make up this Guinean
poultry farming school. Locally
available materials – unfired
stabilized earth blocks, cement
tiles reinforced with sisal fibre,
and woven cane – form the
envelope to an Aaltoesque
structural timber frame.

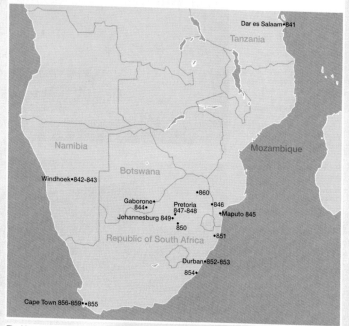

Dar es Salaam •841

Tanzania

Namibia

Mozambique

Botswana

Windhoek •842-843

Gaborone
844•

•860

Pretoria
847-848

•846

Johannesburg 849•

•Maputo 845

•850

Republic of South Africa

•851

Durban •852-853

854•

Cape Town 856-859 • •855

The Manser Practice

Umoja House
Garden Avenue, Dar es Salaam
Tel +255 222 11 0101

841 ◼ ✎ GOV 2002

The open and transparent
facade of this complex
combining European Union and
embassy offices in Dar es
Salaam belies its stringent
security measures. A wave-like
roof with circular cut-outs and
generous overhangs floats
lightly above the building. The
ground floor has pod-like
communal spaces.

Marais Pretorius & Wenhold

Smith House
Windhoek, Khomas

842 ■ RES 1998

A contemporary Namibian farmhouse with a series of floating curved roofs perches on a rocky outcrop in dramatic landscape outside Windhoek. Its typical elements – house, water tower, garages, meat-processing facilities, outbuildings, guest quarters and a caretaker's flat – fan out from a central courtyard.

Architext in collaboration with Charles Delamy Architect

Franco-Namibian Cultural Centre
118 Robert Mugabe Avenue, Windhoek
Tel +264 61 222 122

843 ☐ CUL 2000

This cultural centre is a transparent rectangular box which evolves from a single-storey domestic scale at the back to a three-storey more public urban space at the front. The design was dictated by its site – sloping and restricted.

Rik Leus

National Food Technology Research Centre
Plot 1840, Mputsane Industrial Area, Kanye

844 ▯ EDU 2000

Appearing from the nearby Trans-Kalahari Highway like a giant metal insect asleep in the landscape, this food processing technology research complex is a passive solar building. The barrel-vaulted roofs of its four laboratories allow excess internal heat to dissipate.

Africa

Africa South

José ABP Forjaz

**Mother House for the
Congregation of the Brothers
of the Consolata**
496 Avenida 24 de Julho,
Polana, Maputo
Tel +258 1 490 336

845 □ REL 1999

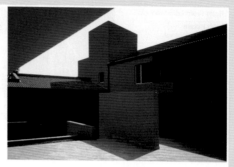

This stunning convent turns its
back on Maputo outside to
create an internal world of quiet
courtyards and cloisters. The
vibrant orange ochre of the
rendered masonry recalls the
natural pigment of the soil and
enhances the volumes.

José ABP Forjaz

Mbuzini Memorial
Komatipoort, Lubombos
mountain range, Mbuzini

846 ◧ CUL 1998

Set in a concrete plinth, 35
Cor-ten steel pipes mark the
spot where a plane carrying 35
passengers, including President
Samora Machel, crashed in
1986. The pipes are filled to
different heights with concrete,
allowing the wind to play a
macabre lament, amplified by a
triangular concrete box below.

Comrie & Wilkinson

House Steyn
Pretoria

847 ■ RES 1999

A suburban family house in
Pretoria combines modern
indoor and outdoor spaces with
African vernacular elements.
Private enclosed spaces are
arranged around a series of
extended thresholds and open-
air courtyards. The formal
cantilevered balcony and glazed
box window contrasts with the
adobe-style balustrade.

Africa

Equilibrium Architects

Equilibrium Studio
694 Downie Street,
Pretoria 0084
Tel +27 12 3292 949

848 □ CUL 2002

Recycled materials were
brought into the suburbs for
this private studio workshop,
an upmarket version of the
township model. Salvaged
office window frames welded
edge to edge form the steel
sub-frames, while the roof is of
corrugated-iron sheets flexed
into an arc.

GAPP Architects, Mashabane
Rose, Britz Roodt, Linda Mvusi

**South African Apartheid
Museum**
Cnr Northern Parkway and Gold
Reef Road, Johannesburg 2001
Tel +27 11 309 4700

849 □ CUL 2001

Seven large concrete columns
representing the seven pillars
of the constitution mark the
entrance. A spiral staircase
descends into the dimly lit main
exhibition space. Finally a large
concrete cube opens to the
elements to celebrate freedom.

Derick de Bruyn

Sue House
660 Twin Rivers Road,
Tshwane 1675
Tel +208 543 0421

850 ✏ RES 2001

Sue House comprises two basic
tin-roofed open sheds placed
side by side, one the main
house and the other sheltered
parking and a studio apartment.
Double-volume living and dining
areas connect directly with the
landscape through fully glazed
walls. Private areas are housed
in a masonry box.

East Coast Architects

**Medical Research Facilities
for the Africa Centre**
R618, Hlabisa, Somkhele 3935
Tel +27 0 35 550 7502

851 ☐ EDU 2002

Research into health and
population is carried out in this
vibrant building, its four pods
containing open-plan offices
clustered around a cruciform
circulation and social space.
Supported by local eucalyptus
timbers, the main tower acts as
a thermal stack.

Soundspace Design

Millennium Tower
Perched high on the Bluff
Peninsula, Durban

852 ☐ CUL 2003

Located at the entrance to
Durban harbour, the Millennium
Tower features a highly visible
kinetic barometer that
communicates sun, wind and
tide fluctuations. The 75 metre
lighthouse, topped by a mesh-
clad cowl and spire, contains
operations rooms and search-
and-rescue functions.

Soundspace Design in
association with Inq Architects

Barrows
17 Intersite Avenue, Springfield
Park, Durban
Tel +27 31 250 8888

853 ☐ COM 1999

This design and manufacturing
facility symbolizes the post-
apartheid flattening of social
hierarchies in its low, elongated
elevations, and integration of
functions. The factory has semi-
public exhibition spaces
animated by video, music and
installations.

Africa

Cohen & Judin

Nelson Mandela Museum
Bunga Building, Owen Street,
Umtata 5100
Tel +27 47 532 5110

854 ☐ CUL 2000

The Mveso monument, one
element of the Nelson Mandela
museum, displays Mandela's
birthplace in a simple open-air
structure of concrete, brick and
gum poles under a steel sheet
roof. Existing fencing and lattice
weaving skills were used in the
project, and training was given
in stone-building techniques.

Piet Louw Architects

**Khayelitsha Service Centres
and Pay Points**
Various sites, Khayelitsha,
Cape Town 7784
Tel +27 21 360 1272 (resource
centre)

855 ☐ PUB 2002

A series of civic centres where
residents can pay rents, these
robust, dignified buildings use
strong forms. Echoing the
informal mono-pitch roofs and
block building of surrounding
shacks, the centres provide a
focus for the community.

Van Der Merwe Miszewski
Architects

Cliff House
40 Glen Crescent, Higgovale,
Cape Town 8001

856 ▮ RES 2000

Perched on densely wooded
land with dramatic views
through glazed facades of Table
Mountain, ocean and city, Cliff
House is a rectangular crate
containing three bedrooms and
a guest apartment. Circulation
is confined to a slot along the
western edge.

Kruger Roos

Unicity Mayoral Chambers
12 Herzog Boulevard, The
Foreshore, Cape Town 8001
Tel +27 21 400 1287

857 ✐ GOV 2002

This extension to a civic centre
adds a floor of chambers and
office space to an existing
podium, a rationalized entrance
and a new pedestrian precinct.
The glazed central chamber has
an inverted steel cone roof
which acts as a city barometer,
its colour changing with the
weather.

Van Der Merwe Miszewski
Architects

Tree House
30 Glen Crescent, Higgovale,
Cape Town 8001

858 ▮ RES 1999

Tree House features five tree-
like structures growing up
through a triple-height void
under a protective canopy roof.
A lightweight steel and glass
envelope sits on a rusticated
slate base; cave-like spaces on
the ground floor contrast with
the volumes above.

CS Studio Architects

**Guga S'thebe Arts, Culture
and Heritage Village**
Washington Avenue, Langa,
Cape Town 8000
Tel +27 21 695 3493

859 ☐ CUL 2000

Set in Langa, Cape Town's
oldest black township, the
colourful pavilions of the Guga
S'thebe cultural centre provide
spaces for arts projects around
an outdoor performance area.
The golden cone recalls the
structures of a semi-mythical
ancient civilization.

Africa

Joubert & Gouws

Nothnagel-Deiner House
Tzaneen

860 ■ RES 2001

Vibrantly painted to mimic the surrounding lush vegetation, this house was designed to protect against heat, humidity and heavy downpours. Timber floors are raised to allow ventilation and a scaffolding-like construction of paired gum poles holds up the insulating aluminium-sheeting roof.

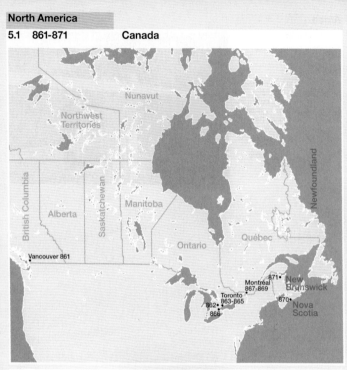

Patkau Architects

Vancouver House
Vancouver, BC

861 ■ RES 2000

The long, narrow floor plan
of this waterfront house in
Vancouver demanded simple
organization. Living spaces are
on the ground floor, private
spaces above and music room
below, with a lap pool
suspended over the entry.
The dining area is fully internal,
rising through the floor above
to a clerestory.

North America

Shim Sutcliffe Architects

Tower House
Stratford, ON

862 ◼ RES 2001

This four-storey town house is
squeezed on to a narrow lot
within Stratford's urban jumble.
The interior expands vertically
with spaces spiralling off a sky-
lit central atrium in two
staggered stacks. The next floor
is always only a few steps up or
down, with movement and light
flowing through the space.

Morphosis

**University of Toronto
Graduate Student Housing**
60 Harbord Street, Toronto,
ON M58 3L1
Tel +1 416 978 2011

863 ◼ ✎ EDU 2000

This student housing containing
119 apartments is a perimeter
block with a large open central
courtyard. Each side differs in
height. The seven-storey west
block contains the recessed
entrance; on the upper two
floors a glazed corridor
continues over the street.

Patkau Architects

Oakdale Community Centre
350 Grandravine Drive, Toronto,
ON M3N 1J4
Tel +1 416 395 0484

864 ◻ PUB 1999

The open facade and linear
organization of this community
centre complements its
function. An angled canopy of
exposed structural steel
supported by yellow pillars runs
the length of the building. A
glazed curtain wall is broken by
infill elements of masonry and
bright yellow ceramic tiles.

Shim Sutcliffe Architects

Weathering Steel House
Toronto, ON

865 ■ RES 2001

This L-shaped house frames a landscape of trees and meadow; pools for plants and swimming provide an internal focus away from the historical pastiche of surrounding suburban houses. The front entry leads to the main living area from where interweaved internal and external spaces unfold.

Kohn Shnier Architects

Student Centre, Erindale Campus, University of Toronto
3359 Mississauga Road, Mississauga, ON L5L 1C6
Tel +1 905 828 5249

866 □ EDU 1999

Located within Erindale College at the crossroads of the site, the simple transparency of this luminous student centre contrasts with the solidity of surrounding buildings. Active spaces, including café and cinema, are on the ground floor. Upstairs are quieter lounges.

Dupuis Le Tourneaux and Menkes Shooner Dagenais

Cité Multimédia Phase 8
31 Duke Street, Montréal, QC H3C 2L8
Tel +1 514 878 1045 x221

867 □ COM 2002

In a dilapidated but historic downtown area of Old Montréal, Cité Multimédia is a public-private enterprise comprising eight office blocks designed by different architects. A huge glass screen attached to the ten-storey west wing acts as an advertising billboard.

North America

Saucier + Perrotte

Gérald-Godin College
15615 Gouin Boulevard West,
Sainte-Geneviève, QC H9H 5K8
Tel +1 514 626 2666

868 ▯ ✎ EDU 2000

The French College in west
Montréal incorporates a Jesuit
monastery built in 1933 into a
new programme of college
buildings. Sports facilities and
a multifunctional theatre are
housed in subterranean spaces.
A slashed black aluminium
facade identifies the main block
of classrooms and laboratories.

Saucier + Perrotte

**First Nations Garden
Interpretive Pavilion**
4101 Sherbrooke Street East,
Montréal, QC H1X 2B2
Tel +1 514 872 1400

869 ☐ CUL 2001

This garden pavilion in
Montréal's Botanical Garden
commemorates a 1701 treaty
reconciling French settlers and
indigenous Quebec peoples.
An undulating concrete roof
on steel columns covers a
promenade of display cases.

Brian MacKay-Lyons

Howard House
West Pennant, NS

870 ■ RES 1999

Like a metal wedge perched on
granite boulders overlooking the
bay, this single-volume, energy-
efficient house has a mono-
pitched roof. Entrance is
through large, sliding metal
doors on either side leading into
a sky-lit courtyard. From here,
a sliding glass door opens into
the double-height room with
exposed steel roof trusses.

North America

Julie Snow Architects

Koehler Residence
Sealy's Cove, NB

871 ■ RES 2000

On a granite cliff overlooking the Bay of Fundy, strong geometry anchors this isolated, modernist house to the dramatic landscape. Glass walls frame views in all directions. Sliding doors transform transparent bedrooms into private cabins. Elegant yet robust, the house can be battened down in severe weather.

5.2   872-917   USA West

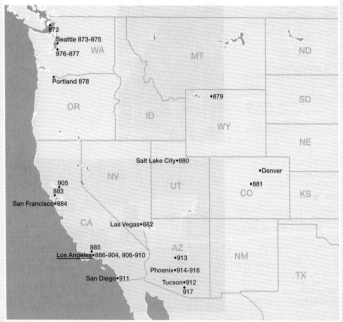

North America

Patkau Architects

Agosta House
San Juan Island, WA

872　■ RES 2000

Stretching across the ridge of a meadow and creating a forecourt with panoramic views to the islands of British Colombia, a simple extrusion forms this combined work and living space. The extrusion is manipulated by intruding exterior spaces and the insertion of non-structural bulkheads.

Steven Holl Architects

Bellevue Arts Museum
510 Bellevue Way, NE
Bellevue, WA 98004
Tel +1 425 519 0770

873　□ CUL 2000

The organizing concept of this museum with an educational rather than a collecting focus is 'tripleness': three slightly warped main lofts contain dramatically curved volumes with distinct lighting conditions. The outer walls, in a 'shotcrete' construction, support the lightweight steel framework.

Gehry Partners

Experience Music Project
325 5th Avenue North, Seattle, WA 98109
Tel +1 206 367 5483

874　□ CUL 2000

The Experience Music Project at the Seattle Center, which celebrates the history of American popular music, inhabits a cluster of fragmented and undulating forms suggesting a trashed Fender Stratocaster guitar. Looping steel cables are reminiscent of guitar strings.

Miller/Hull Partnership

Seattle Center Fisher Pavilion
220 Harrison Street, Seattle,
WA 98109
Tel +1 206 684 7200

875 □ CUL 2002

Providing exhibition space, the
Fisher Pavilion is partly sunk
into a 1 hectare green at the
heart of the Seattle Center. A
glazed facade allows views
through the building. A
rooftop plaza displays a
pattern of water droplets when
viewed from the adjacent Space
Needle.

Antoine Predock Architect

Tacoma Art Museum
1701 Pacific Avenue, Tacoma,
WA 98402
Tel +1 253 272 4258

876 □ CUL 2003

The two wings of the Tacoma
Museum hover on slender *piloti*,
mediating the vehicular scale of
the adjacent freeway with the
pedestrian scale of the
immediate context. Stainless
steel and smoked glass evoke
grey skies. Fissured openings
connect the interior galleries to
the urban environment outside.

Arthur Erickson with Nick
Milkovich Architects

Museum of Glass
1801 East Dock Street, Tacoma,
WA 98402
Tel +1 866 468 7386

877 □ CUL 2002

The Museum of Glass presents
a public space that visitors can
walk through, around, over and
under. Entry is via a bridge that
leads on to the roof, from where
a staircase radiates around the
iconic cone-shaped stainless
steel tower. Inside, public
spaces are on a single level.

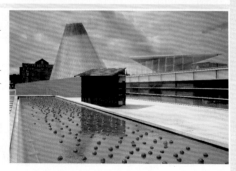

Allied Works Architecture

2281 NW Glisan Street Building
2281 NW Glisan Street,
Portland, OR

878 ▯ COM 2000

On an urban site in north west Portland, this mixed-use building contains retail and office space, with a penthouse apartment. A tight skin of glass, metal mesh and stone tile wrapped around a simple frame adds a pleasing composition to the streetscape.

Charles Rose Architects

Paint Rock Camp
Hyatt Ranch, Hyattville,
WY 82428
Tel +1 818 703 6334

879 ✎ TOU 2001

Sixteen separate structures clustered around the mouth of a canyon in the legendary landscape of Wyoming make up this camp for teenagers from inner-city Los Angeles. Sleeping cabins are built on steel platforms supported by stilts, while communal buildings are grounded more firmly.

Machado and Silvetti Associates

Marcia and John Price Museum Building, Utah Museum of Fine Arts
410 Campus Center Drive,
Salt Lake City, UT 84112
Tel +1 801 581 7332

880 ▢ CUL 2000

A series of prismatic volumes step up and around the tall central space of the Grand Gallery, crowned by green glass, the centrepiece of this museum within the University of Utah's hillside campus.

Forsythe + MacAllen Architects

House and Stable
Cherokee Meadows, Colorado

881 ■ RES 1999

Deceptively simple and romantic, this house clad in unseasoned local pine is located in wild, rolling Colorado. Kitchen and sleeping loft are on the first floor with a glazed roof ridge offering dramatic views of the ever-changing sky. A bedroom and bathroom on the ground floor give way to stabling.

OMA

Hermitage Guggenheim
3355 Las Vegas Boulevard South, Las Vegas, NV 89109
Tel +1 702 414 2440

882 □ CUL 2001

This understated Cor-ten steel vault gallery with superscaled signage confronts the ostentatious Las Vegas casinos. Designed to exhibit artworks from the Hermitage in St Petersburg, internal space is divided into several galleries. Paintings are mounted on steel walls with magnets.

Fernau & Hartman Architects

Napa Valley Museum
55 Presidents Circle, Yountville, CA 94599
Tel +1 707 944 0500

883 □ CUL 1998

Financial constraints called for an imaginative approach to a new Napa Valley Museum; located in a mature redwood grove, the curved aerodynamic roof belies the simple open shed that houses the galleries. The concrete, wood and metal structure is interwoven with indigenous gardens.

North America

Stanley Saitowitz Office/
Natoma Architects

Yerba Buena Lofts
855 Folsom Street,
San Francisco, CA 94107

884 ▯ RES 2001

Referring to San Franciscan
Victorian detailing in its bay
windows, the overall form of
this housing loft block recalls
the chaos of the contemporary
world. Cut-outs and set backs
create outdoor space for each
loft. By night the facade
appears as glowing lanterns.

Barton Myers Associates

**House and Studio at Toro
Canyon**
Toro Canyon, Montecito,
CA 93108
Tel +1 310 208 2227

885 ✎ RES 1998

A series of four buildings
following the site contours
make up this residence in a
picturesque canyon with
panoramic views of islands and
mountains. Rooftop reflecting
pools and galvanized steel
shutters protect the property
from bush fires.

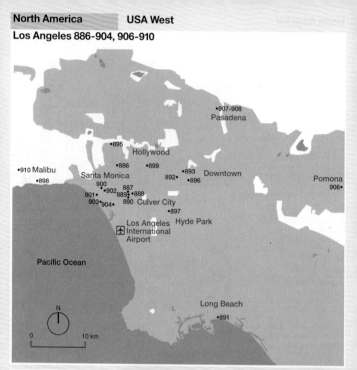

- •907-908 Pasadena
- •895
- Hollywood
- •886 •899
- •910 Malibu
- •898
- Santa Monica
- •893 Downtown
- 892• •896
- Pomona
- 906•
- 900
- 887
- •902
- 901• 889• •888
- 903• 904• 890 Culver City
- •897
- Hyde Park
- ✈ Los Angeles International Airport
- Pacific Ocean
- N
- 0   10 km
- Long Beach
- •891

Michael Maltzan Architecture

Hergott Shepard Residence
1261 Shadowhill Way,
Beverly Hills, CA 90210

886 ❘ RES 1999

Composed of a series of
volumes closed to the street,
the solidity of this house
overlooking Los Angeles gives
way to transparency around
living spaces and pool at the
rear. Two zinc-clad elements
hold together its composition.
Entry is via a gallery space
within the central volumes.

North America

Eric Owen Moss Architects

3535 Hayden Avenue
3535 Hayden Avenue,
Culver City, CA 90232

887 ☐☐ COM 1998

The headquarters of a media
company incorporates exposed
timber bowstring trusses,
rescued from old warehouses,
within a four-storey steel frame
of wide-flange beams and
tubular columns. Inside space is
organized around a three-storey
combined circulation and
gallery entrance lobby.

Eric Owen Moss Architects

Beehive
8520 National Boulevard,
Culver City, CA 90232
Tel +1 310 839 1334

888 ☐☐ ✦ COM 2001

This distinctive sculptural
form attached to existing
warehouses contains a
reception area, conference
room and exterior staircase.
Set on an equally sculptural
bed of grassy landscaping, the
Beehive's skeleton comprises
hoops of steel pipes around
four columns.

Eric Owen Moss Architects

Umbrella
3542 Hayden Avenue,
Culver City, CA 90232
Tel +1 310 839 1334

889 ☐☐ ✦ COM 1999

On a former industrial site
in Culver City, now home to
many of California's creative
industries, the Umbrella
functions as bandstand, seating
area and viewing deck. Glass
panels mounted over an open-
air platform and stairway make
up this apparently chaotic
structure.

Eric Owen Moss Architects

Stealth
3528 Hayden Avenue,
Culver City, CA 90232

890 ▯ COM 2001

Lifted up on steel struts to accommodate on-grade parking and spanning a below-ground-level outdoor theatre and garden, Stealth is a high-specification office space. A glass-enclosed elevator leads across bridges into the building's two wings. In section Stealth evolves along its length.

Morphosis

International Elementary School
450 Long Beach Boulevard,
Long Beach, CA 90802
Tel +1 562 436 4420

891 ▯ ✏ EDU 1999

Stacked up on just half the land needed for a suburban equivalent, International Elementary School provides a stimulating three-dimensional learning environment. A metal screen bends and folds around the top of the facade, enclosing the rooftop playground.

Daly Genik Architects

Camino Nuevo Charter Academy, Elementary and Middle School
697 Burlington Avenue, Los Angeles, CA 90017
Tel +1 213 483 2000

892 ☐ EDU 2002

Located in a low-income area of Los Angeles, this project transformed an abandoned mini-mall into a neighbourhood school, by reconfiguring interior space into 12 classrooms and wrapping a bold and protective structure around it.

North America

Rafael Moneo

Our Lady of the Angels Cathedral
555 West Temple Street, Los Angeles, CA 90012-2707
Tel +1 213 680 5200

893 ☐ REL 2002

The third largest cathedral in the world, this complex stretches over an entire city block with two buildings framing a plaza. A concrete cross cut into a box of alabaster announces the cathedral's presence to the city. Within the polished interior, no two walls meet at a right angle.

Pugh + Scarpa in collaboration with OMD

Portable Construction Training Centre
Los Angeles, CA

894 ▌ EDU 2001

One long wall of this revamped mobile home, or trailer, is rebuilt from translucent panels that pivot upwards and open to create a canopy and extend the usable interior space. A metal grid defines an entrance area. Cost-effective materials, such as corrugated steel, are used.

Michael Maltzan Architecture

Feldman-Horn Center for the Arts
3700 Coldwater Canyon, North Hollywood, CA 91604
Tel +1 818 980 6692

895 ✎ CUL 1998

A plaza and white-stuccoed bell-tower provide a new landmark for the Department of Art at Harvard Westlake School, which now accommodates classrooms, studios, lecture theatre and large gallery space, and doubles as a transitional public entry to the campus.

Gehry Partners

Walt Disney Concert Hall
111 South Grand Avenue, Los
Angeles, CA 90012
Tel +1 323 850 2000

896 ☐ CUL 2003

The billowing forms of the new
permanent home of the LA
Philharmonic Orchestra are a
unique addition to Los Angeles.
Inside, the timber walls and sail-
like ceiling express acoustic
parameters, while natural light
flowing in through skylights and
a large window enhances
daytime performances.

John Friedman Alice Kimm
Architects

Los Angeles Design Center
5955 Western Avenue, Los
Angeles, CA 90047
Tel +1 323 778 8612

897 ☐ COM 2003

Part of a regeneration plan in a
furniture-manufacturing area of
Los Angeles, this pedestrian-
orientated showroom complex
incorporates two existing brick
warehouses. A car park has
become a public event space,
animated by projections on a
polycarbonate-panel screen.

Moore Ruble Yudell Architects &
Planners

Yorkin House
Malibu, CA

898 ■ RES 1999

This house presents a solid but
sculptural presence to the
Pacific Coast Highway with its
streams of traffic on one side,
and an open, extensively glazed
facade to the Pacific Ocean on
the other. Private family spaces
at the front lead to light-filled
social spaces, terraces and
courtyards at the back.

North America

Neil M Denari Associates

I.a. Eyeworks Showroom
7386 Beverly Boulevard, Los
Angeles, CA 90036
Tel +1 323 931 7795

899 ☐ COM 2002

The interior design of this shop
for a cutting-edge eyewear
company uses a continuous
suspended surface of aqueous
blue to shape space and
movement. The shop cuts into
the existing building's curved
exterior, and features an eye-
catching information and
signage system.

Koning Eizenberg Architecture

**25th Street Mixed-Use
Building**
1454 25th Street, Santa Monica,
CA 90404
Tel +1 310 282 6131

900 ☐ COM 1999

Functional and ecologically
aware, these new offices blend
into the residential landscape of
Santa Monica. Small windows
punctuate the metal cladding to
prevent unnecessary heat gain,
while vents and a pivoting glass
door maximize the benefit of the
ocean breeze.

Pugh + Scarpa/Kodama
Architects

Colorado Court
502 Colorado Avenue, Santa
Monica, CA 90401

901 ▮ RES 2002

Energy independence is the key
to this affordable housing
project in the wealthy coastal
city of Santa Monica; Colorado
Court provides 44 single-room
units with kitchen and bathroom
for low-income residents. A grid
of solar panels covers the
western facade.

Pugh + Scarpa

Bergamot Artist Lofts
2525 Michigan Avenue, Building
J, Santa Monica CA 90404
Tel +1 310 829 5854

902 ☐ CUL 1999

This conversion project within
an artistic community includes
a ground-floor commercial
gallery with three live/work lofts
for artists above. Formerly an
industrial warehouse, swathes
of angled steel cladding and
translucent panels unfold
across the facade. The lofts
have polished concrete floors.

Daly Genik Architects

Slot Box House
653 Raymond Avenue, Santa
Monica, CA 90405

903 ▮ RES 1998

The boxy form of the house is
slotted into its sloping site on
a hill in Santa Monica. Parking
and kitchen are on the lowest
level, with living spaces and
outdoor patio above. The walls
include opaque polycarbonate
sliding panels. The box-like top
floor appears to float above
the site.

Marmol Radziner and
Associates

Glencoe Residence
2125 Glencoe, Venice,
CA 90291

904 ▮ RES 2002

On a narrow site in a popular
Los Angeles beach area, this
house presents a single-storey
facade to the street. A recessed
L-shaped second storey
maximizes interior space. The
short leg of the L creates a
covered patio area and divides
the garden in two.

North America

Stanley Saitowitz Office/
Natoma Architects

Lieff House
40 Auberge Road, Rutherford,
Napa, CA 94573

905 ▮ RES 2002

Two courtyards carved out of a
long block divide this low-lying
guesthouse overlooking the
vineyards of the Napa Valley. A
largely closed Cor-ten steel wall
is separated from the glazed
interior by clerestory windows.
Views are shaded and framed
by an arcade of stucco walls.

Morphosis

Diamond Ranch High School
100 Diamond Ranch Drive,
Pomona, CA 91766
Tel +1 909 397 4715

906 ▮ ✎ EDU 2000

Built on a steep gradient in
Pomona, Diamond Ranch High
School presents an interaction
of architecture and topography.
Edgy geometries and unlikely
cantilevers articulate the
campus. Sports areas are at the
top and bottom of the hill, with
two rows of buildings and a
pedestrian street between.

Pei Cobb Freed & Partners
Architects

**Broad Center for Biological
Science**
360 Wilson Avenue, Pasadena,
CA 91125
Tel +1 626 395 6811

907 ▮ ✎ EDU 2002

On a campus gateway site
among new buildings, this
facility accommodates
laboratories and semi-public
spaces. Etched stainless-steel
wall panels clad the laboratories
on three sides and a travertine
facade identifies public areas.

Hodgetts & Fung

Sinclair Pavilion, Art Center College of Design
1700 Lida Street, Pasadena, CA 91103
Tel +1 626 396 2260

908 □ EDU 2001

Designed as a casual diversion to Craig Elwood's iconic 1969 Miesian structure next door, the Sinclair Pavilion provides a relaxed setting for student activities. A succession of light and airy interior spaces are sheltered from the hot sun by a large steel-framed roof.

Richard Meier & Partners

Southern California Beach House
CA

909 ■ RES 2001

This pristine white house is arranged around an interior L-shaped courtyard connecting the road to the ocean. The house frames views and controls light as the space unfolds. The two-storey entrance leads to a double-height living room that looks directly out over the ocean.

Hagy Belzberg/George Wittman Collaborative

BRM Residence
Yellow Hill Road, Ventura County, Malibu, CA

910 ▮ RES 1999

On an environmentally sensitive site next to National Park land, this house camouflages itself by wrapping round a granite outcrop. A south-facing butterfly-shaped roof is angled to achieve maximum solar exposure and collect and channel rainwater.

North America

Daly Genik Architects

Valley Center House
Valley Center, San Diego, CA

911 ■ RES 1999

In the tradition of Californian domestic modernism, this concrete and aluminium single-storey guesthouse sits quietly within its granite landscape. Two splayed ranges of bedroom accommodation flank a living space and look on to a central courtyard. Perforated vertical and horizontal screens shield the building's glazed envelope.

Rick Joy Architects

Rubio Avenue Studio
400 South Rubio, Tucson,
AZ 85701
Tel +1 520 624 1442

912 ✏ COM 1999

A deeply recessed double gate is the only interruption in a massive 4 metre high rammed earth wall that forms the front boundary for this architectural office. A long glass wall separates the spacious interior from the courtyard, with its reflective pool, single mesquite tree and framed sky.

Gluckman Mayner Architects

Mii Amo Spa, Enchantment Resort
525 Boynton Canyon Road,
Sedona, AZ 86336
Tel +1 520 204 6260

913 ☐ TOU 2001

Surrounded by the red rock walls of Boynton Canyon, the main building of this resort is organized along a horizontal circulation corridor. A grand hall lit by a continuous skylight runs along one side; on the other side, five adobe-brick towers contain the treatment rooms.

North America

USA West

Will Bruder Architects

Byrne House
Scottsdale, AZ

914 ■ RES 1999

On a steep site, in the cactus-studded terrain of the high desert, a series of abstract canyon walls of concrete masonry and metal-clad frame walls, enclosing main entry, living areas and circulation gallery, make up this vertiginous house. Brackets attach the roof to the central spine of the building.

Will Bruder Architects

Scottsdale Museum of Contemporary Art, Gerard L Cafesjian Pavilion
7374 East Second Street, Scottsdale, AZ 85251
Tel +1 480 994 2787

915 □ CUL 1999

The new wing of this centre for art adapts an existing cinema complex into versatile exhibition galleries. A rectangular corrugated-steel service pod and curved galvanized-steel arrival pod embrace the mass of the building.

Wendell Burnette Architects

Schall Residence
Phoenix, AZ

916 ■ RES 2000

The sinuous form of this house in a nondescript development on the outskirts of Phoenix wraps around the edges of its site. Living areas on the first floor above a walled courtyard take advantage of carefully framed desert views. Spiral procession through the house can be on foot or via custom-made elevator.

North America

Rick Joy Architects

Tubac House
Tubac, AZ

917   ■ RES 2000

Two shed forms cradling a
courtyard rest on a shallow
shelf carved into the desert
hillside. Exterior walls and roofs
are clad in rusted steel, echoing
the surrounding red ochre
landscape. Inside, slivers of
light add to a palette of white
plaster, steel, maple and glass.
Protruding steel boxes form
windows.

MN   952•

Minneapolis
953-954•

WI

Milwaukee 959•

MI

920•

922• NY

923•

Chicago 961•

Cleveland 949•

IA

Iowa City 960•

NE

Omaha 955•

IL

IN

OH

PA

918, 9

951•

948• Ph
MD   • NJ
•Baltimore

KS

MO

•962-963
•950

WV

965•

DE

KY

VA

969•

967•

OK

•968

TN

NC

966•

AR

977• Dallas 979
Fort Worth 978•

MS

973-975•

•970
Atlanta
971-972•

SC

GA

AL

TX

LA

Houston 976•

•980

New Orleans•

FL

981-982•

•983

•Miami 984

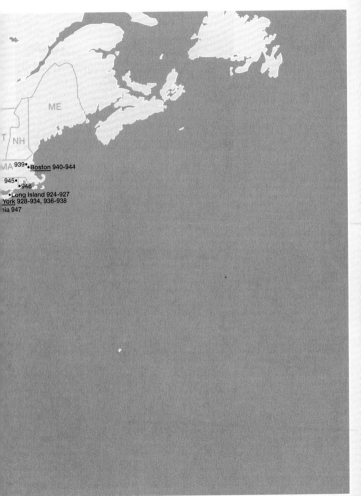

ME

T NH

MA 939• •Boston 940-944

945• •946
•Long Island 924-927
York 928-934, 936-938
nia 947

Robert Irwin/Open Office

DIA Center for the Arts
3 Beekman Street, Beacon,
NY 12508
Tel +1 845 440 0100

918 □ CUL 2003

Three buildings and a train
shed are joined into a single
structure, transforming a 1920s
printing plant in upstate New
York into a striking art gallery.
Approach is through a car park
planted with fruit trees into a
new sculpted pavilion. Excellent
lighting enters through factory
window skylights.

Steven Holl Architects

Y House
Catskill Mountains, NY

919 ■ RES 1999

In a remote mountain area, the
Y House climbs its hill site, its
red-iron-oxide and red-stained
cedar form splitting into two
arms culminating in deep south-
facing balconies. The Y shape
draws light into the heart of the
house and creates an unlikely
interior dynamic. Interlocking
grids characterize the glazed
facades.

Archi-tectonics

Gipsy Trail Residence
Gipsy Trail, NY

920 ■ RES 2003

The bipartite structure of the
Gipsy Trail Residence is clearly
visible, with a steel, wood and
glass box perched above a
base of stone collected on the
site. A generative core,
containing domestic services
and a music system, channels
circulation and is distorted to
create organic winding interior
shapes.

North America

Antoine Predock Architect

Tang Teaching Museum and Art Gallery
815 North Broadway, Saratoga Springs, NY 12866
Tel +1 518 580 8080

921 ☐ CUL 2000

This modest-sized building placed against a tight semi-circle of pine trees at Skidmore College serves as both gallery and classroom. Three wings interact in a central atrium, while stone ramps emanate from the earth and culminate in a single ivory tower.

Simon Ungers with Matthias Altwicker

Cube House
61 Makarainen Road, Ithaca, NY 14850
Tel +1 607 256 8651

922 ✏ RES 2000

The Cube House, set in a field in upstate New York, reduces the elements of 'home' to essentials; devoid of ornament, it is a statement of principle. A studio takes up the ground floor with living quarters above. Artfully composed facades belie its rationalist bent.

Smith-Miller + Hawkinson

Corning Museum of Glass
One Museum Way, Corning, NY 14830
Tel +1 607 937 5371

923 ☐ CUL 1999

This project involved refurbishing a glass museum, renovating a glass-blowing factory and designing a new entrance pavilion to connect the two. Different grades of glass are used to create varying levels of depth and transparency in a three-dimensional interlocking set of planes.

Richard Meier & Partners

Federal Building and United States Courthouse
170 Federal Plaza, Central Islip, NY 11722
Tel +1 631 853 6321

924 ◻ ✎ GOV 2000

This New York government building dominates its coastal landscape. The rectangular main volume has a curtain wall with *brise-soleil* and balconies, arranged with a rhythmic delicacy that balances the hefty sculptural form of the conical drum enclosing the entrance.

Tod Williams Billie Tsien Architects

Rifkind Residence
Long Island, NY

925 ◼ RES 1998

Surrounded by mature pines beside a pond, this quiet weekend retreat is on one level, apart from a reading loft and balcony. Its four volumes include communal living spaces, master bedroom suite and guest wing, all connected by glass passageways, and storage shed.

Gluckman Mayner Architects

Matchbox House
4630 Orchard Street, Orient, NY 11957

926 ◻ RES 2001

A weekend beach house designed to maximize views at the water's edge on Long Island. Spread over three floors, the interior is fully integrated with the outdoors; living areas open onto decks, encouraging the sea breeze into the house. The triple-height section contains vertical circulation.

Rafael Viñoly

Piano House
South Hampton, NY

927 ■ RES 2000

This summer and weekend residence is a piano rehearsal studio and intimate recital hall. The steel structure, finished in cedar outside and maple inside, is in a clearing surrounded by dense vegetation. An inverted roof composed of three planes sloping from front and side walls enhances the interior acoustics.

New York 928-934, 936-938

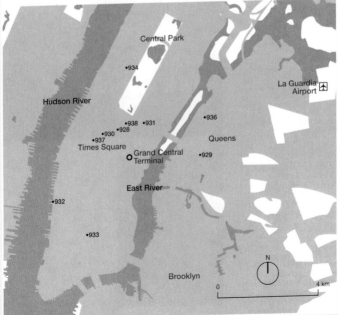

Atelier Raimund Abraham

Austrian Cultural Forum
11 East 52nd Street, New York,
NY 10022
Tel +1 212 319 5300

928 ▮ ✏ CUL 2000

A slim 24-storey tower sits on a
7.5 metre wide Manhattan plot,
its upper levels stepping back
to satisfy street-level daylight
zoning requirements. A vertical
window slit and a solid crown
with horizontal cut-outs give a
robotic quality to the top of the
building.

Michael Maltzan Architecture

MoMA QNS
33rd Street, Long Island City,
Queens, NY
Tel +1 212 708 9400

929 ☐ CUL 2002

MoMA QNS was the temporary
home of the Museum of Modern
Art in New York until the main
building, in Manhatten, re-
opened in November 2004. The
painted equipment boxes on
the roof top declared its identity
to passing trains, with the
letters disappearing as the train
travelled by.

Arquitectonica

Westin Hotel, Times Square
270 West 43rd Street at 8th
Avenue, Times Square, New
York, NY 10036
Tel +1 212 201 2700

930 ☐ TOU 2002

On Eighth Avenue at Times
Square, the striking 863-room
Westin Hotel sits on top of E
Walk, a retail podium. A
recessed curve in the south
facade incorporates a slit of
moving light that appears to
split the building in two and
transforms a rectangular tower.

North America

Christian de Portzamparc

LVMH Tower
17–21 East, 57th Street, New
York, NY 10022
Tel +1 212 758 8877

931 □ COM 1999

The New York headquarters of
the luxury goods group LVMH
(Louis Vuitton-Möet Hennessy)
accords with the setback
requirements for all Manhattan
buildings; two sections touch
the setback line asymmetrically.
A three-storey glass cube on
top of the building is used for
fashion shows.

Richard Meier & Partners

Perry Street Apartments
173/176 Perry Street, New York,
NY 10014

932 ▮ RES 2002

The minimalist transparent
forms of two residential towers
in Greenwich Village overlooking
the Hudson River make a
striking addition to the skyline.
Flat glass facades to the street
are interrupted by blocks of
corner balconies. Floor-to-
ceiling windows afford
panoramic views of Manhattan.

Aldo Rossi Studio di
Architettura

Scholastic Building
557 Broadway, Soho, New York,
NY 10012
Tel +1 212 343 6100

933 ▮ ✐ COM 2001

The rear of this headquarters for
publishing company Scholastic
responds to surrounding cast-
iron warehouses with industrial
arches; the Broadway elevation
exhibits the monumentality of
classical organization. Primary
red steel lintels support bright
white columns.

Polshek Partnership

Rose Center for Earth and Space
Central Park West at 79th
Street, New York, NY 10024
Tel +1 212 769 5000

934 ☐ CUL 2000

A spherical planetarium floating
within a glazed cube has turned
the American Museum of
Natural History into a new night
time landmark. The Hayden
Planetarium is the most
powerful virtual-reality simulator
in the world. Tubular steel wall
trusses support spider fittings.

Rafael Viñoly

**Columbia University
International Research
Institute for Climate
Prediction**
61 Route 9W, Palisades,
NY 10964
Tel +1 212 854 4920

935 ☐ EDU 1999

Composed of two long,
overlapping curved wings, this
single-storey building sits on
the edge of a steep gorge. The
point of overlap marks the
entrance and space for formal
and informal interaction.

Greg Lynn Form

Korean Presbyterian Church
43–23, 37th Avenue, Long
Island City, NY 11101
Tel +1 718 706 0100

936 ☐ REL 1999

This project converted and
extended the 1930s
Knickerbocker Laundry factory
into a multi-function church and
community centre for a primarily
Korean-American congregation.
A new sanctuary located on the
factory roof is enclosed by a
monumental long-span roof;
telescopic shells allow in light.

North America

ARO: Architecture Research Office

US Armed Forces Recruiting Station
Times Square, New York, NY

937 ☐ GOV 1999

In the extraordinary location of a narrow traffic island in Times Square, the US Armed Forces Recruiting Station's east and west facades display large illuminated American flags. Surrounding skyscrapers dwarf the tiny building, which houses four desks and a bathroom.

Tod Williams Billie Tsien Architects

American Folk Art Museum
45 West 53rd Street, New York, NY 10019
Tel +1 212 265 1040

938 ☐ CUL 2001

Sculptural facades on the east and west elevations of this eight-storey museum announce its independence from its busy Manhattan context. Natural light floods through a skylight into four upper floors of galleries; auditorium, library and archive are on lower floors.

Will Bruder Architects

Private House
MA

939 ■ RES 2000

Situated on granite ledges on the Atlantic coast, this extensive family home is radially organized in a series of interacting crescent shapes. Curving stone walls define the spaces. The outer arc is the main living pavilion with master bedroom, while the secondary crescent contains children's and guests' rooms.

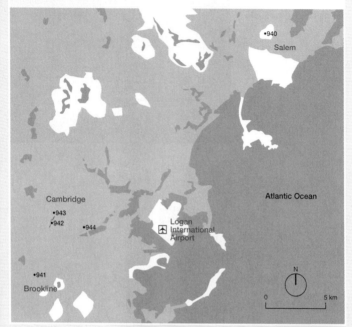

Moshe Safdie and Associates

Peabody Essex Museum
East India Square, Salem,
MA 01970
Tel +1 978 745 9500

940 ☐ CUL 2000

The complex project to rethink
America's oldest operating
museum unifies disparate
buildings, adds new gallery
spaces and brings coherence
to the whole. A curved, glazed
arcade forms the spine of the
new wing, and with a courtyard,
joins a row of house-like
galleries to existing buildings.

North America

Mack Scogin Merrill Elam
Architects

Private House
Brookline, MA

941 ■ RES 1999

A family house in a quiet suburb
presents contrasting facades:
the entry courtyard has a formal
face with undulating curves
flanked by symmetrical
pavilions, while the rear is open-
plan, with the office cantilevered
out over the gardens. The
design is anchored around a
two-storey unifying central wall.

Machado and Silvetti
Associates

**Honan-Allston Branch of the
Boston Public Library**
300 North Harvard Street,
Allston, MA 02134
Tel +1 617 787 7313

942 ☐ CUL 2001

This library in a one-storey
configuration is divided into
three parallel bands. The front
zone contains the book stacks.
Gardens and glass reading
pavilions alternate in the central
void, with community functions
at the back.

Machado and Silvetti
Associates

**Harvard University, One
Western Avenue**
1 Western Avenue, Harvard
University, Allston, MA 02163

943 ■ EDU 2003

Containing graduate
apartments, One Western
Avenue sits next to the Charles
River, creating a gateway to the
Harvard Business School.
Materials contrasting in colour,
texture and pattern soften the
unrelenting volumes.

Steven Holl Architects

Simmons Hall, Massachusetts Institute of Technology
229–43 Vassar Street,
Cambridge, MA 02139
Tel +1 617 452 2415

944 ◼ ✆ EDU 2002

This ten-storey dormitory resembles a slice of the city within MiT, with light and movement circulating horizontally and vertically. Five large-scale openings provide entrances and outdoor activity terraces. Wide interior corridors are more street than hallway.

Polshek Partnership

Mashantucket Pequot Museum and Research Centre
110 Pequot Trail, Mashantucket, CT 06338
Tel +1 800 411 9671

945 ☐ CUL 1998

While documenting the history of the Pequot Indians, this building portrays an advanced society. The limestone-clad observation tower surveys the wooded site and the curvilinear glass atrium balances the low-slung body of the centre.

TEN Arquitectos

Princeton Parking Structure
Princeton University, Princeton, NJ 08544
Tel +1 609 258 6115

946 ☐ EDU 2000

An aesthetically contentious multi-storey car park demanded modification in this historically sensitive part of the Princeton campus. The pre-cast concrete structure was tinted black and a wrapping veil of mesh hung over it. Embedded steel brackets hold the stainless-steel chain-mail to the wall.

North America

Rafael Viñoly

Kimmel Center for the Performing Arts
123 South Broad Street,
Philadelphia, PA 19109
Tel +1 215 772 2446

947 ☐ CUL 2001

A shimmering glazed barrel-vaulted roof balanced on steel columns is the new home for the Philadelphia Orchestra. An atrium connects two sculpted steel-framed auditoriums. One is clad inside with mahogany, the other mixes black granite with gold corrugated steel.

Wesley Wei Architects

Media House
Media, PA

948 ■ RES 2001

A sensitive addition to an eighteenth-century farmhouse in a Pennsylvanian forest setting provides a house to display the client's extensive art collection. A timber volume contains the kitchen, while the main living areas present a solid facade with a band of windows. In contrast, the rear elevation is generously glazed.

Gehry Partners

Peter B Lewis Building, Case Western Reserve University
10900 Euclid Avenue,
Cleveland, OH 44106
Tel +1 216 368 2030

949 ◐ ✎ EDU 2000

Accommodating administrative and educational facilities for a management school, the red-brick volumes of this building are apparently engulfed by steel towers erupting from the surface. Ground-floor facilities are arranged around a canyon-like atrium with curving bridges.

Zaha Hadid

**Rosenthal Center for
Contemporary Arts**
44 East 6th Street, Cincinnati,
OH 45202
Tel +1 513 345 8400

950 ☐ CUL 2003

On a corner site in Cincinnati,
this arts centre hosts temporary
exhibitions and performances.
The circulation system curves
slowly upwards as it enters the
building, rising up to become
the back wall. Gallery spaces
appear on the outside as black
and white overlapping volumes.

Arata Isozaki & Associates

**Center of Science and
Industry (COSI)**
333 West Broad Street,
Columbus, OH 43215
Tel +1 888 819 2674

951 ☐ CUL 1999

This comparatively low-rise
facility features two vast curving
wings clad in pre-cast concrete
panels anchored in a central
entrance cylinder. Stainless-
steel joints animate the facade
in the sun. Inside, interactive
themed Learning Worlds are
arranged along a central spine.

Salmela Architect

Emerson Sauna
5524 White Pine Drive, Duluth,
MN 55803
Tel +1 218 721 4922

952 ✿ RES 2002

Suggesting a child's abandoned
building blocks, this sauna sits
quietly within a grove of trees.
A brick box punctured by
square openings and a chimney
contains sauna and changing
rooms; a large semi-circular wall
supports a steeply pitched roof
containing a relaxing area. The
triangular area holds stairs.

Vincent James Associates

Rowing Club
Minneapolis, Minnesota,
MN 55458

953 ■ SPO 1999

The roof of this elegant
boathouse on the banks of the
Mississippi tips up at diagonally
opposite corners representing
the full arc of an oar moving
through water. Clerestory
windows separate the dynamic
roof from its static base, a barn-
like box faced in timber strips
with copper-clad sliding doors.

Antoine Predock Architect

**University of Minnesota
Gateway Center**
200 Oak Street SE,
Minneapolis, MN 55455
Tel +1 612 624 7570

954 ☐ EDU 2000

Architectural references to the
Minnesota landscape, evoking
a rock face or farmstead, invite
the visitor into this gateway
centre, which combines a
ceremonial gathering place and
office block. The Memorial Hall
is an irregular polyhedron of
granite and glass planes.

Randy Brown Architects

120 Blondo Building
1925 N 120th Street, Omaha,
NE 68154
Tel +1 402 551 7097

955 ☐ COM 2000

Deliberately adopting geometric
collisions and unexpected
asymmetries as a challenge to
the bland suburban office, this
project asks people to look
again at their built environment.
Construction is of familiar
industrial materials. A metal-
clad first-floor structure housing
a library doubles as a canopy.

Steven Holl Architects

Cranbrook Institute of Science
39221 Woodward Avenue,
Bloomfield Hills, MI 48303
Tel +1 248 645 3200

956 ▯ ✎ EDU 1998

An uneven U-shaped extension is linked to the existing science museum via a sloping science garden with outdoor exhibits. A new entrance tower includes a south-facing wall made of a complex system of types of glass used to explain light phenomena.

Tod Williams Billie Tsien Architects

Williams Natatorium, Cranbrook Educational Community
Williams Natatorium, Bloomfield Hills, MI 48303
Tel +1 248 645 3724

957 ▯ ✎ SPO 2001

Integrated with the rich fabric of the existing Cranbrook campus, the new indoor swimming pool is approached via a ramp. Blue-green ceramic tiles line the pool, while vertical mahogany panels in the walls open up the interior.

Rafael Moneo

Studio Addition for Cranbrook Academy of Fine Arts
39221 Woodward Avenue,
Bloomfield Hills, MI 48303
Tel +1 248 645 3300

958 ▯ EDU 2001

This new building for ceramics, fibre and metalworking stands next to the iconic Saarinen Art Museum. Four volumes include exhibition areas, student studios, artists-in-residence spaces and workshops. Warm red brick and glass walls house the studio section.

North America

Santiago Calatrava

Milwaukee Art Museum addition
700 N Art Museum Drive,
Milwaukee, WI 53202
Tel +1 414 224 3220

959 □ CUL 2001

Three elements make up this project: a low-slung gallery extending southward from an existing Saarinen building, a cable-stayed pedestrian bridge linking the museum to the city of Milwaukee, and the soaring *brise-soleil* made up of 72 paired steel fins.

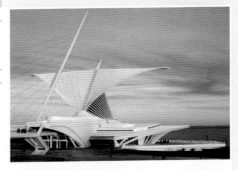

Gwathmey Siegel & Associates Architects

Levitt Center for University Advancement, University of Iowa
1 West Park Road, Iowa City,
IA 52244
Tel +1 319 335 3305

960 ✏ EDU 1998

Visible from much of Iowa city, the limestone-clad Levitt Center articulates the functions within the building. A curvaceous stair within the five-storey glazed rotunda leads to the public spaces on the top floor.

Garofalo Architects

Markow House
300 North Elm Street, Prospect Heights, Chicago, IL 60070

961 ❚ RES 2002

A provocative renovation of an existing 1960s split-level house in suburban Chicago involves three new elements providing 185 square metres of additional space. A tubular structure is perpendicular to two original gables, and an organic form cantilevers out over the building line.

USA East

Carlos Jimenez Studio

Cummins Child Development Center
650 Pleasant Grove Street,
Columbus, IN 47201
Tel +1 812 378 5833

962 ✐ EDU 2001

A centre providing childcare facilities for employees of the Cummins Engine Company, modular classrooms are placed around a central playground bordered by a continuous single-loaded corridor. This arrangement fosters a sense of community.

Carlos Jimenez Studio

Irwin Mortgage Corporate Headquarters
10500 Kincaid Drive, Fishers,
IN 46038
Tel +1 317 537 3900

963 ✐ COM 2003

An uninterrupted flow of natural light permeates each floor of this four-storey office building beside an interstate freeway. The offset fenestration pattern is interrupted only by a triple-height portal entrance. Inside, textures and colours animate the neutral open-plan volumes.

Tod Williams Billie Tsien Architects

Mattin Arts Center, Johns Hopkins University
3400 North Charles Street,
Baltimore, MD 21218
Tel +1 410 516 8064

964 ☐ EDU 2001

This modernist arts centre is composed of one short and two long sides around a grassy piazza. Ramps and decked areas inside and out encourage student interaction. The sturdy red-brick bases contrast with the sandblasted glass panels.

North America

Robert AM Stern Architects

Robert C Byrd United States Courthouse and Federal Building
110 North Heber Street,
Beckley, WV 25801
Tel +1 304 253 1519

965 ☐ GOV 1999

Beckley's new courthouse, representing civic pride and the dignity of law, is constructed from angled brick, with pre-cast concrete blocks. A simple brick portico leads to the civic lobby. Inside are modern architectural features and classical murals.

Marlon Blackwell Architect

Moore Honey House
Little Terrapin Mountain,
Cashiers, NC 28717
Tel +1 479 973 9121

966 ⌁ COM 1998

An addition to an existing house on a smallholding on Little Terrapin Mountain, the Honey House is a combined carport and honey store. A butterfly roof shelters a timber box containing workbench, storage and parking space. A grid-like display wall made from glazed steel plates holds honey jars.

Mario Bellini Associati

Natuzzi America Headquarters
2200 South Main Street, High Point, NC 27260
Tel +1 336 841 8599

967 ☐ COM 1998

This new headquarters on a triangular urban site features a large burnished-copper curved wall with a large porthole window like the prow of a ship. Inside, a full-height gallery runs the length of the building and is constructed from a quadruple order of pillars and beams.

Marlon Blackwell Architect

Tower House
Old Missouri Road, Fayetteville,
AR 72702
Tel +1 479 973 9121

968 ✆ RES 2000

A holiday retreat with views over the tree canopy to the Ozark Mountains recreates childhood treehouse experiences. An open-air sequence rotates up the tower arriving at the foyer/kitchen level. Above is the sleeping/living level, from where a stair leads to the skycourt with its primary view of the sky.

Maya Lin Studio

Langston Hughes Library
1000 Alex Haley Lane, Clinton,
TN 38152
Tel +1 865 457 6466

969 ✆ CUL 1999

An abandoned barn has become a library for African-American studies, retaining the existing structure of a shed perched on log cribs. Now with frosted glass walls and a slate floor, the cribs accommodate the entry and shop. A skylight and window bring light into the reading room.

Mack Scogin Merrill Elam Architects

Mountain Tree House
Dillard, GA

970 ■ RES 2001

This tiny building comprises garage, bedroom and bathroom. The steel-and-glass bedroom, with contrasting solid rear wall and roof, cantilevers over the garden. A slate-covered terrace stretching away from the house into the forest has slots cut in it for bamboo to grow through.

North America

Mack Scogin Merrill Elam
Architects

64 Wakefield
64 Wakefield, Atlanta,
GA 30309

971 ▮▮ RES 1998

The rebuilding and insertion of a
lap pool into an existing house
was constrained by the
narrowness of this site. The
second-floor pool, constructed
of poured-in-place concrete, is
shielded from the street by a
translucent glass wall but is
open to the sky.

Mack Scogin Merrill Elam
Architects

Lee B Philmon Branch Library
414 Valley Hill Road, Riverdale,
GA 30270
Tel +1 770 472 8100

972 ☐ CUL 1998

On a triangular site within
sprawling suburbs, the library
has thin walls and flat facades
terminating in a conical meeting
room to the south. The pennant
shapes of the giant windows are
echoed in the interior roof
trusses, which are installed with
alternating slopes.

Rural Studio

**Mason's Bend Community
Center**
Mason's Bend, Hale County, AL

973 ☐ PUB 2000

Students from Auburn
University designed this open-
air community centre on an
unpaved road lined with
shanties, using found, recycled
and donated materials.
Rammed-earth walls taper to a
point at one end of the pavilion,
which serves as chapel,
meeting hall and playground.

Rural Studio

Antioch Baptist Church
Perry County, AL

974 □ REL 2002

Community engagement and
inventive recycling have
produced this small Baptist
church in one of the poorest
areas of the USA. Materials
salvaged from the previous
building are reused, including
corrugated metal and wooden
panelling. Two interlocking
wrapping elements make up
the body of the church.

Rural Studio

Lucy's House
Mason's Bend, Hale County, AL

975 ■ RES 2002

Enlivening the rural vernacular
of the Deep South with its
simple sheds and trailers,
students from Rural Studio
stacked 72,000 donated carpet
tiles into a colourful, striated
enclosure. Steel rods within the
carpet walls support the pitched
overhanging roof. The faceted
tower contains dining room,
tornado shelter and bedroom.

Rafael Moneo

Museum of Fine Arts
1001 Bissonnet Street, Houston,
TX 77005
Tel +1 713 639 7300

976 □ CUL 2000

This four-storey limestone
addition fills its available site,
more than doubling the
exhibition space of the existing
museum. The facade is
fragmented by the skylights on
the roof which reflect the
arrangement of galleries inside,
including the first-floor
sculpture court.

North America

Hardy Holzman Pfeiffer
Associates

**Lucille 'Lupe' Murchison
Performing Arts Center**
1200 North Texas Boulevard,
Denton, TX 6203
Tel +1 940 369 7802

977 ☐ CUL 1999

This performing arts centre,
with its distinctively shaped
zinc-clad roof on a rusticated
stone base, acts as gateway to
the University of North Texas.
The glazed and tiled lobby is a
curved enclosure leading to the
concert hall and lyric theatre.

Tadao Ando Architect &
Associates

**Modern Art Museum of Fort
Worth**
3200 Darnell Street, Fort Worth,
TX 76107
Tel +1 817 738 9215

978 ☐ CUL 2002

Five rectangular volumes in a
row, surrounded by reflective
water, make up this new
museum. Cantilevered concrete
roofs supported on Y-shaped
columns protect the buildings
from sunlight. Each block is a
concrete box within a glass box.

Renzo Piano Building Workshop

Nasher Sculpture Center
2001 Flora Street, Dallas,
TX 75201
Tel +1 214 242 5100

979 ☐ CUL 2003

Five connected two-storey
pavilions defined by parallel
stone walls, linked to the
gardens through glazed
facades, take up little of this
extensive green Dallas oasis.
Glass roofs screened against
direct sunlight provide perfect
viewing conditions for the
sculpture collection.

Studio Atkinson

Zachary House
Zachary, AL
Tel +1 650 321 6118

980 ✆ RES 1999

Like the Louisiana 'dog trot' house, this building consists of two simple structures joined by a roof, with a freestanding hearth and chimney. Roof and wall materials are merged and external openings suppressed. The house sits in a grove of pecan trees and takes maximum advantage of the prevailing breezes.

Toshiko Mori Architect

House of the Gulf of Mexico
Casey Key, FL

981 ■ RES 1999

This guesthouse located on a sandbar east of the Gulf of Mexico is raised on *piloti* 5 metres above sea level to withstand storm surges, flooding and hurricanes. Different types of glass protect against heat and glare. The modernist T-shaped design features protective roof planes and coloured concrete masonry.

Toshiko Mori Architect

Compound on the Gulf of Mexico
Casey Key, FL

982 ■ RES 2002

The main house in this residential compound on a narrow strip of land sits on tall piers within a tropical garden. Fully glazed along the east and west, the house is divided through the centre by cores of utility spaces. Double-height rooms take advantage of views and breezes.

North America

Richard Meier & Partners

Neugebauer House
Naples, FL

983 ■ RES 1998

Looking across Doubloon Bay,
this pavilion is a substantial
family house reached via a
winding avenue of palm trees.
Its linear organization consists
of four parallel layers, stacked
from front to back. The
asymmetrical butterfly roof
creates a high wall of glazing to
all living areas, including
bedrooms.

Arquitectonica

**American Airlines Miami
Arena**
601 Biscayne Boulevard, Miami,
FL 33132
Tel +1 786 777 3865

984 □ SPO 1999

This elliptical multipurpose
arena has a commanding
presence on Miami's old
harbour site, its white cladding
echoing the yachts. Seating can
be configured to suit the scale
of the event. Illumination and
bright signage turn the arena
into a beacon at night.

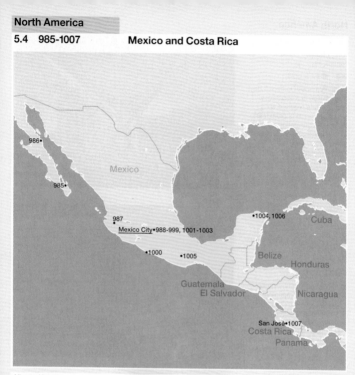

Mexico

986•

985•

987
•

Mexico City•988-999, 1001-1003

•1000   •1005

•1004, 1006   Cuba

Belize

Honduras

Guatemala
El Salvador   Nicaragua

San José•1007

Costa Rica
Panama

Alberto Kalach

Augen Opticos
Ensenada 3ra #1282, 22800
Ensenada, Baja California
Tel +52 646 1758 0319

985 ▮ ✎ COM 2001

The project adds a research
tower, offices and workshop
space to an existing production
complex and provides a new
landmark. Clad in a series of
scale-like steel panels that allow
slits of natural light into the
work spaces, the research
tower is designed to withstand
seismic movement.

North America

Steven Harris Architects

Weiss House
Cabo San Lucas, Baja
California

986 ■ RES 2002

Built into a rocky headland, this
is the southernmost private
house on the Baja California
peninsula. The approach is
down steps carved out of rock
and through an entrance
pavilion. Wings to the sides of
an internal courtyard house
living spaces and a pool
cantilevers along the cliff edge.

TEN Arquitectos

**Sports Facilities Area,
Educare School**
Madero 5850, Jocotán,
Zapopan, Jalisco
Tel +52 36 27 36 66

987 □ EDU 2001

This sports complex contains
gymnasium, outdoor pool,
exercise rooms and changing
facilities in simple volumes that
exploit natural light. The lower
facade consists of metal louvres
that regulate ventilation, with
sandblasted glass above. The
aerobics block is a glass box.

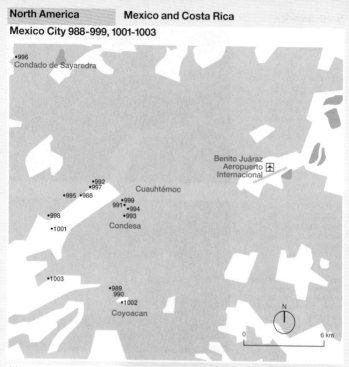

•996
Condado de Sayaredra

Benito Juáraz
Aeropuerto ✈
Internacional

•992
•997
Cuauhtémoc
•995 •988
991• •999
•994
•993
•998
Condesa
•1001

•1003

•989
990
•1002
Coyoacan

N

0   6 km

Adriana Monroy Noriega

Pedernal House
Pedernal 240, Jardines del
Pedregal, 01900 Mexico City

988 ☐ RES 2000

Functionality and purity of form
characterize this renovation of a
1955 house. The rectilinear style
of the interior facade is softened
by use of varied materials and
by merging interior spaces with
the landscape. Differently
coloured wood and stone walls
give a sumptuous feel to the
minimal interior.

Migdal Arquitectos

Las Flores Corporation
Boulevard Adolfo López
Mateos 2009, Los Alpes, 01010
Mexico City

989 ▯▮ COM 2002

On an awkward site beside a
busy street in Mexico City, this
long rectangular office building
is supported 10 metres above
ground level by a concrete
plinth. Blue tonal figures on the
front elevation disguise a
complex glazing system, while
a dramatic white wing protects
the roof terrace.

Mario Schjetnan and José Luis
Pérez

Siglum Office Tower
Avenida Insurgentes Sur 1898,
Florida, 01030 Mexico City
Tel +52 5 555 312 48

990 ▯▮ ✎ COM 2001

A symbol of prosperity, the
landmark Siglum Office Tower
is built of overhanging slabs
arranged in concentric rings set
back from the edge. The lobby,
with a curved glass facade and
aluminium-clad concrete
columns, is contained in a
double-height pediment.

TEN Arquitectos

**Parque España Apartment
Building**
Parque España 47, Condesa,
06140 Mexico City

991 ▯▮ RES 2001

Clad in translucent plastic
panels, this striking building
contains five apartments and a
ground-floor art gallery. Interior
space is flexible: apartments
can be open or divided. A
laminate stairway zigzags up
the sealed plane of a plastic
panel on the east facade.

Mexico and Costa Rica

TEN Arquitectos

Hotel Habita
Avenida Presidente Masaryk
201, Polanco, 11560 Mexico City
Tel +52 55 5 282 3100

992 ☐ TOU 2000

A renovation of a five-storey
1950s apartment building, the
Hotel Habita is on a busy street.
Its translucent glass skin is
interrupted by horizontal bands
of transparent glass. Sports and
restaurant facilities are at the
top of the hotel, floating on
projecting platforms.

TEN Arquitectos

Amsterdam Residential Building
Amsterdam 67, Condesa,
06140 Mexico City

993 ▮ RES 2001

Only six storeys high, this
apartment block takes account
of its immediate environment,
addressing its corner site with
a curved facade. On one side,
balconies are screened against
traffic by translucent panels.
The apartments enjoy views of
nearby Parque Mexico.

Central de Arquitectura

Amsterdam-Sonora Apartment Building
Sonora 144, Condesa,
06100 Mexico City
Tel +52 55 3640 1800

994 ☐ RES 2002

This corner apartment building
presents a gently curving glass
box suspended over the
pavement. A concrete volume
fragments the lateral facade
and confers weight on the
block. 26 residential units are
arranged over six floors with
two parking levels.

Teodoro González de Léon
Arquitecto

Arcos Bosques Corporation
Paseo de los Tamarindos
400-B, 05120 Mexico City
Tel +52 55 52 86 54 60

995 ✆ COM 2003

Situated on the western side of
Mexico City and of unparalleled
scale, this office and retail
complex is an urban precinct,
visually isolated from its
surroundings. Three low-volume
buildings contrast with the
monolithic arch, positioned on
an inclined plane.

Adriá+Broid+Rojkind

F2 House
Rio Lancaster 12, Condado de
Sayavedra, 52938 Estado de
Mexico

996 ▮ RES 2001

This L-shaped house sits on
a triangular plan within a
development of conventional
houses, orientated away from
its neighbours. The solids and
voids interact on all three levels
with the landscape. Materials
are restricted to exposed
concrete, steel columns and
aluminium and glass partitions.

LEGORRETA + LEGORRETA

House of the Fifteen Patios
Mexico City

997 ▪ RES 1998

An oasis of domestic calm
within the chaos of Mexico City,
this house steps around its site
in a series of semi-articulated
pavilions separated by
courtyards and layered planes
of water that make enough
noise to drown out the city.
From the street, the house
reveals nothing of its openness
within.

LEGORRETA + LEGORRETA

Los Patios 1 Residential Complex
Mexico City

998 ■ RES 1998

This residential block addresses the need in Mexico City for affordable, quality housing. Standard components are used to create high-ceilinged spaces lit with natural light. Each apartment has a private patio and looks out onto a pool. The simple shapes and hot sun complement the bright colours.

Sanchez & Higuera

Veracruz Apartment Building I–IV
Avenida Veracruz 79, 81, 83, 85, Condesa, 06140 Mexico City

999 ▯ RES 2001

These apartment buildings redefine the local urban fabric. One building takes the form of a curved sheet; a series of openings in the concrete form half-covered balconies. In the second, individual apartments are articulated on the facade.

LCM Laboratory/Fernando Romero

Ixtapa House
Ixtapa, Guerrero

1000 ■ RES 2002

In a private resort on the Pacific coast, Ixtapa House epitomizes the dream of escape. The upper floor houses bedrooms and bathrooms. The downstairs public space is framed at the rear by the wall enclosing the private areas, but is otherwise uncontained, giving directly on to the terrace and pool.

North America

Billy Springall & Miguel Angel Lira

Center for Economic Investigation and Instruction
Carretera México-Toluca 3655,
01210 Mexico City
Tel +52 55 5727 9801

1001 ☐ EDU 1998

A box-like building on a sloping site, the classroom building for the Economic Investigation Center stands near the middle of the campus. A light aerodynamic roof appears to hover above the top-floor terrace and auditorium.

Adriá+Broid+Rojkind

Videoteca Nazionale Educativa
Canal de Coyoacan 2040,
04810 Mexico City
Tel +52 555 6 796 603

1002 ☐ EDU 2000

This new complex housing the national educational video centre incorporates a stripped-down existing building. A glass-and-steel volume placed at right-angles to the old forms the new facade. Interior open mesh walls allow the centre to be visible from the outside.

LCM Laboratory

Anexo D
Mexico City

1003 ■ RES 2001

Annexed to an original 1950s modernist post-and-beam house, this snail-shaped space bursts into the garden. The skin folds back on itself so that a stepped winding ramp can climb inside. The curve of the facade is mainly blind, with small light apertures accentuating the cave-like nature of the interior.

Augusto Quijano Arquitectos

Casa de Huéspedes
Mérida, Yucatán

1004 ■ RES 1998

The strongly horizontal design of this guesthouse adjacent to both the main house and pool is dominated by roof and floor planes. Two volumes are under a single roof. One, shown here, housing the bedrooms and a bathroom pod, is isolated from the public area. The other houses social spaces.

Torres + Velázquez

Reforma House
306A Reforma, Oaxaca, 68000 Oaxaca

1005 ◨ RES 2001

This project in the heart of Oaxaca remodels the interior of an old house, retaining the original walls. Materials used include adobe and wood, alongside steel and glass. Water recurs through the space as a motif or for swimming. Here a sunscreen on pulleys is suspended over a pool.

Augusto Quijano Arquitectos

Bacsa Corporation
Calle 60 Diagonal 496, Mérida, 97300 Yucatán
Tel +52 999 9 300 400

1006 □ COM 1999

On an industrial estate to the north of Mérida, this two-storey complex for a construction and engineering company houses offices in an L-shaped block and services and storeroom in a larger, parallel structure. A curved wall and a freestanding wall bisecting a pool transform it into a sculptural statement.

North America

Guillermo Garita and
Athanasios Haritos

Achio House
200 mts North, 200 mts West,
lot 34, Rio de Oro, San José

1007 ◼ RES 1998

Two volumes suspended at
an angle to each other and
connected by a bridge contain
the programme for this house.
With the pool as central focus,
the house is a three-
dimensional composition of
coloured cubic forms. A high
boundary wall ensures privacy.

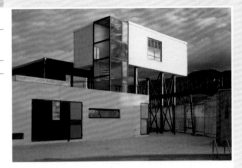

1008
•1009-1011
Bogotá•1012-1013
1015
1014•

Colombia

1016•
•Quito1017
Ecuador

Perú

Lima•1018-1020
•1021-1022

Bolivia

Brazil

Salvador•1025

•La Paz
•1023

•Brasilia

•1024

Grupo de Arquitectos

Court House
Carrera 47, Calle 62, Rionegro
Tel +57 4 562 5593

1008 ▮ ✏ GOV 2000

In Antioquía, Columbia's
second largest region, this court
house expresses the Corbusian
ideal of 'justice that covers all'
in its monumentality and
dramatic winged roof. The
glazed public entrance
modulated by the concrete
structure expresses the idea of
judicial transparency.

Uribe de Bedout Arquitectos

Interactive Museum
Carrera 57, 42–139, Medellín
Tel +57 4 380 6956

1009 ☐ CUL 20000

Part of the urban regeneration package for Medellín, the museum explores four areas of interactivity: water, energy, telecommunications and the internet. A timber and glass portal reached via a raised landscaped plaza announces the entrance. Interior exhibition spaces are finished in timber.

Uribe de Bedout Arquitectos

Cremation Unit and Ashes Temple
Calle 2 Sur, 65–263, Medellín
Tel +57 4 285 3300

1010 ☐ REL 1998

Two elements make up this monolithic slab structure in limestone and granite in Campos de Paz cemetery. The narrower end of the wedge is the Cremation Unit, with a monumental stairway leading to a roof terrace. The Ashes Temple is accessed from here.

Grupo de Arquitectos

School of Architecture and Design
Circular Primera No. 70–01, Avenida Bolivariana, Medellín
Tel +57 4 415 9070

1011 ☐ EDU 1999

Completing a triangle of buildings at the University of Pontificia, one side of the new school faces a busy avenue; a high brick wall is interrupted by the white volume of classroom and studio. Brick spaces at either end contain auditorium and exhibition spaces.

Daniel Bonilla Arquitectos

Los Nogales School Chapel
Calle 202 #58-50, Bogotá
Tel +57 1 676 1128

1012 ✆ REL 2002

The chapel of Los Nogales School in Bogotá is an abstract prism with smaller volumes added and subtracted, and a freestanding slender bell-tower. Timber doors on the northwest wall can swing open, transforming the paved terrace into a congregational space. Inside, a shaft of light falls on the raised altar.

Daniel Bonilla Arquitectos

Los Nogales Academic Resource Centre
Calle 202 #58-50, Bogotá
Tel +57 1 676 0123

1013 ✆ EDU 1999

Connecting previously isolated buildings, this new elbow-shaped resource centre creates open and enclosed outdoor spaces. Glazing characterizes the lower floor, with cantilevered window boxes above. Inside, the library forms the functional core, with bridges, stairs and mezzanine levels.

Giancarlo Mazzanti

Red Cross Headquarters
Avenida Bolivar, Calle 23 Norte, Armenia, NO, Armenia-Quindio
Tel +57 7 674 93991

1014 ☐ PUB 2001

Part of the reconstruction plan for Armenia following the 1999 earthquake, the concrete exterior relates this building to its institutional neighbours, but belies its spacious interior. An internal ramp links the ground-floor blood bank and training rooms with first-floor consulting rooms.

South America

Juan Pablo Ortiz

Historic Archive
Calle 5TA 5–75, Bogotá,
Cundinamarca
Tel +57 1 381 3000 ext. 4113

1015 ☐ COM 1998

Within an area of urban renewal
in Bogotá, the Historic Archive
acts as a container for the city's
past. Highly restricted
documents are housed in a
coffer-like volume of pre-cast
concrete elements at the centre
of the building. Public areas are
expressed by the two-storey
opening in the main facade.

VERS

**Altamar at –1° latitude, 81°
longitude**
Avenida Favio Reyes,
Barbasquillo, Manta, Manabi

1016 ■ RES 2001

On a cliff-edge overlooking the
Pacific, this house responds to
a challenging site. The
fragmented design minimizes
the effects of likely seismic
movements. A high-tech fabric
skin stretched over the land
contains erosion and supports
a garden of native plants.

Wood & Zapata

Private House
Quito

1017 ■ RES 2002

Views of Cotopaxi Mountain,
an active volcano, dominate
the inclined site of this house,
a tangle of fluid, puzzle-like
fragments. Presenting a solid
curved facade to the street,
double-height battered glazing
opens up the rear elevations.
Shallow curves and tight angles
characterize the dynamic
interior arrangement.

Ruth Alvarado-Pflücker

Las Lomas Beach House
Playa Las Lomas del Mar, Km.
122, Cerro Azul, Cañete, Lima
Tel +511 477 1749

1018 ◼ ✎ RES 2001

This beach house in the popular resort of Las Lomas del Mar is open to the surrounding landscape of cliffs, rocks, sea and desert. A white planar volume over a stone base, the house is constructed in two sections joined by an open gallery which brings cool air inside.

Hans Hollein

Interbank Headquarters
Paseo de la Republica at
Avenida Javier Prado, Lima

1019 ◼ COM 2001

Set between two highways, the Interbank Headquarters comprises a sculptural high-rise element. The tower stands behind a dramatically curved screen of steel tubes and contains offices, auditorium and bank branch. The surface patterning of the stone blocks echoes the Inca heritage.

Cooper Graña Nicolini
Arquitectos

Colegio San Pedro
Calle Hurón 409, Rinconada del
Lago, La Molina
Tel +511 368 1010

1020 ▢ EDU 2001

The first phase of a project to accommodate 1,000 students at La Molina, a new desert settlement near Lima, caters for children. Classrooms are laid out diagonally in a staggered arrangement along the sloping ravine site and linked to public spaces by ramped walkways.

Barclay & Crousse Architecture

Casa Equis
Cañete

1021 ■ RES 2003

Perched precariously above the Pacific, this solid rectangular volume has a large entrance patio on the land side with access to upper-floor living areas. An external staircase follows the topography down to the lower bedroom level. Sliding doors extend compact living rooms on to the large terrace, with its dramatic ocean views.

Barclay & Crousse Architecture

M House
Cañete

1022 ■ RES 2001

An outer enclosure of simple walls gives this house next door to Casa Equis a fortress-like shell of privacy. Three volumes follow the slope of the ground: carport and entrance, secondary bedrooms and main living areas. Planes of colour articulate the spaces and refer to traditional Peruvian domestic patterns.

Jae Cha

Church
Urubo

1023 □ REL 2000

Simple circular structures made from pressure-treated timber and polycarbonate sheeting provide the village of Urubo with a combined community centre, school, market and church. Careful positioning of the polycarbonate sheets prevent glare and create a changing rhythmic pattern of light and shade during the day.

Maia Arquitectos Associados
with Jô Vasconcellos

Wanda Bambirra Academy
Avenida Uruguai 473, Sion,
30310-300, Belo Horizonte
Tel +55 31 3281 2633

1024 ☐ REC 1998

Squeezed into a small site in
Belo Horizonte, this compact
gymnasium extends over five
floors. A striking shell protects
the main volume from the
strong sun and is moulded from
bamboo, rendered with iron-
coloured concrete and covered
with a fabric of iron lattice.

João Filgueiras Lima

**Regional Electoral Tribunal of
Bahia**
Avenida 1a, Salvador,
41746-900, Bahia
Tel +55 71 373 7000

1025 ☐ GOV 1998

Four elements make up this
complex: the main two-storey
office building, the auditorium,
a circular volume containing the
Register's office and a single-
storey service building. The
gleaming wave-like roof of the
main building makes this a
striking addition to the city.

•1031

Brazil

Rio de Janeiro•
São Paulo•1026-1030

•1044

1032•

1043•

Chile

Córdoba•1033-1034
•1035
1036
1037
Santiago•1045-1048
•1051
•1052
Buenos Aires•1038-1042

1049
•
1050

Argentina

...ulo Mendes da Rocha

...nacoteca do Estado
...Praça da Luz, Luz, 01120-010,
...o Paulo
...l +55 11 228 1148

...26 ☐ CUL 1998

...e redesign of São Paulo's
...te art museum reorientates
... existing building. The main
...ance is now at right angles
...e primary axis and the
...ding looks inward. Internal
...tyards form the central
...e of the reorganized interior.
...zed roof sections flood the
...eum with light.

MMBB Arquitectos

House in Ribeirão Preto
184 rua Guarantã, Ribeirão
Preto, 14040-190, São Paulo
Tel +55 16 630 2069

1027 ✆ RES 2001

Four columns sunk into the
rocky subsoil carry the
apparently weightless concrete
container of this house. Stand-
up beams protrude above the
roof and support the horizontal
slabs that define the levels. The
interior is free of columns and
sheets of mullion-free glazing
encase the living area.

UNA Arquitectos

Pavilion House
São Paulo

1028 ■ RES 1998

Situated outside São Paulo, the
Pavilion House consists of a
single raised volume with a
single pitched roof of laminated
metal sheeting. A stone-paved
patio, entrance area and
balcony at tree-top height form
an axis perpendicular to the
main volume. Inside is open-
plan, with only the private areas
closed off.

Ruy Ohtake

**The Child and the Sea
Community Centre**
220 Estrada do Pasto Grande,
Ubatuba, São Paulo

1029 □ PUB 2001

Set in a nature reserve on the
Atlantic coast, this children's
educational complex has a
wide-ranging brief including
ecology and indigenous crafts.
The centre has a concrete arch
framing a brick vault, bamboo
walls and a circular window as
decorative eye.

MBB Arquitectos

ntal Clinic
5 rua 10, Orlândia, 14620-000,
o Paulo
+55 16 3826 2077

30 □ PUB 2000

s dental centre on the
tskirts of São Paulo takes
ccount of adjacent houses
d the regular grid pattern of
e streets. A box of wood and
ass houses the upper-level
nic and lower-level laboratory.
separate concrete wall forms
 portico and frames the
ternal entrance.

sé Tabith

**azilian Bar Association and
rristers' Welfare Fund
adquarters**
00 Avenida Mato Grosso,
mpo Grande, 79031-001,
ato Grosso do Sul,
+55 0 21 67 31 84700

31 □ GOV 2000

blic and private areas
erweave on this site next
a large city park. A shopping
ntre links the two main blocks
d provides access to an
ditorium. A multipurpose
blic plaza unifies the site.

car Niemeyer

seu Oscar Niemeyer
9 Marechal Hermes Street,
530-914, Curitiba, Paraná
+55 41 350 4400

32 □ CUL 2002

s dramatic annexe to the
ginal museum building is
nstructed from reinforced
crete and mounted on a
ic plinth. Designed for
ibitions and multimedia
sentations, the ceiling height
es by 9 metres. Diagonal
ting reveals the interior
ce at night.

Miguel Angel Roca

School of Arts, Córdoba University
Ciudad Universitaria,
5000 Córdoba
Tel +54 351 433 4080

1033 ☐ EDU 1999

Arranged like the arms of a windmill, four volumes centred on a glass foyer accommodate the departments of Film, Music, Drama and Set Design. While each building is tailored to its specific needs, from theatre to production workshop, the programme remains cohesive.

Miguel Angel Roca

Aeropuerto Community Centre
4500 Avenue Monseñor Pablo Cabrera, Córdoba
Tel +54 351 433 5459/63

1034 ☐ PUB 1999

A circular concrete envelope containing a cylinder and two rectangular prisms makes up the unusual plan of this community centre. The saw-tooth roof is the primary light source for the council offices, exhibition hall, auditorium, library and community spaces.

Miguel Angel Roca

Weekend House
Ruta Nacional 36, Calamuchita Valley, Córdoba
Tel +54 351 469 9346

1035 ☐ RES 1998

A composition of bridges, galleries and towers allows this house in a wooded valley in the Córdoba hills to preserve and amplify its spectacular views. The long, low form of the living room is the main 'bridge' element. Four towers constructed of local grey stone contain all service facilities.

Rafael Iglesia

Altamira Building
70 San Luis, 2000 Rosario

1036 ▮ RES 2001

Responding to the varying size
of the modern family unit, this
city block in Rosario offers
varied apartment types. Inside,
neutral finishes including white
walls, large windows and plank
floors add to the versatility.
Outside, the luminous white
punctured facade appears
weightless, a sense enhanced
by the slender street profile.

Rafael Iglesia

Paraná River House
Barrancas del Río Paraná,
2128 Arroyo Seco

1037 ▮ RES 1999

This pavilion house stands
beside the wide Paraná River,
its lower plane exposed in mid-
air and suspended above the
water with views all round.
Structure is the principal feature
of this project: beams, columns,
partitions and floors literally
unfold, becoming walls, roofs
and railings.

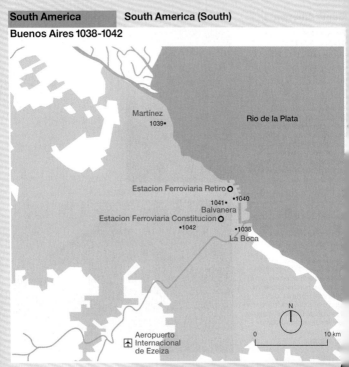

Martínez
1039•

Rio de la Plata

Estacion Ferroviaria Retiro O
•1040
1041•
Balvanera
Estacion Ferroviaria Constitucion O
•1042
•1038
La Boca

N

0   10 km

Aeropuerto
Internacional
de Ezeiza

Aja Espil – Cobelo Arquitectos

OMBU Metrogas
1360 Lamadrid, Federal,
1267 Buenos Aires
Tel +54 11 4515 0790

1038 ☐ COM 1999

The new Central Building joins
two existing buildings on this
complex. The street facade is
virtually unbroken with a facing
of Paris stone pierced by
narrow strip windows, and the
building almost seems to
recline. Inside, there are five
floors of offices including one
underground.

Lier & Tonconogy Arquitectos
and Manuel Glas Arquitectos

IBM Argentina Headquarters
2149 Hipolito Yrigoyen,
Martinez, 1640 Buenos Aires
Tel +54 11 4319 7141

1039 ✆ COM 2001

This IBM Headquarters,
incorporating existing buildings,
has transformed a Buenos Aires
industrial estate. A cantilevered
entrance canopy welcomes
visitors into a spacious atrium
with a triangular plan. Stone
and wood inside contrast with
the aluminium and steel.

FT Arquitectos

**Museum of Latin American
Art**
Avenida Figueroa Alcorta 3415,
425 Buenos Aires
Tel +54 11 4808 6500

040 ☐ CUL 2001

A pale stone-clad wedge with
cantilevered box houses this
new museum, now a lively
cultural centre. Circulation
routes inside begin in a glass-
covered double-height atrium.
Ground-floor gallery spaces are
by a glazed walkway opening
to a landscaped area.

brindo Testa and Juan
ntana

**Headquarters of the
ssociation of Notaries**
33 - 1° piso, Avenida Las
eras, 1127 Buenos Aires
+54 11 4801 1023

41 ☐ GOV 1999

commodating the Notaries
adquarters, this office
lding becomes part of the
eet. Metal sunshade
ments on curved steel
mes echo the next-door
conies and falsely imply
essiveness.

Faivre, Román & Lavaselli

Monasterio Santa Monica
3905 Nazca, Barrio 'Villa
Devoto', 1419 Buenos Aires
Tel +54 11 4571 9498

1042 ☐ REL 2001

The organizing elements of this
monastery in Buenos Aires are
the Chapel and Library, each set
in a tower of concrete and stone
porphyry. Domestic spaces
complete the site, creating a
modern, open cloister. Double
walls protect from external
noise; interior facades are open
to bring in light.

German del Sol

Hotel Explora
San Pedro de Atacama, Ayllú de
Larache, Atacama
Tel +56 55 85 11 10

1043 ☐ TOU 2000

Within the Atacama Desert, one
of the hottest and driest places
on the planet, this low-level
hotel complex with riding
stables is arranged as an oasis
settlement. Gently arching
overhanging roofs protect
terrace areas from solar glare.
Materials are left rough to allow
the buildings to mature.

Auer + Weber Architekten

**ESO Hotel and Information
Centre for the European
Southern Laboratory**
Cerro Paranal, near Antofagasta
Tel +56 5543 5000

1044 ☐ TOU 2001

Within the immense scale and
harsh environmental conditions
of the desert, a unique habitat
has been created; a landscape
wall embedded below the
horizon line contains the entire
programme, using small
modules with flexible links to
withstand earthquakes.

José Cruz Ovalle, Juan Purcell
Pena

**Centromaderas Timber
Processing Plant**
s/,100 Avenida Eduardo Frei
Montalva, Lampa, Santiago
Tel +56 2 425 8000

845 ☐ COM 2000

Standing adjacent to the Pan-
American Highway which runs
the length of Chile, this plant
includes production, storage
and offices. A single curved roof
covers the entire plant. Pine is
used throughout, demonstrating
its flexibility and elasticity.

Alejandro Aravena

**Faculty of Mathematics,
University of Chile**
Vicuña Mackenna 4806,
Santiago
Tel +56 2 354 4000

846 ☐ EDU 1999

Connecting two existing
buildings, this new element is
geometrically articulated to
withstand earthquakes, cleverly
juxtaposing materials to avoid
monotony. A covered atrium in
exposed concrete and glass
announces the entrance. Inside,
skylights illuminate three levels.

Mathias Klotz

Altamira Secondary School
El Acueducto, Peñalolen,
Santiago, Region Metropolitana

847 ☐ EDU 2000

This large secondary school
with its mountainous backdrop
provides a landmark for the
surrounding residential area.
Two parallel volumes, closed
against the extreme climate,
enclose a central ramp. A
gymnasium beneath the ramp
is used as a community space.

José Cruz Ovalle

Adolfo Inbañez University
2640 Diagonal Las Torres,
Peñalolen, Santiago
Tel +56 2 369 3660/2

1048 ☐ EDU 2002

Dramatically located in the foothills of the Andes, the elements of this university campus are scattered across the site. The buildings are linked by esplanades, patios, ramps and amphitheatres. Inside, mezzanines, ramps and galleries continue the idea of layers and connections.

Eduardo Castillo Ramirez

L'Animita Chapel
Camino a Bulnes, Concepción,
Provincia del Bio-Bio
Tel +56 4 164 5247

1049 ☐ REL 2002

This project provides a poor agricultural area near the town of Concepción in southern Chile with a small chapel for bi-weekly mass. Cheaply and elegantly clad in local radiata pine, it is a prototype for chapels across the countryside. A sliding panel reveals a glazed pivot door.

Mathias Klotz

Casa Reutter
Cantagua, Comuna de Zapallar,
V Region

1050 ■ RES 1998

In a pine forest near to the beach, this summerhouse consists of two rectangular boxes balanced above a wall. The bedroom box penetrates the living room box, and sliding walls replace doors. Services, kitchen and study are within a third concrete volume. A timber overhang covers a terrace.

South America

José Cruz Ovalle

Bodega Viña Perez Cruz
Camino Los Morros w/n
Huelquén, Paine
Tel +56 2 639 9622

451 ☐ COM 2002

This winery in the foothills of the
Andes features two parallel
barrel-vaulted volumes unified
by a sweeping roof. The timber
building is broken into three
zones by two wedge-shaped
entrance spaces. A central
route along each vault provides
access. A bridge in the spandrel
leads to the fermentation tanks.

Mathias Klotz

Viña Las Niñas
Apalta, Santa Cruz, VI Region

452 ☐ COM 2000

A series of boxes of varied
shapes and materials make up
this winery in the dramatic Valle
de Colchagua. The north
elevation of the main building
containing the fermentation
tanks is clad in timber strips
and features a continuous
ground-floor window; the south
elevation is of full-height
polycarbonate sheeting.

Index of Architects

Note: Key words are printed in bold type for the sole purpose of indicating alphabetical order. Surnames beginning with 'de' or 'd' are listed under the letter 'D'; surnames beginning with 'van' or 'von' are listed as appropriate under the letter 'V'.

Practice Page number

Index of Architects

Index of Architects

Index of Places

Index of Places

Index of Places

Index of Places

Picture Credits

H Abadie: 487. Acconci Studio: 739. ADP: 120. George Aerni: 672. Søren Ågard: 340. Ejaz Ahed: 079. Kim Ahm: 317. Aires Mateus & Associates: 583; 589. Aker/Zvonkovic: 976. Ole Akhøf: 316. Fernando Alda: 548; 550. Roos Aldershoff: 430. Luís Ferreira Alves: 581; 586. Brit Andresen: 011. Arcaid/Richard Bryant: 243; 327; 333; 375; 382; 792. Arcblue/Hélène Binet: 366; 385. Arcblue/Peter Durant: 332; 737. Arcblue/Keith Hunter: 325; 328. Archipress: 485. Archipro: 212–3. Architects 49: 225. ©Thomas Dix/Architekturphoto: 678. Arfo/Snøhetta: 266. Arkibulian: 254. Remco Arnold: 435. Artur/Roland Halbe: 657. Artur/Jochen Helle: 628. Artur/ Tomas Riehl: 612. Satoshi Asakawa: 098; 100. Emilie Maximilian Ezuka Ashley: 268. Luís Asin: 529; 568–9; 575. Asin & Megias: 555. Erieta Attali: 826. Javier Azurmendi: 563. Alejo Bague: 540. Barefoot Photographers of Tilonia: 084. Barnes, Pfeiffer, Ueda: 886. Richard Barnes: 918. Guido Baselegia: 685. Peter Bastianelli-Kerze: 952. Peter Bennetts: 042. Mary Berkhout: 417. Jordi Bernado: 561. Hélène Binet: 339; 347; 351; 392; 479; 516; 707. Patrick Bingham-Hall: 001–2; 007; 012; 016; 022; 051. Bitter & Bredt: 578; 631. Craig Blackmon: 977. Anna Blau, Markus Pillhofer, Gerald Zugmann: 723. Bleda y Rosa: 559–60. Sarah Blee: 476. Brett Boardman Photography: 025–6. Peter Lind Bonderup: 309; 315. Tom Bonner: 887–91; 895. Nicolas Borel: 493; 495; 514; 931. Pierre Boss: 670. Aljosa

Brajdic: 819. Anthony Browell: 009; 028–30. Geraldine Bruneel: 065; 069–70. Alex Bryce: 1018. Angela Buckland: 851. Angela Buckland/Elle Deco/Sean Lorenze: 852. Melinda Buie: 926; Friedrich Busam: 698. Jean de Calan: 765. Peter Campbell: 354. Enrico Cano: 700; 746. David Cardelus: 571. Roberto Cardenas: 1004; 1006. Kraig Carlstrom: 019. Earl Carter: 041; 054. Lluís Casals: 541–2; 1035. Antonio Castañeda: 1015. Raffaele Cavadini: 693. Martin Charles: 358. Joe Chartouni: 067. Myung Whan Cho: 135. Chuck Choi Architectural Photography: 879. Finn Christoffersen: 621. David Churchill: 329. Mario Ciampi Fotografo: 751. Tom Cohen: 894. Keith Collie: 608. Coop Himmelb(l)au: 722. Bruun Corfitsen: 275. Roderick Coyne: 345, 371. Marc Cramer: 867–9. JP Crousse: 1022. José Manuel Cutillas: 527; 531. José Manuel Cutillas/César San Millán/Hisao Suzuki: 546. Paul Czitrom: 1005. Kristien Daem: 455; 469–70. Nils Petter Dale: 261. Richard Davies: 365. JC Decaux: 617. Andreas Deffner: 088. Michel Denancé: 175. Jan Derwig: 418. Simon Devitt: 060. Lyndon Douglas: 343. James Dow: 862; 864–5; 872. dRMM: 353. Peter Durant: 388. Gerda Eichholzer: 706. Gerrit Engel: 639; 659. Torben Eskerod: 277. Esto/Peter Aaron: 965. Esto/Scott Frances: 909; 924; 932; 983; 986. Esto/ Jeff Goldberg: 230; 934–5; 945. Esto/Tim Griffith: 064; 247. Esto/Peter Mauss: 486; 490. Esto/Lara Swimmer: 882. Esto/ Bill Timmerman: 917. Steven Evans: 863. Gilbert Fastenaekens: 460. Ralph Feiner: 688. Georges Fessy: 426; 501; 504. Thomas Flechtner: 702. Alan Forbes: 323. José Forjaz: 845. Foto Facciata: 467. Fotoworks/Benny Chan: 131; 146; 897; 899–900; 904. Klaus Frahm: 591. Willem Franken: 456. Esquias Freitas: 1025. Gustavo Frittegotto:

1036–7. Felix Fuentes: 564. Mitsumasa Fujitsuka: 190. Fabio Galli: 272. Gartner Photography: 119. Andreas Giakoumakatos: 822. Gigantes Zhengelis Architects: 222. Richard Glover: 367. Silvia Gmür: 831. Eujin Goh: 242. Michel Goiffon: 503. John Gollings: 003; 006; 010; 015; 032; 034; 039; 045; 047; 049; 055–6; 123; 125. Stephen Goodenough: 063. Luís Gordoa: 994. David Grandorge: 368. Peter Grant: 269. Tomaz Gregoric: 812. Tim Griffith: 043; 245–6; 884; 905. Paul Groh: 889. P Gumuchdjian: 391. Kaid Haagen: 767–70. Roland Halbe: 466; 499; 517; 521; 532–3; 545; 556; 558; 573; 613; 618; 627; 638; 641; 644; 647; 649; 653; 656; 661; 682; 709; 950; 1044; 1051. TR Hamzah & Yeang: 232 Rob't Hart: 161; 420; 448; 452–3. Ester Havlová: 789; 794. Jiri Havran: 257. Hectic/Hans Werlemann: 507. Michael Heinrich: 666; 668. Heinrich Helfenstein: 597. Heinrich Helfenstein/Gaston Wicky: 687. Heinrich Helfenstein/Valerio Olgiati: 689. Joerg Hempel: 609. HG Esch, Hennef: 605. Hannes Henz: 673. Herik Hesmergy: 473. Chris Hill: 389. Javier Hinojosa: 1000; 1003. Hiroyuki Hirai: 153–4; 166–7; 180–1; 192; 206; 208. Kotaro Hirano/Karoku Kato: 201. Pedro Hiriart: 990; 995. Kazunori Hiruta: 221. Knut Hjeltnes: 263, 265. H Lin Ho: 231. Helga Hohl: 843. Jaro Hollan: 256; 258–9. Maija Holma: 285. Carl-Viggo Hølmbakk: 267. Florian Holzherr/Jens Passoth: 660; 663. Ross Honeysett: 018; 020; 024; 036. Chris Honeywell: 342. R Huarcaya: 1021. Eduard Hueber: 664; 701; 703; 705; 708; 922. Keith Hunter: 330. Hertha Hurnaus: 719. Timothy Hursley: 862; 876; 907; 916; 921; 940–1; 954; 968–75; 980. Werner Huthmacher: 279; 630; 635. Marko Huttunen: 290; 696. Juha Ilonen: 839. Bastiaan IngenHousz: 454. Kerun Ip: 117. Ole Jais: 276. Tadeuz Jalocha:

Picture Credits

434

The Phaidon Atlas of Contemporary World Architecture
Comprehensive Edition

450 x 310 mm, 17 5/8 x 12 1/8"
812 pp
Hardback
ISBN 0 7148 4312 1

If you would like to know more about the buildings featured in the Travel Edition of *The Phaidon Atlas of Contemporary World Architecture* then the Comprehensive Edition of the book is essential. The scope and extent of this highly acclaimed book make it an invaluable tool in understanding the state of contemporary architecture, as well as a source of inspiration and pleasure. A unique resource, the Comprehensive Edition of *The Phaidon Atlas of Contemporary World Architecture* is an indispensable addition to the libraries of architects and all those who appreciate the importance of our built heritage, past, present and future.

• Features the same 1,052 buildings by 656 architects in 75 countries as the Travel Edition

• Contains over 4,600 colour photographs, 2,400 line drawings and 62 specially commissioned maps

• Each project is fully illustrated with photographs that document the building as a whole, as well as plans, elevations and cross-sections

• Descriptive texts provide contextual background, an appreciation of the particular qualities that mark each building and essential data for professional users

• For ease of use, the same project numbers are used in the Comprehensive Edition and the Travel Edition

• Full indexes and a comprehensive cross-referencing system allow the reader to access the information by building type, building name, architect and location

• World data pages illustrate the global, economic, demographic and environmental context of the practice of architecture

• A detailed world map indicates the distribution of buildings in the book shown in conjunction with population density

• A series of charts set out the area of each country and the current as well as projected population figures

• Country-by-country tables set out gross domestic product, annual expenditure on construction, literacy and environmental sustainability rankings

• Includes data on the numbers of registered architects, architecture students and schools of architecture in each country to illustrate the relationship between wealth and the profession of architecture

Phaidon Press Limited
Regent's Wharf
All Saints Street
London N1 9PA

Phaidon Press Inc.
180 Varick Street
New York, NY 10014

www.phaidon.com

First published 2005
© 2005 Phaidon Press Limited

ISBN 0 7148 4450 0

Designed by Hamish Muir and
Lisa Drake
Printed in China

Acknowledgements
The Publishers would like to
thank the architects who appear
in this volume for their time,
resources and enthusiasm for
the project. Thanks are also due
to Lise Connellan, Gary Gravatt,
Ian McDonald, Kim Richardson,
Jane Rollason and Ann
Simmonds.